Long Shadows of Yesterday

India and the Middle East Seen from the Perspective of a Young British Officer from 1945 – 1949

Cyril J.M. Branson

MERRIAM PRESS

MILITARY MEMOIR
BENNINGTON, VERMONT
2016

First published in 2016 by the Merriam Press

First Edition

Copyright © 2016 by Cyril J.M. Branson
Book design by Ray Merriam
Additional material copyright of named contributors.

The views expressed are solely those of the author.

ISBN 9781576384725
Library of Congress Control Number: 2015959958
Merriam Press #ME3-P

This work was designed, produced, and published in
the United States of America by the

Merriam Press
133 Elm Street Suite 3R
Bennington VT 05201

E-mail: ray@merriam-press.com
Web site: merriam-press.com

The Merriam Press publishes new manuscripts on historical subjects, especially military history and with an emphasis on World War II, as well as reprinting previously published works, including reports, documents, manuals, articles and other materials on historical topics.

Prologue

BY late 1945, the movement for independence in India was coming to a head. In Palestine, the conflict between the majority Arab population and the ever-increasing Jewish settlements was intensifying. The political situation in Egypt was deteriorating; in Greece, the government was facing a civil war; and in Trans-Jordan, King Abdullah was trying to save his throne. British influence (the old Raj and previous political leverage) in these areas was declining fast and the vestiges of "Empire" were fading rapidly.

During the period of 1945-1949, I served as an army officer in India and a number of Middle-East countries. This provided me the opportunity to see, at first hand, some of the miseries inflicted on hundreds of thousands of people as a result of bad decisions made by politicians sitting comfortably in their offices in Westminster and Washington, D.C., whose major concerns seemed to have been guided mainly by the patronizing party politics and nationalistic arbitrary needs.

Wherever I was stationed, the Union Jack was about to be replaced by the flag of the mother nation. After a while, this became discouraging; somewhat similar to being engaged in a continuous withdrawal action. My brother officers and I were constantly reminded of the political need for the actions being taken. We were also lectured about the importance of considering the situation from the perspective of the "other person." To place oneself in the shoes of the "other person" is easier said than done. For example, in India, who was the other person? Was it the Hindu or the Moslem? And in Palestine, was it the Arab or the Jew? Living in such proximity to the people who were suffering the consequences of political decisions, it became increasingly difficult to remain unbiased, and not let your emotions dictate empathy, anger, or discrimination, especially towards those who tried to be exonerated from acts of terrorism.

In each of the countries I served, the local situation varied necessitating a different set of behavioral rules. Though this caused preliminary problems, it also provided a welcome change to what would otherwise have become routine work. I have felt compelled to recount my experiences that took place during a seminal period. But to write such an account poses a number of problems. In the first place, the incidents occurred almost seventy years ago and to recall one's thoughts at that time without recourse to retrospect is almost impossible. In the second place, I was very young and my views were based on first impressions (some of which were later proved false.) Given these problems, I decided to write a number of short sketches of what life was like for a young officer serving in India and the Middle East during those turbulent times. To give the picture some background, I have included my earlier training period in England that led to a commission in the Indian Army.

—C.J.M. Branson

Chapter 1

My Early Days

WHAT are the forces that direct us along a certain path as we journey through life? Some might say it is ambition while others might argue that envy and greed play a prominent part. Those who circumscribe it as mere circumstances may be closer to the truth. In its formation during our childhood, our basic character is strongly influenced by a number of factors: the atmosphere at home; peer pressure; the education one receives at home, at school and , in my case, by the Church of England; and like a surge of force building up, by the sinews of society. Considering this variety of guidance, I actually had, within reason, a happy and carefree childhood, and was left to do whatever I wanted. I don't think that I was particularly spoilt, my father made sure of that. My parents were very good to me – loving but firm – showing me the way to behave in all manner of circumstances. I received a good education at private schools, though I was by no means a studious pupil and much more an athlete, nevertheless I managed to pass the compulsory examinations. My friends and acquaintances were, for the most part, from the upper-middle class and consequently, the values I learned to respect were those of that class.

My father was an officer in the Royal Navy who was more often abroad than at home. In order to be close to him, my mother dragged myself, and my older brother, Peter, around the globe, making us a home wherever father was stationed. This constant uprooting of the family must have been most unpleasant for my mother, but it must have given me a taste for travelling and since those early days, I have been happiest when visiting new locations. I have never had an interest in establishing grass roots.

The atmosphere at my preparatory school was closer to that at home than that normally associated with a boarding school.

The Masters exercised common sense when dealing with the boys rather than brute force. It was a mixture of kindness blended with firmness. I had enormous fun at this school and was often in trouble for misbehaving or breaking the rules for which I would be caned. I enjoyed playing all types of sports and due to being a good athlete, quickly attained the captaincy of both the soccer and cricket teams. In this capacity, I enjoyed my first taste of being in a position of command and even popularity. During my final term, I was made Head Boy, a figurehead position with no responsibilities over others; however, the status of the position was pleasing to my ego and confidence.

My parents and brother was somewhat extrovert in their manner, whereas I was much less so for I was terribly shy. I had an aversion to being centre-stage, preferring to watch others act their parts. Children notice everything and remember much of what they have seen. I was no exception and due to this propensity, I became quite good at analyzing individual characteristics. It is uncanny that my shyness never intimidated me from speaking my mind when annoyed, but if I was asked to speak, sing or play the piano in front of a group, I would be struck with stage-fright. Strangely enough, I never had any problems when commanding troops.

The values learned in my youth, that I still find difficult to abandon today, are those associated with honesty, fairness, decency and sportsmanship. It surprises and saddens me how few people appreciate these values, today. We have become a rather delinquent and nihilistic society. My parents would have been considered high-middle class and most of their friends certainly were. The circle in which the family moved was very much "Navy" at a time when the Navy was one big family; the officers coming from the same social caste. I became used to seeing or hearing about senior officers who were friends of my parents and consequently, was rarely in awe of similar exalted persons in later life.

As a young adolescent, I had been accustomed to the Navy way of life since my father and Peter were both in the Royal Navy, so it is not unexpected that I should also want to serve in that illustrious career. At the age of 13½, I sat for, and passed, the entrance examination to the Royal Naval College Dartmouth as well as the subsequent interview. Unfortunately, of all things, I failed the medical examination. I had to have an eye operation to set matters right, but by the time I was fit again, the term had started and all the vacancies were filled. This was my first major setback in life and I took it badly. My small world was utterly shattered. I blamed myself for being a failure. Luckily, my father was still at home and he encouraged me to face facts and to be more positive for, after all, there were many other interesting careers that would surely fit me.

Since Dartmouth was out of reach, it was decided that I should attend Bedford School as it offered an alternative and special entry to the Navy. Bedford School also prepared would-be officers for the Colonial Civil Service and the Indian Army. I was thus given the choice of studying alternative careers as a safeguard. Bedford School, established in 1552, was a Public School similar to Dulwich, Oundle, and the school of Rugby. It operated on the "perfect" system whereby senior boys were made responsible for the correct conduct of the other boys. This system proved particularly useful in the training of young men in the art of leadership and people-management. When I became a senior student, I was assigned to the position of Junior Prefect and was responsible for such matters as facilitating the running of different sporting events, the control of a dormitory, and overseeing evening homework classes. I became aware for the first time of some of the pitfalls, benefits and a certain omnipotence associated with having legitimate authority over others.

World War II was in progress while I was at Bedford School. In Britain, conscript was at 17½ years of age, young men were being called-up to serve in one of the branches of the armed forces. On reaching 17, I had to decide on which branch to join. I realized that I had little hope of passing the difficult examination for special entry into the Navy and I was not interested in joining the Air Force. This left me with the choice of serving with the British Army, the Colonial Civil Service, or the Indian Army. Still impressionable, I had heard that life in the East African

Police Force was both interesting and challenging, and I approached the Deputy Headmaster offering my services as a possible candidate. He urged me to look elsewhere as he saw little prospect of any of the British Protectorates in Africa remaining under British control following the end of the war. He was also of the opinion that India would soon obtain its independence following which most of the other colonies would also demand theirs. Such advice, though well meant, was discouraging to say the least. My career prospects were diminishing leaving me the option of the British Army or the Indian Army. At that time, should you wish to become an officer in either of these armies, you could only obtain a short service commission (for hostilities/emergency only). There was always the off-chance of obtaining a regular commission should you show extraordinary promise but the competition would be fierce.

The idea of serving in the British Army, whether in Europe or the Far East, did not particularly appeal to me. What I had seen of the British soldier during the war years had been somewhat off putting. On the other hand, to serve with the Indian Army, even for a short period, could be a unique experience that would never again present itself and, should certain regiments be transferred to the British Army following India's independence, there was the chance of a permanent commission in one of those units. Moreover, I was drawn to the Indian Army by family ties with India itself.

John Edward Branson was the first of the family to land in India in 1780. He was followed by many other Bransons, most of whom did well in their different endeavours from being merchants to judges. Several were in the legal establishment, such as James Charles Emerson Branson, who became the Advocate General of Bombay and later the position of Treasurer of India during the period of the British Raj. When he was Advocate General, an Indian Prince offered the equivalent of $105,000 in rubies to my great-grandfather for a day's work. A few Bransons went into business, one of whom by the name of William Powell Branson, helped in introducing coffee with the brand name, a Spade Is A Spade Coffee, to East Africa. There were also a dozen

Bransons who had joined the Indian Army, including a favourite uncle of mine who had served with the 16th Rajputs. He had also been to Bedford School and when in India, was noted for his pranks, including sending an elephant to the Headmaster back home.

Prior to finally deciding to join the Indian Army, I thought it wise to first learn more about their conditions and habits. Any mental image I then had of life in India was loosely based on stories I had heard from members of the family who had served in or visited the country, and from books that glamourized the British Raj during the reign of Queen Victoria. The picture painted was pure Kipling and had little resemblance to the India of the mid-1940s. During a recruitment campaign at our school, a much more vivid portrayal of India was revealed by several British Indian Army officers. In their presentations, they candidly expressed the conditions we would have to endure should we serve with the Indian Army. They emphasized that the gilt of the Indian Empire had tarnished considerably and that the pomp and ceremony, where the British were concerned, was a thing of the past. India was entering the twentieth century even if it was at an elephant's pace. Given that many Indian soldiers had served overseas, coming in close contact with European men and women whose behaviour was quite different to that of the Sahibs and Memsahibs, the sepoys no longer held the "whites" with the same reverence, awe and esteem as before. Nonetheless, many Indians retained a lingering admiration for the British Indian Civil servant; their railway engineering, their educational system, the British law, and for the British officers in the Indian Army.

In my research into the Indian Army, I learned that it was manned by both Hindus and Muslims and officered by British and Indian officers. The British officers, and some Indian officers, were appointed to the senior ranks (commanding officers and company commanders), and the junior ranks (Company Seconds-in-Command and Platoon Commanders), were Viceroy Commissioned Officers (VCOs), who were Indians with long service in their respective regiments. It was quite normal for a VCO with fifteen or more years of service to be under the command of a young British subaltern who was his Company Commander.

I decided not to wait for my call-up and instead made the necessary application to join the Indian Army. This decision must have been a relief to my parents as my mother was patiently waiting for me to join-up so that she could leave England and join my father who was stationed in Canada. In March 1945, I was invited to London for an interview and on arrival at the appointed place, was surprised to find the "Board" consisting of one, an ancient Brigadier with several rows of medals, who immediately made me feel at ease. On learning of my family's history in India, and after hearing my pathetic reasons for wishing to join, he kindly accepted my application. He appeared almost apologetic as he explained that Indian Army applicants had to undergo basic infantry training as privates rather than as officer cadets, as was the case for those undergoing officer training for the British Army, mumbling about the "infernal discrimination." We discussed the future of the Indian Army which he thought was nil in the long run, at least where the British officers were concerned. Some senior officers would be required to stay on for a while to ensure an effective handover to the Indians, but the majority of officers would be returned to England before independence took place. The only regiments that might be retained or transferred to the British Army were the Gurkha units since the terms of agreement for their existence was made primarily between the governing bodies in Britain and Nepal.

While waiting to receive my joining instructions, I tried to visualize the life of a recruit. I had seen films depicting training at "boot camp" and had heard enough gossip to realize that life as a recruit was generally considered to be a period of sufferance for all concerned. My training with the Bedford School Junior Training Corps had accustomed me to the utter boredom of foot drills and to the more arduous effort expected when on field training exercises. I was sure that I could meet the physical demands but was uncertain of being mentally prepared for the living conditions and the frustrations that each recruit had to accept. Maybe my ignorance was a blessing for had I known what life as a recruit was going to be like, I might never have volunteered. The one thought I kept at the back of my mind was that I would be training with a group of people who had much the same background as myself all of whom had the same aim – a commission in the Indian Army.

Chapter 2

Basic Training, England

A few weeks following the London interview, I received "joining instructions" ordering me to report to the Royal West Kent Regimental depot at 1400 hours, June 1, 1945. Parting from my mother was a sad occasion for neither of us could foretell when we would meet again. With a sense of uncertainty as to the future, I set off by train for Maidstone in Kent, where the depot was located. I tried to feel excited in the fact that I was on my way to join the army, and for a short space of time, was wrapped in thoughts of adventure to come, but the closer I came to the depot, the greater my sense of apprehension. On arrival at Maidstone station, I took a taxi for I had no idea as to how to get to the depot. When I got out of the taxi at the main gate, the sentry on duty, seeing the taxi, must have thought I was an officer and was in the process of coming to a salute when I asked him where I was to report. On realizing his mistake, the sentry became embarrassed and confused, and in annoyance, grumpily pointed the direction I was to take. With suitcase in hand, I took a shortcut and strolled across the parade ground. Unbeknownst to me the parade ground was hallowed ground and this, I was soon made to realize when a very loud voice from goodness knows where, bellowed "March to attention you 'orrible little man and get off the parade ground!" I guessed rightly that this order had been directed at me and moved about in lively fashion in spite of the suitcase banging against my left knee. As a welcome address, it certainly prepared me for what was to come.

On entering the main reception room I was glad to see that other members of the Indian Army draft had arrived ahead of me. There was the usual nervous chatter and uneasy smiles associated with people meeting for the first time though, in this instance, I recognized several boys from different public schools;

individuals with whom I had previously competed in a number of sporting events. There was even a friend of mine from Bedford school. I was considerably heartened at the sight of these acquaintances and felt much less alone in this unfamiliar world. Eventually an immaculately dressed Sergeant-Major entered the room. He was a tall, well-built man with a face that wouldn't accept fools lightly attached to a massive, square jaw that, no doubt, was accustomed to barking. However, he spoke quietly and immediately received our full attention. He divided the eighty of us into two large platoons and allotted each a separate barrack room. We then shuffled off to our assigned areas like a flock of sheep to find a tall, cheerful Sergeant waiting for us. The Sergeant informed us that he was our Platoon Sergeant and that the three Corporals standing beside him were the Section Commanders come instructors. One was of medium size, ruddy-faced Irishman with a large, liquor induced red nose. His nose was as straight as a bobsleigh course, and by his pugnacious-looking demeanour, had walked into several fists in the past. Another was a lean, gaunt-looking man with an expression like a curate just beginning to have doubts. And the third Corporal was a small individual with a perpetual smile on his pockmarked face. All these non-commissioned officers (NCOs) had seen action with the 8th Army in North Africa and Italy. They looked remarkably tough yet managed to appear quite human.

The Sergeant assigned us beds according to alphabetical order. I was to share the second bunk with John, a quiet individual from the city of Bath who had been to Stowe school. The wooden bunk was a two-tier contraption with thin metal trellises serving as bedsprings. This type of bunk was anything but sturdy, and in fact, was apt to sway dangerously whenever one of the occupants moved too abruptly. John and I tossed for who would get the lower and more secure bunk. I won. Our first task was to get "fitted-out." We were marched to the Quartermaster's store where we collected clothing, equipment and bedding. Once inside the store we moved as if on a conveyor belt, stopping every so often to receive some item of clothing or equipment from different storemen who never inquired as to your measurements, preferring to use their own judgment with a perfunctory glance. Typically, the last item to be issued was a large kitbag into which all items had to be placed. You can imagine the chaos at the end of the line as individuals, encumbered by a mass of clothing and equipment, harassed by lack of space and urgent demands to "move along" tried to pack their gear without losing or misplacing any of the issued items. As to bedding, we were each issued with a canvas palliasse that we later half-filled with straw. It was only half-filled so that it could be folded into three for stowing during the day.

On returning to the barrack room, the NCOs showed us how to store our under-clothing in the individual metal locker above each bunk. Each item had to be squared-off to a precise measurement using cardboard as a stiffener. After some effort, we attained the required standard. Most of us decided to leave the contents of the locker undisturbed for the duration of our stay at the depot, preferring to purchase extra clothing rather than have to go through the laborious process of squaring-off each item every time we had to change our underclothes. We were also shown how to place our equipment and bedding for the daily inspection. Lastly, we were shown the most effective way to fold two blankets so as to provide maximum warmth and comfort for sleeping. We were then told to dress in our issued uniforms and to pack our civilian clothes in our suitcase that was to be sent home. From that moment on, I was never in civilian clothes until I reached India. The issue battledress uniform had been treated with some form of anti-gas chemical that gave it the feel and appearance of used cardboard. In addition, the material was thick, rough and extremely durable. It took several weeks of continuous wear before the body accustomed itself to the peculiarities of such coarse texture. My tunic was too large and the trousers were inches too long. I exchanged the trousers with John, who was taller than I, but the result was still unsatisfactory. With needle and thread from the "Housewife" we had been issued, I was able to shorten the trouser legs as a temporary measure until I was able to exchange the trousers at the Quartermaster's store. On trying the boots, I noticed that they were one of two sizes too big. With three pairs of socks, they fitted quite well. I prayed that I wouldn't get blisters. We were later told that our feet would soon harden and fill-out, hence the need for the oversize.

Prior to being marched to supper that was served at the incredibly early hour of 5:30 p.m., our Platoon Sergeant briefed us on the daily routine we could expect. Not so interesting was the news that we were to be confined to barracks for the first week or until such time as it took to make us at least look like soldiers. After further advice about saluting officers, marching about rather than walking and how to address officers and NCOs, we were sent to the kitchen for our fist experience of army cooking. One word would describe it, horrible. It was inedible. That first night I slept badly. Here we were forty young lads, who would be normally in their bedroom or in a university or college dorm, instead were packed closely together in uncomfortable bunks and feeling cold and hungry in Gulag-like surroundings and feeling distinctly lonely. I was surprised at the number of lads who snored; the room sounded like an orchestra out of tune without a conductor to syncopate the sound.

At 6:00 a.m., we were awakened by one of the Corporals who, after we had washed and shaved in lukewarm to cold water, had us clean the barrack room and prepare our bunks and kit for the morning inspection. Having swept the floor and polished everything in sight (and out-of-sight), we then stretched a cord from one end of the room to the other and aligned the separate items on each individual's bed with that of the other bed layouts. The daily morning inspection was carried out by the Platoon Sergeant who inspected each man, his dress, his bed layout, and his locker. Following this inspection, the Corporal marched us at the double to the kitchen for breakfast. We seemed to do everything at the double. There was at that time a radio program called *Double to Victory* that our NCOs must have assessed as their patriotic duty to conform according to their interpretation of the phrase. Anyway, we arrived at the kitchen ahead of the other groups, passing by them on the way – at the double. This did little to endear us to them and the food was still repulsive. The food was like poison. The army was killing us.

Immediately following breakfast came the Company Parade that was conducted with the utmost punctilio; there seemed to be a liturgical solemnity about it, possibly because all the company officers were present. I disliked such parades from that day forward. The rest of the morning was spent doing foot drills, physical training and weapon handling. In the afternoon, we were taught basic battle drills (attacking and self-protection) as well as field craft. The day's formal work finished at 4:30 p.m. after which we were free to do what we liked but still had to clean our kit and uniforms in readiness for the next morning inspection. It was also standard for a number of the lads to sweep the barrack room on a rotational basis. A similar routine to that of the first day continued throughout our four weeks at the depot. The only major change occurred on Friday mornings when a full kit inspection was held with the Platoon Commander in attendance. Every single item of clothing and equipment had to be lined up, including razor blades. Everything had to be clean or highly polished, even the nails on the soles of the boots had to be shined. All in the name of discipline.

Any infraction of the rules such as failing to salute an officer, no matter how far in the distance he was, or having a speck of dust on some part of your rifle, resulted in some form of punishment. The penalty, depending on the seriousness of the alleged violation, and on who charged you, could be any of a variety of punishments such as fatigues (cleaning out lavatories, helping the kitchen staff, extra duties in the evenings or on weekends, etc), or extra drill with full marching order or extra guard duties. I spent several fruitless hours on "Jankers" as punishment was called, all for ridiculous misdemeanours.

The physical training program was strenuous but well planned to gradually bring us up to the desired standard of fitness. We went through the normal daily physical jerks to loosen up the muscles and also went on marches, the distances increasing daily till we reached ten miles. At first, we were made to run wearing shorts and singlets and our oversized boots without socks. Naturally, we developed blisters but these soon disappeared to be replaced by calluses. You can imagine what an amusing sight we must have created as we clattered down the city streets having to halt and retrace our steps every so often to collect a boot that had slipped off. Rain or shine, we continued these marches adding more distance each day as well as more clothing and equipment. In this way, we became accustomed to the weight and fit of each added item. By the end of the fourth week, most of us were able to cover ten miles in full marching order even when having to alternate between walking fast and running. Although I had no trouble with the weight of the equipment on my back, I never became accustomed to the weight of the rifle. I found it awkward to carry and a heavy burden to hold in my small hand. I also had a great deal of trouble with the ghastly steel helmet that didn't seem to fit the shape of my head and either slipped forward to rest on my nose or fell back causing the chin strap to half throttle me. I have worn all manner of steel helmets since those early days and harbour a loathing of them all.

The handling and firing of the different weapons added zest to an otherwise dull routine. To start with, we practiced firing the .22 rifle to learn how to aim and fire the rifle correctly. We soon graduated to firing the .303 rifle outdoors. I will always remember my first shot with this rifle; the enormous kick left me with a bruised cheek for a week. Obviously, I wasn't holding the rifle properly; my arms were too short or the rifle too long. The rifle range was situated several miles out of town, and instead of being transported there by motor transport, we were required to march to the range in tactical formation, no matter the weather conditions. By the time we reached the range, we were tired and often wet through. The purpose of this exercise was to accustom us to shooting under battle weary conditions. To obtain a pass mark on each weapon, you had to reach the level of at least a second-class shot as applicable. Of all the practices I found the most difficult to be that of firing the rifle at one thousand yards while wearing a gas mask. As I wasn't a particularly good shot with the rifle, I was certain that I would fail this practice. When it came my turn to shoot at this ridiculous distance, there were thirty people on the firing point and I found myself positioned somewhere in the middle of the group. I had no idea as to my number in the group as there were no ground markers and, consequently, had difficulty identifying my own target, let alone seeing it for the eyepieces of the gas mask had started to fog-up even after having been defogged. Luckily for me, the fellow on my left was an excellent shot and, in confusion, must have fired on my target. I'm sure that I missed all the assigned targets, especially my own. At any rate, I was given the necessary pass mark that I gladly accepted.

Though there were some teething problems to begin with, I became a marksman with every automatic weapon. On the occasion of my first practice with the STEN sub-machine gun, we were located in a quarry, slippery with mud. I slipped and in trying to regain my balance, happened to pull the trigger that resulted in a burst of shots, several rounds coming close to hitting not only my own foot but also that of the instructor close by. He took the incident remarkably calmly, and resorting to some dry humour, advised me to accompany him in saying the Lord's prayer. In somewhat of a panic, my next burst cleared the top of the quarry disturbing some sheep grazing. I remember a certain absurd incident when firing the pistol. The ammunition must have been defective for of the six shots fired, only two reached the target a mere thirty paces away. A few rounds landed softly between me and the target and one pathetically rolled out of the barrel, landing at my feet. The instructor, noticing this remarkable performance, suggested I use a sub-machine gun rather than the pistol if I ever found myself in a close combat situation though he probably had his doubts as to who I would hit more: the enemy or my own men. I've never liked the pistol nor the revolver for two reasons: I have a small hand and find it difficult to hold the weapon correctly, and even more annoying, I found that the weight of the weapon when carried on the web-belt would pull down the belt on one side and sometimes my summer shorts with it.

Another weapon that had to be mastered was the grenade that could be thrown or, for added distance, fired from a grenade launcher attached to the rifle. The priming and throwing of the grenade is at first quite an experience, but it is perfectly safe as long as you follow the given instructions. Even so, it is not uncommon to have one's adrenalin pumping when you stand in the throwing bay and are about to throw a "live" grenade. After tossing the grenade, the thrower must check where it lands before ducking behind cover so that should it not explode, its whereabouts is known. When a thrown grenade does not explode, the officer-in-charge of the practice has to detonate the dud using a time-charged slab of gun cotton or similar explosive. Since the dud grenade might have a mind of its own and go off at any moment, this "for officers only" detail is one of the least amusing. Though we were not yet officers, we nonetheless had to practice blowing up dummy grenades. When using live explosives, there is a natural tendency to get undercover as quickly as possible once the fuse has been lit. You are taught never to run after lighting the fuse. Instead, you should walk quickly to the nearest shelter. I have always found that particular requirement is a very long drawn out affair.

Occasionally it is necessary to remain at the firing range for more than one day. In such cases, we bivouacked overnight in a field nearby. Warm meals were brought to us for supper and breakfast – the only time we had good food. For cover, each man was given two ponchos that, when tied together, could be used as a tent and for warmth. Each individual was issued a blanket. Was it malice aforethought or for just a joke that we always seemed to bivouac on the side of a hill used by a herd of cows? When it rained, which was often, the water would flow down the hill by way of our pup tents. Since we were on an incline, the tendency was for the body to move downhill every time you moved and in the morning, you often found yourself a few feet removed from your temporary cover and quite likely lying on a cow pat.

All this physical exercise and training resulted in our having healthy appetites. Unfortunately the meals served were badly prepared. Given the shortage of food in Britain at that time, the immense wastage of food due to the disregard by those in charge to employ incompetent cooks was not only folly but downright criminal. Someone was making a tidy profit selling the waste food as pigswill. In lieu of butter, we were served Trex; some form of grease. The vegetables were overcooked and tasteless, and the meat was mainly fat and grizzle. The bread was often stale and the fruit over-ripe or spoiled. Only the pangs of hunger forced me to eventually swallow some of the garbage served. To add insult to injury, the cooks and servers were some of the ugliest, dirtiest, laziest, slovenly and surly creatures imaginable. Though complaints were made to the Duty Officer on his rounds at mealtime, little was ever done to improve the deplorable conditions. To keep up my strength, I would nip into town and buy myself a dish of fish or sausages and chips at a soldiers' canteen run by civilian volunteers or, if short of sufficient funds, I would go to the depot's canteen and buy a bar of chocolate. I have rarely had a big appetite; however, I remember being always hungry during my days at the depot.

THE INDIAN ARMY CADRE

The officers of the Indian Army cadre at the depot were rarely seen; goodness knows what they did. Those with whom we did come in contact were officious and disagreeable. The senior officers were pompous and lacked the basic principles of man-management. The subalterns were young, inexperienced and officious martinets who took little or no notice or care of the men under their command. My own Platoon Commander would hand out punishments for the most trivial things and seemed to take a certain glee in our discomfort. The officers were all too aware of their own importance and in their condescending vanity, insisted on being saluted no matter what they were doing; failure to this resulted in punishment. As a result, recruits could be seen marching about the depot, saluting officers hundreds of yards away, saluting the Officers' Mess and Headquarters' building in case an officer was at a window looking out. Recruits resembled wound-up toy soldiers with their right arms continuously moving up and down from the salute position.

As for the non-commissioned-officer instructors, we rarely came in contact with them other than those in our own Company. We came to like these men and much appreciated the concern they demonstrated in the business of making us into soldiers. There was never any bullying nor any use of threats or profanity when giving orders. For all their outward hardness, they showed an admirable sense of tolerance and good humour. By means of using a firm hand when necessary and encouragement at all times, they received in return our full cooperation. Whenever we found the time to go to the local pub or cinema, one or more of the NCOs would accompany us and it was at such times that they would let their hair down and recount some of their battle experiences. We made sure never to abuse this off-duty friendship and thus preserved a friendly but professional bond of respect between the two groups.

The members of the Indian Army draft were boys who came mainly from the upper-middle class and the majority had been educated at English public schools. Several were from families with a background linked to India. Though a few left their school in a blaze of glory, the majority would not be regarded as intellectuals, rather as a result of their upbringing at home and at private schools, they demonstrated a self-confidence, a significant degree of independence, an inner and outer toughness that enabled them to face life's hardships with equanimity and a rough sense of justice that restrained their otherwise uncontrolled shenanigans. They were in all respects boys who had yet to grow into adulthood. Not the most likeable of individuals yet totally reliable when the occasion so demanded. I was used to their behaviour and felt at ease among them, but for the NCOs and other recruits, we must have been a puzzle.

At last our four weeks of basic training came to an end. Those who had failed to meet the set standards were relegated to the draft of new intakes and had to repeat the whole program. I never saw any of them again. The others prepared to move to the 13th Infantry Training Corps for the final training phase conducted in England. Not one of us was sorry to leave the depot. At the outset, the novelty of army life had maintained our interest but on realizing how the system severely curtailed all freedom of action and thought, our mood soon changed from one of interest to one of frustration. Life became a routine, and like most routines, engendered at times the wish to rebel; a small exercise in wishful thinking.

While at the depot, I had no occasion to visit the Infantry Training Corps (ITC), and therefore knew little about it. I had learned that the establishment was but a temporary one built at the beginning of the war for the purpose of training men and women in Special-to-Corps subjects prior to their being posted to operational or base units. As the camp was but a few miles distance from the depot, we were marched there, our kitbags being moved by motor transport. The layout of the ITC was quite different to that of the depot. Each training Company was located in a separate and self-contained unit area (i.e. offices, stores, training and accommodations buildings were close together). Many of the original trees had been left standing thus providing a pleasant landscape. Living conditions were rudimentary. We were housed in small wooden huts tucked in among the trees. Even in summer, the huts were permanently cold and humid with icy draughts circulating everywhere. Though each hut contained a pot-bellied stove, there was no coal or coke with which to fuel it. We would gather any loose pieces of wood or branches whenever the opportunity presented itself such as when on field exercises, but these few bundle of sticks were insufficient to heat the hut for any worthwhile period of time. A certain heat was generated when thirty human beings were tightly packed in the limited space. Though I lived in several school boarding houses, nothing really prepares you for the perpetual dampness of such conditions. As a welcome change, we had hot water in which to shave and shower. There must have been at least fifteen hundred men and women at the ITC. We saw little of these other trainees since much of our training took us outside the camp where we would spend the better part of the day. In one respect, being out of camp at lunchtime was an advantage as we often had our lunch at some local country pub that served a far better meal than that served at the camp kitchen.

The Indian Army draft remained grouped as two platoons: one per hut and with the same NCOs as before; however, we were immensely pleased to have as our new Platoon Commanders two British Indian Army officers. These two officers were an odd pair: one was tall and thin and had a permanent serious expression stitched to his face. He reminded me of Charles de Gaulle. The other was short and muscular and had a ready smile. Both had been wounded in action and had been returned to England to recuperate from their wounds and from the affects of malaria or dysentery. This rest period actually amounted to their having to train potential Indian Army officers, such as us. They were anything but in good health and during exercises, would occasionally feel faint and have to lie down awhile. The Commanders were excellent instructors, and in spite of their condition, were full of good humour. Their presence had a significant effect on our morale. For the first time since joining the Army, we were made aware of our status as potential officers and treated as such by our officers and NCOs. The taller of the two officers was a Lieutenant in the Baluchistan Regiment and the other, who was my Platoon Commander, was a Lieutenant in the Sikh Regiment.

If only the ITC's staff and the other trainees could have treated us fairly and decently, our existence at the camp would have been tolerable. As it was, both the staff and the other inmates took exception to our special group and went out of their way to be unpleasant. For example, whenever a particularly undesirable duty was called for, it was invariably given to us; we were never granted weekend passes though all the other trainees received this privilege. We were also singled out for a harsher form of discipline than was called for. The most officious and unpleasant group, other than the kitchen staff, was the military police (MPs). Rarely human at the best of times, the MPs would revel in frustrating our attempts to get to town when off-duty. It required a pass to get in and out of camp and had to be shown to the MPs at the main gate. If you were on your own, the MPs would inspect your turn-out and find all manner of fault and told to return to your hut. Should you argue with an MP, he would place you on a charge for insubordination. To get around this treatment, we decided to always arrive at the main gate in strength so as to have witnesses to the bullying tactics of these cretins. In the dining hall and canteen, many of the other trainees would make loud and obscene comments about us, but we soon became immune to such boorish behaviour, and since we ignored it and the others were unable to goad us into doing something stupid, they eventually stopped their spiteful foolishness. These antics demonstrated the existing class discrimination within the army as well; envy or prejudice of anything associated with the Indian Army. Our Platoon Commanders were aware of the situation and could do little about it. They advised us to take whatever came our way for the few remaining weeks and to consider the experience as a good lesson in behavioural attitudes. This we had to accept, and anyway, we had little or no time in which to fraternize with the other trainees. Moreover, we were quite content with our own company.

The advanced training consisted of field training exercises that tested us both mentally and physically. We would march in tactical formation to a selected area where we would undergo one or more battle manoeuvres. Wearing battle dress in hot weather is uncomfortable and the exertion required in field training brought on a heavy sweat that resulted in itching and sores wherever equipment rubbed against the uniform or against the skin. We would leave camp around 7 a.m. and return at 5 p.m. or later, sometimes missing dinner. As of the second month, we started night training that consisted of navigation exercises, patrols, and night attack manoeuvres. These night exercises would last anywhere up to five hours and we would get back to camp between midnight and 2 a.m. Regardless of the time we finished, parade the next morning was at the usual early hour followed by the morning inspection. Such training taxed our endurance to the limit and I, for one, was always tired.

We were taught Urdu by our Platoon Commanders. To graduate from the ITC, you had to prove by way of an oral test your ability to understand the fundamentals of this language, failure to do so meant relegation to the next incoming group of recruits from the depot. We received three hours formal tuition per week and had a further four hours of evening homework, some of which had to be completed during the weekend. Urdu is not an especially difficult language to learn and I found it quite fascinating. My major problem was in getting the correct inflections for these sometimes changed the meaning of the word.

Our marches to the different training areas were pleasant enough and they helped to build up a remarkable team spirit. We would march in "ack-ack" formation; that is, with one section of ten men in single file on one side of the road followed by another section on the opposite side of the road, the pace often in synch by having us sing in unison. Once your feet have adapted to the boots and the body to the marching pace, the cadence of the marching feet has a hypnotic effect and you feel you could go on marching indefinitely. The men would cover between fifteen and twenty miles each time we undertook field training and during these marches, the pace would occasionally be raised to 5 mph. It may not sound like much, but a forced pace of 5 mph when carrying full equipment is very tiring, especially to the legs, and to alleviate the soreness of the leg muscles, we were made to run for a few minutes every twenty minutes or so. It was only natural that some of the lads had difficulty in keeping up with the others and needed assistance from the fitter men. To relieve the monotony of the long march, we were put through action scenarios, such as scattering on the "enemy aircraft" alert or procedures taken when confronted by an obstacle. Every time we came to a bridge over a shallow river or stream, we had to wade across the water rather than use the bridge, which for exercise, had been declared unusable.

Our Platoon Commanders managed to arrange our lunch stops in some delightful place, ostensibly for their training facilities, but more likely than not, because of the nearness of some country pub. It was while visiting one of these pubs that we came to know a very fat publican who wagered that he could blow a dart from his mouth and split a match four feet away, one out of three tries. To our amazement, he rarely lost. These pub lunches not only helped us relax, they also provided us the opportunity to discuss India with our Platoon Commanders. They painted a picture of a vast land mass, the size of Europe, peopled by hundreds of millions of people – a mosaic of race and creed separated by a babble of tongues (845 language groups). We were to expect the plight of stinging insects, atrocious diseases, abject poverty, and an all-encompassing corruption. We could count on unrest among the people with increasing acts of civil disobedience; however, as long as the Indian Army remained disciplined, most of the riots could be controlled. Both our officers were wedded to their regiments. The Sikh officer, in a semi-humourous manner, explained that the behaviour of his Sikh sepoys was never entirely predictable; therefore, to be on the safe side, he would select what he hoped was a reliable man to spy on the others thereby obtaining advance warning of trouble and the chance to quell it. He went on to explain that Hindus and Sikhs had never been friends and he saw trouble ahead for the Sikh communities once the British were gone from India. I later encountered many Sikhs, military and civilian and, quite frankly, never felt at ease with them. It was not that they were particularly unfriendly, but rather not amicable. What I remember about them is their haughtiness and uncooperativeness. They could be as stubborn as a mule and seemed constantly on the defensive as if suspicious of non-Sikhs.

When on field training exercises, trainees were assigned the job of Platoon Sergeant or Section Commander on a rotational basis. This practice taught us leadership and the basic elements of command. In the knowledge that your turn would come to take command in one of these positions, you made sure to cooperate with those in temporary command lest they in turn retaliate for any trouble you might have caused. This system allowed each individual to try out his own ideas without fear of making a real fool of himself or damage to anyone. Each successful exercise served to increase the confidence of the individuals in command. Following each exercise, all experiences and experiments were analyzed and faults in techniques could thus be studied and remedied while the correct procedures were learned and remembered. It soon became apparent which individuals had the potential to become good officers and which were likely to fall by the wayside. The process of sorting and weeding-out the weak students had started.

On one particular exercise, I was the platoon signaller and had to carry on my back a heavy box-like wireless set, the dimensions of which were 3 feet high by 2 feet wide. The extended aerial added another 3 feet to the height of the contraption. The exercise in question required the platoon to cross an open gap and then get through a wire obstacle while under enemy fire. This action, at the best of times, is fraught with problems and when encumbered with an awkward wireless set, becomes suicidal. "There's not to reason why..." Anyway, I managed to get across the gap without mishap but became inextricably entangled in the wire fence that contained concertina wire as well as strands of horizontal barbed wire. The strands caught in my equipment, clothing and the wiring of the damned wireless set. I tried removing the set off my back but as I was about to accomplish this, two students threw themselves on the wire to make a bridge over which the others could cross. This action pinned me to the ground and as a consequence, the wireless was unserviceable. My temper, raging, was only subdued when a couple of instructors felt I had made their day.

THUNDERSTRUCK

Rarely does one choose a frontal attack against a well dug-in opponent. The norm is a flank attack using dead ground or woods to cover your approach while artillery and mortar shells rain on the enemy to keep their heads down. A flank attack sounds simple; just a matter of going left or right and attacking the enemy where he can bring the least amount of firepower against your force. Well, it's not necessarily so. The enemy realizes the options open to you and will have mines sown in the dead ground and other obstacles to stop or slow your approach. Furthermore, his artillery and mortars will be directed at the most likely routes of your advancement. During exercises, thunderflashes were used to simulate artillery fire. The thunderflash is a powerful cracker about twelve inches long that, when exploding, gives off a flash and makes a tremendous bang and billows of smoke. During one such exercise, I was a temporary Section Commander. With one section giving us cover fire, my section plus another, were to attack the enemy on its left flank approaching by way of the woods. Artillery smoke shells were to cover our advance. As we were traversing the woods, we heard the simulated artillery open fire and, almost immediately, were enveloped in dense, blinding and choking smoke. An instructor had lit a twenty minute smoke-pot without first checking the direction of the wind and instead of the wind drifting onto the enemy, it had blown towards the woods where it remained suspended. I couldn't see where I was going and was sure the others were equally incapacitated. I shouted for my platoon to link up by holding hands and then set about finding my way out of the woods. This took me about ten minutes only to find myself where I had originally started. It was futile. There was one casualty that day; a thunderflash exploded close to one of the trainees and the blast burst his eardrum.

NIGHT PATROL

It was when we were introduced to night training and, in particular, to the navigational skills required in carrying out a patrol, that I became horribly aware of my complete lack of sense of direction. Though I quickly learned how to navigate using alternative methods, this inability to naturally orient myself was to plague me whenever I was on field operations. To this day, I have a terrible time with directions. Night patrol exercises are an excellent means of cementing an individual's self-confidence. Any form of patrol, be it a reconnaissance patrol, consisting of but a few men or a fighting patrol of platoon strength, is far from easy to accomplish successfully. My first effort as commander of a reconnaissance patrol had me in fits of self-doubt. Not only did I have to navigate correctly to pass through our own minefields and other obstacles, I also had to reach the appointed destination according to a set route and time program. Using a compass to guide me accompanied by one man to keep track of distance covered (by counting his steps), I managed to get to the destination on time. My mission was to find a fordable place to cross a river. I divided the area into three; one per individual in the patrol, and we set off on our search. To ascertain the depth and base of a possible ford required that we enter the water that was positively icy cold. I divided the area into three sections to scan for the ideal ford. Though the water was frigid, a spot was found to proceed. However, we would use a different route to return. I realized that the exercise would call for an ambush to be set on our return, so I spaced my small party well apart with me in the middle. By looking at the map, I made an assessment at the likely ambush areas and these we bypassed, but one such bypass led me directly into a marked minefield and while skirting this obstacle, we walked straight into a well-planned ambush. We scattered as previously planned and individually, returned to our lines where we were fired upon by our own side who were not expecting us and took us for the enemy. At night, "fire first and ask questions later" is often the rule. While at the ITC, we were put through many such exercises as a means of training us to work effectively in small groups and to test our initiative and reactions when suddenly faced with a difficult situation.

ANYTHING FOR A BREAK

Our constant use of the training areas soon familiarized us with their respective peculiarities such as: the location of villages and farms; where there was bogland, and most importantly, where orchards were. Whenever possible, we would choose a route that led past an orchard where we would eagerly stuff our tunics with whatever we could eat. The farmers, not surprisingly, took unkindly to our presence and, on hearing the dogs bark, would come out with their shotguns and fire in our direction to warn us off. This encouraged us to improve our stealth tactics but did nothing to arrest our nocturnal visits.

Part of our training included communications. We were shown how to operate the different wireless sets that were in use by the infantry. Having calibrated the sets, we would be sent off in pairs to various locales where we were to follow given instructions in sending and receiving messages. Either the area was prone to static or the sets had been misused or the trainees weren't interested, whatever the reason, the aim of the exercise was rarely achieved. Oddly enough, it was easy to tune in to the BBC and, after attempting to contact other stations without success, we would all tune in to the BBC and spend a pleasant hour or so relaxing in the sun until some frustrated signals NCO would find us and tell us to head for home – in no diplomatic terms.

V.I.P.s

Being one of the few training centers of its sort in Southern England, it was to be expected that military VIPs would occasionally visit the camp for inspections. Each time this happened, we would stop all routine work and clean the camp till it shone; every stone, brass button, boot, and attitude was whitewashed to perfection. A parade would be held with all personnel present. After hearing rather than listening to the address given by the VIP, we would carry out the usual march past and that would be it.

One day, General Auchinleck visited the ITC. He arrived in a jeep and was dressed in battledress. Had he followed the normal pattern for such visits; however, he chose to visit the camp kitchens that had not been prepared for such an occasion. It was only a matter of minutes before the General's jeep came roaring down the road with him in it and out through the main gate, taking the quarter-guard by surprise. The General was obviously not amused nor was the ITC's Commandant, for we spent the rest of the morning trying to make the kitchens presentable; an impossible task, yet more useful than parading about like robots.

I might add that we weren't particularly sorry to hear that the camp staff had received a good dressing-down from the General, not that it improved their manners.

SEX EDUCATION

For recreation, we sought our escape from military life by experiencing whatever the city of Maidstone had to offer. Maidstone was a medium-sized city dating back several centuries and must have been a pleasant place to live in during its pre-war days, but now it was filled with soldiers from the many units stationed close by. Most of the soldiers were young and inexperienced in the ways of the world. Though the bars were full of soldiers, there were few drunks to be seen, maybe this was due to lack of money, for the soldier only received the equivalent of about 15¢ a day. With such a concentration of young men in one area, it drew opportunists to the city; the most threatening being prostitutes, many of who were diseased. We were constantly warned by the staff to avoid sexual contact with these young women as the VD rate among them was exceedingly high. If in the cinema by yourself, it wasn't uncommon to draw several women to your side, suggesting all kinds of promiscuous innuendos. For someone inexperienced in these matters, it was more embarrassing than titillating. There was one theatre in town that catered to the vaudeville audience where you could always get a seat and a good laugh. Other than the cinema, the theatre and the pubs, there was little else of interest. As I was always hungry, much of my pay and allowance went on food, including buying food from local farmers where I could buy a substantial (black market) meal.

I was most fortunate in that very good friends of my parents lived close to Maidstone. They lived in a beautiful large house from which radiated a lush, plentiful garden. I was invited to spend weekends there whenever I could get leave to do so. I managed to get two weekend passes through the manipulations of my Platoon Commander and made full use of the open invitation. It was glorious to once again live like a civilized person with no one to order me about and to have space in which to move. Other than the splendid meals, the thing I appreciated the most was privacy when I wanted it and pleasant company the rest of the time. I slept well, ate like a hippopotamus, swam like a seal and enjoyed every moment of this bliss. Those visits were a tremendous tonic in keeping up my spirits.

FLAG DAY

To mark the occasion of the capitulation of Germany, a Victory Parade was held in Maidstone. Naturally, many of the trainees at the ITC, including the Indian Army contingent, were called upon to participate in the march through town. As I disliked marching with the rifle at the slope, I volunteered to be a flag-bearer and ended up carrying the Free-French flag. In all, there must have been a dozen or so flag-bearers. The flags, measuring about six feet across and, with strong gusts, became somewhat of an effort to carry. At one point in the program, the flag bears formed a victory "V" close to the city's cenotaph. The Mayor and dignitaries then moved unexpectedly to the centre of the "V". When the Last Post was sounded, the dignitaries doffed their hats and the flags were lowered. As can be imagined, many of the dignitaries became tangled and enfolded in the flags. In some cases this was an improvement. My own flag came to rest in the outstretched hand of one of the municipal politicians and, since I was tired of carrying the heavy thing, I saw no point in moving it and he, poor man, was too embarrassed to drop it. To end the parade, there was a march past the saluting Mayor. To our embarrassment, women who had lined the road, cheered us on for our bravery during the war. Oh well, why not, for Japan was still in the fight.

About mid-October, the second phase of our training came to an end. Of the 80 Indian Army recruits who had started the program, only 49 graduated. Following the final kit inspection and graduation parade, we were officially appointed to "Officer Cadet" status and were permitted to wear the white shoulder flashes denoting the fact. We celebrated our success with a night on the town only getting back to camp the following morning in time to collect our gear and embark for the railway station. We were off to London.

LONDON

On arrival in London, we were taken to the Marylebone Staging Centre where we were to wait for our sailing orders to India. During our short stay at the Centre, we again encountered the Colonel Blimp attitude. The staff considered it proper that we continue our physical training program starting each morning with a run in Green Park. Our two Indian Army officers, who were to travel with us to India and who, for the present, were still in charge of us, arrived at a satisfactory solution. Instead of the ridiculous "run" each morning, they went through the procedure of having us march in the direction of Green Park wearing "walking out" dress (instead of shorts and singlets). Once out of sight of the Centre, they dismissed us for the day. The staff must have realized what was going on but chose to look the other way. It was amusing to march along the streets of London and have the police hold up traffic to let us pass, especially since we were not on official duty. At such moments, you couldn't help remembering the delays you had to endure when held up in a taxi to let a Guard's unit pass.

A few days after our arrival, we were sent on several days embarkation leave. Since my parents were in Canada and my brother at sea, I decided to remain in London and it turned out to be a good choice. Three other cadets also chose to stay in the city and so we remained together. The over-riding problem was money, or more precisely, the lack of it. Though I was still in receipt of a small monthly allowance this, plus my pay, was insufficient to paint the town red. We decided to stay well clear of all military establishments for obvious reasons; though we did check in at a Serviceman's Club to see what accommodation and entertainment could be had at a reasonable price. Armed with this information, we discussed our coming agenda. One of the cadets said that he wanted to attend the final Royal Academy of

Dramatic Arts examination that was in progress at the Albert Hall. Truth be told, his pretty cousin would be on stage. The rest of us, hoping that there would be other pretty "cousins" at this event, willingly agreed to join him.

We were delighted with the performance given by these budding actors and, following the final curtain, went backstage to meet the performers. As is common with actors/dancers after a show, our new acquaintances were in need of strong ammunition – the replenishing from drink - and so we accompanied this happy and lively group to the nearest pub. In the course of the evening, we explained that we were on embarkation leave prior to sailing to India and were wondering where to stay and what to do during our leave. While ideas were being tossed about, the girls congregated together to talk in whispers. When they returned, to our surprise and delight, they suggested we accompany them to their dorms, as they were sure some form of accommodation could be arranged. Now we were really intrigued. The place where they were staying had been damaged during the bombing raids but still had a graceful appearance. After some haggling between the girls and the manageress, we were found rooms. The girls had very generously agreed to double-up leaving us two vacant rooms. We gave the manageress our meal coupons and everyone seemed satisfied.

It was during the first evening meal taken in the main dining room that I noticed an aunt of mine and her two daughters at an adjoining table. I had not seen them since our annual holidays in Brittany during pre-war days when members of the Branson family would gather together at St. Servan near St. Malo. They were living in an apartment at the hotel where they were awaiting my uncle's return from overseas somewhere. The three of them looked terrible and, at first, I wasn't sure if they were my relatives. Apparently they had been captured by the Germans during the Polish campaign and had been interned. They had suffered considerably while imprisoned; their health, complexion and mental attitude reflecting their ordeal. I spent several evenings with them during which they recounted some of their traumatic experiences, such as being confined to a small, filthy cell with seven other women, sharing a bucket as the latrine. I don't recall how they managed to get to England.

Since our female acquaintances were awaiting the results of the finals and had time on their hands, they volunteered to show us around town. We went to out-of-the-way pubs for lunch, saw numerous exhibitions and art galleries and, in the evening, saw a number of shows and plays at no cost thanks to the girls getting us in through the stage door. We could not have enjoyed ourselves more had we had the funds to do so and we owed it all to those generous, agreeable and charming young women. I wrote to one of the girls for about six months. Distance may make the heart feel stronger, but it can also alienate the passion.

Though the time spent at the Maidstone training establishments had been exhausting, and in many ways frustrating, it would be incorrect to view it as having been useless. Individually, we had grown up a little and had considerably more knowledge and skill in soldiering then before, but more importantly, we had been given a view of how, and how not, to behave as officers. We were also very much aware of the dull and unglamourous life of the poor private soldier and that he should be treated as a human being rather than as a mere number or mule. My thoughts and those of my comrades were now concentrated on the forthcoming long passage to India. I, for one, was looking forward to it but many others, who had never been to sea (or out of England), weren't so keen. We all hoped for the best.

Chapter 3

Passage to India

THE day arrived for our departure. I was to ship out from Liverpool for passage to Bombay in company with forty-eight other officer cadets. During the train journey from London to Liverpool, much of the conversation centred around our impending sea journey that naturally had captured our imagination. None of us had any idea of what the living conditions on a troop ship would be like and we consoled ourselves with the thought that nothing could be worse than the conditions we had had to endure at the 13th ITC. How wrong we were. As the train pulled into the Liverpool dock area that evening, we were delighted to see several large, brightly lit ocean-going liners moored alongside the pier thinking that one of them was sure to be our troopship, but this was not to be. On leaving the train, we were marched down the deserted wharf to an ancient ten thousand ton ship that had obviously seen better days. The ship, with only dim lights showing, looked as inviting as a closed pub. This was to be our home for the next month. In single file, we nervously climbed the slippery gangway, dragging our kitbags behind us wondering if this wasn't the biggest mistake of our lives.

We were led to our mess deck along narrow alleyways, round sharp corners and up and down numerous ladders. Every footstep, every movement, created a banging sound off the ship's metal interior that seemed to reverberate throughout the deck. As we descended to the mess deck, a stench of nauseous, fetid fumes hit us like a hammer: a mixture of stale air, cooked food, engine grease and oil, body odour, urine, and the sour smell of vomit. This pong permeated the lower decks and remained for the whole journey, sometimes becoming worse and only occasionally improving depending on the weather conditions. The decks between the upper deck and the engine room were divided into open mess decks resembling the car storage space on a ferry, except that six foot tables and benches were bolted to the floor. All scuttles were closed and the glass of the portholes painted over as a blackout precaution. It was a depressing and thoroughly cheerless, though practical, environment. Our particular quarters measured 50 X 25 feet and had eight tables with benches to accommodate forty-nine men. Each man was issued a hammock and one blanket. When not in use, the hammocks were stowed at one end of the mess deck, reducing the limited space even further. Without lockers, all our gear had to be stowed in our kitbags; this was more of an inconvenience than a hardship. Most of the other eighteen hundred passengers on board were faced with the same living conditions. It was living in a sardine can.

We had nothing to eat since breakfast and there were some cadets who were looking forward to an evening meal. It seemed that we had come aboard too late for dinner and would have to do without. I have to admit, I was quite thankful for this as the thought of food was far from my mind, but those with iron stomachs went searching for the ship's canteen only to find it closed due to being in harbour.

Soon the rattle of steam winches loading cargo ceased and the ship slipped her lines and threaded her way down the Mersey. As many men possible clambered on deck to watch the diminishing view of Liverpool slowly blot out due to a downpour of rain, was soon blotted out. It was a miserable evening as the wind blew the rain stingingly into our faces. To add to the discomfort, the ship began to roll sickeningly even in the protection of the estuary. There was not much choice between getting soaked among a lot of people vomiting in a high wind and returning below where the odour churned your stomach. I remained on deck till the wet and cold sent me below where utter confusion reigned as hordes of soldiers moved about the ship looking for their respective mess deck.

On reaching my mess deck, I noticed that some intelligent fellows had used the occasion, when the area was more or less deserted, to sling their hammocks. To do this when few are about, is a simple matter, but when forty-nine try to do so simultaneously, chaos reigns. After a few hilarious moments of pushing and shoving, reason prevailed. It was obvious that not all the hammocks could be slung at the same level within the restricted space and that an alternative had to be found. We ended up with a three-tier level system with some hammocks only a couple of inches above the tables. Since those sleeping at the lower levels had the more uncomfortable positions, it was agreed that individuals would alternate levels on a weekly basis. Once settled in my hammock, it was quite comfortable, even during rough weather, though I had to put up with the closeness of the hammock above me being a few inches from my face. Anyone wanting to get in or out of a hammock created a domino effect of discord. This was even worse during rough weather. You could be halfway into the hammock and, at that precise moment, the ship might roll badly and you found yourself dumped onto the iron deck or hanging grimly with one arm caught in an upside-down hammock while your other arm caught in someone else's hammock, causing a chain reaction.

The feeding arrangements on board were very basic. The men were assigned to eat on a rotational schedule whereby three lads from our mess deck would collect food in large cannikins from the gallery and bring them back to the mess deck where the food was then distributed to each individual who would use his mess tins as plates. We ate at the tables or sitting on kitbags. During stormy weather, the ship would pitch and roll to such an extent that serving the food efficiently became an art. Occasionally a portion of food would miss the proffered mess tin and land on someone's lap or onto the deck to add to the smell and mess already there. The daily routine was boring. Up at 6 a.m., wash and shave in cold salt water, stow hammocks and get dressed, have breakfast, clean the mess deck after which you were free for the rest of the day.

The ship creaked and groaned the whole passage from Liverpool to Gibraltar. She would reach the apex of a wave, pause for breath, shake herself and slide helplessly into the next trough. For the first few days I was unable to hold down much of the food I had eaten. I spent most of the time somewhere between the open deck and the "head." The ship hardly seemed to be making any headway and the noise of the masses of men trapped in this floating prison, together with the loud metal groans, gratings and creaks of the old vessel, was disheartening.

After a couple of days I thought that I had found my sea legs; however, I continued to feel poorly. When this condition continued, I became concerned, though I put it down to lack of food and sleep, and the violence of the storm and seasickness. When nothing had changed for the better by the fourth day, I knew I was suffering from something serious and decided to check in at the sick bay. I wasn't the only one as many other cadets were complaining of stomach cramps. Before I could reach the sick bay, the intercommunication PA crackled the alert that dysentery was rapidly spreading among the passengers onboard and that those suffering from the disease were to report to the sick bay according to times set for each mess deck. When the time came for those on my mess deck to report, we were unable to get anywhere near the sick bay for the queue stretched endlessly. To add to the problem, you had to leave the queue from time to time and rush to the toilet, otherwise known as "the head," where of course, there was an even longer line up, only to return to the end of the queue at sick bay. This coming and going would occur several times until you were lucky enough to reach the head of the queue. I recall during these days of misery taking several cold, saltwater showers in an attempt to cool off. I would be only semi naked since I was too ill to get undressed. These showers did help to reduce my temperature and make me feel somewhat better though it didn't do much for my uniform. When I eventually reached the medical orderly, I was given a quantity of white powder to take there and then. Within hours, I felt much better. A bout of dysentery, no matter how short the duration, is both incapacitating, painful and soar on the posterior. When combined with the unpleasant conditions we had to endure, the overall effect is apt to affect your thinking process. I remember quite clearly looking at the lights of villages when passing close to the Portuguese coastline and being strongly tempted to jump overboard and swim ashore, but obviously did nothing other than think longingly about it.

Among those onboard was a large number of paratroopers on their way to Palestine. They were young fellows who had come straight from their training depot. These men shared the same discomforts as everyone else onboard only they took exception to the living conditions and started a mini riot. An armed guard soon had the situation in hand and moved all the rioters to F Deck, the lowest deck of the ship, where they were kept incarcerated under armed guard. The conditions on F Deck were paralyzing; twice as hot with a feverish stench with little clean air to breathe. The Executive Officer ordered us to send a small party to F Deck four times a day and report on their condition. Naturally, we were anything but pleased with this order; however, officer cadets had no standing being neither officer nor other ranks. In the event of trouble, we would be faced with a Catch 22 scenario. In discussing the matter among ourselves, we agreed with reason for the riot but not with the mode of conveying the message. To carry out the checks, we decided that two cadets were required; one to check the conditions and the other to alert the guard should there be trouble. In true democratic fashion, the largest and toughest in the group were chosen to be the first checkers. When these two cadets entered F Deck, they were appalled at the state of the men and shocked at the terrible smell. Though the detainees had only been locked up for twenty-four hours, the smell of vomit and urine was overpowering. The men were exhausted from seasickness and from the heat. The reason for our visits was explained to the men and they were asked whether they needed anything within reason. They asked for cigarettes and a means of getting some cool fresh air. We kept the Executive Officer informed of the conditions below and of the request for fresh air, the latter being immediately seen to. During each visit, we brought packets of cigarettes and chocolate bars to the men who paid us in return for favours received. In this way, we got to know many of the men and a good rapport was established that lasted until the men were disembarked. I don't know whether our reports, which may have been exaggerated here and there, made any impression on the ship's captain, but shortly before reaching Gibraltar, he allowed the detainees to return to the mess deck.

At some spot in the Bay of Biscay, the ship's engine was stopped for a while to allow the ship's surgeon to carry out an emergency operation on a member of the crew. Without some forward movement, the ship seemed to rock and twist that much more, yet the operation was a success. We had expected to stop at Gibraltar if for no other reason than to take on fresh food and fruit; however, we sailed past Gibraltar at night. Perhaps the riot aboard had something to do with this decision. On entering the Mediterranean, the weather improved considerably. Even though it was October, the sun came out occasionally and at such times the troops would sun themselves on the open decks. This change in weather helped to air-out the between deck areas, making conditions more livable. We were also made to thoroughly clean our mess decks to remove the filth that had accumulated during the voyage.

BEATING BOREDOM

The improved weather conditions brought on restlessness among the troops. There simply weren't sufficient diversions to overcome the insufferable boredom. The ship's captain suggested a sports program be organized and a Major in the Black Watch was chosen to arrange the affair. Shortly thereafter, the Major asked me whether I would assist him in this endeavour. He told me that in looking for an assistant he had studied the list of officer cadets onboard and on seeing my name, decided to see me first since he was familiar with the family name. It turned out that he knew and got on well with an uncle of mine when the two of them were serving with the British Missions in Budapest and Bucharest immediately after the war in Europe.

After some preliminary thoughts concerning the program, we decided to recruit additional assistants to help in the planning and conduct of the different events. There was no lack of volunteers and a team was soon established. We proceeded to hammer out the rules, conditions and penalties under which the contests would be conducted and, with the help of several whiskies furnished by the good Major, we arrived at an excellent program consisting of every imaginable game and sport. The program would take six days to complete and would require most of the available deck space aboard the ship. To encourage maximum participation, each mess deck was asked to produce a team for each event. The team scores were to be posted on notice boards around the ship to alert and maintain a competitive spirit. Almost all the troops onboard participated and the competitive spirit remained in spite of poor showing results by some teams. During the closing ceremony, the captain presented each member of the organizing group with a scroll expressing his thanks for a job well done.

Included in the sports program was boxing. Boxing matches were arranged for the officers as well as for the other ranks, these being separate events as decreed by army sports regulations. The ring for the officer's matches was located in the stern section of the ship and for the other ranks, a ring at the bow. I was interested in watching our team of cadets compete against the officers, and together with some other cadets, made my way to the ring. It was only after having got settled that I realized someone had switched the rings around and we were at the other ranks' ring. A well-muscled individual had entered the ring and was going through some warming up exercises prior to the start of the fight. No one seemed in a hurry to challenge him for the other team. I suggested to my companions that we move to the other boxing ring and stood up. The next thing I knew I was being manhandled to the ring accompanied by such encouraging remarks as "Watch yerslf, mate" and "Give it to 'im, Titch." My tunic was removed and gloves put on. The referee looked rather concerned; perhaps it was my startled expression that had him worried. Anyway, he asked me whether I'd ever boxed before and, on being informed that I knew the rudiments of the sport, he wished me luck. I could see that I would need more than luck.

On the sound of the bell, I approached my opponent and, without further ado, landed a very satisfactory punch on his nose. Instead of the desired effect, this brutal act of mine brought immediate retribution and the fight was on. Luckily for me, my opponent had as little experience in the art of boxing as I, consequently there was much flailing of arms and several beautiful uppercuts, but few decisive blows. At the end of the regulated three rounds, we were both exhausted. The onlookers seemed to have enjoyed the spectacle and, though no amount of blood was spilt, were appreciative of our efforts. That evening, as I was getting some fresh air on deck, a few paratroopers joined me and complimented the officer cadets for boxing with the other ranks. I did not explain the circumstances. Surprisingly, one in the group quite seriously asked me whether I needed an agent to arrange further boxing matches. This did my ego a power of good and I thanked him saying that I would consider the matter.

MINED YOURSELF

Close to Malta, we encountered a number of loose mines bobbing on the sea's surface. Volunteer sharpshooters were called upon to destroy these mines. All of the mines were eventually sunk by rifle fire except one which exploded with a tremendous noise as a lucky shot hit one of the mine's horns. It was difficult to forget those mines as we bedded down that night, especially as our mess deck was at sea level.

SUEZ CANAL

After what seemed like an eternity at sea, we arrived at the Suez Canal and proceeded to its southern end, Port Suez, where the paratroopers were disembarked. The Nile Delta and the Canal itself provided an interesting change of scenery, especially Great Bitter Lake, where several other ships were anchored waiting their turn to journey northwards. The Canal is so structured that it takes but little imagination to conjure up the immense human endeavour and engineering feat that went into its construction. As we travelled along its length, I couldn't help but think of the thousands of men who had helped build the Canal and the unpleasantness of the work considering the antiquated equipment and rampant disease.

Those troops remaining onboard were relieved to see the paratroopers disembark thinking that we would now have extra space in which to spread ourselves in anticipation of a much warmer climate ahead. To our chagrin, hundreds of Muslim Indian Army troops were embarked. These newcomers kept very much to themselves during the rest of the journey but you couldn't help bumping into them. When it came time to say their prayers, which was five times a day, they could be seen in the most odd places, in narrow passageways, under ladders and close to the lifeboats. You often had to step over them in order to pass, though this didn't seem to bother them.

As is the custom in many ports of the Middle East and Asia, visiting ships anchor to a buoy in mid-stream rather than tie up alongside a dock. This practice could be due to the lack of suitable docks or to minimize the cost of port dues. Whenever this occurs, the local merchants arrive in their boats, better known as "bum boats," to sell their wares. Merchandising is conveyed by means of a rope and basket; the product moving up the line and the money down. Starved of fresh fruit and vegetables, we welcomed such produce and made complete pigs of ourselves. For amusement, coins were thrown into the water and young native boys would dive in to collect them; they rarely missed and would come to the surface with a huge grin on their bright little faces, clutching the coin in their upturned hand.

We remained at Port Suez for the better part of a day and then proceeded down the Gulf of Suez. The passage down the Red Sea was very boring. The ship continued its slow progress at ten knots that was hardly sufficient speed to cause a breeze to counter the heat to which we had yet to become accustomed. The heat clung to the skin like shaving cream. The majority of the troops would spend the day sunbathing and playing cards on deck. Every inch of the open deck was covered with bronzed bodies. To find an ideal spot on deck, you had to get up very early in the morning and then remain in that location otherwise lose your place. I spend much of the time with an group who enjoyed playing contract bridge and one of the players kindly offered to teach me how to play. He was an excellent teacher and by the time we reached Bombay, I was able to play with some confidence. It was just as well I learned to play for the game of bridge was *de rigeur* in most officers' messes.

Once past Suez, a philosophical change occurs. The ties to Europe weaken and those to Asia begin to be felt. It's as if you have entered a completely new way of life, requiring some social and behavioural transition. As we slowed down to approach the port of Aden, where more troops were to be disembarked, we passed quite close to some barren hills and were immediately struck by the heat reflected from the shore that was like the blast from a furnace. Unfortunately, the ship chose this moment to run aground. Without a whisper of wind, the atmosphere became stifling. There were no tugs available to drag the ship off the sand bar and so we had to wait several hours for the next tide before we were once again afloat. Meanwhile, those that had to disembark were transported to shore in lighters. My father, who had been stationed at Aden in pre-war days, had thoroughly enjoyed his posting there that seemed to have consisted of sailing, swimming, tennis, parties and, from time-to-time, a little work. I could well understand his feelings but, under the prevailing conditions, I was ready to say goodbye to the place.

BOMBAY

We departed the hellish heat of Aden and once again put to sea. I had been told that the waters close to Aden abounded in sharks, yet I never saw one. I did see a pod of dolphins skimming near the bow of the ship and making torpedo motions from abeam. They are beautiful and graceful creatures that one never tires of watching. On reaching the Arabian Sea and changing course for Bombay, the ship's roll and pitch also changed, and this inclined me to miss the next meal until I became accustomed to the new gyrations. The closer we came to Bombay, the greater our impatience to arrive. We had endured an uncomfortable and very long journey, and any attraction there might have been in travelling through the sunny seas had long worn off. About a day's journey from Bombay, we became conscious of a new smell in the air; one that was coming from the land. It was the smell of India; a mélange of dust, open drains, of things rotting, all counterbalanced by the pleasing aroma of spices.

Early next morning, there was a rush to obtain the most advantageous point from which to view our first sight of India. I had read and heard a great deal about Bombay: how Vasca da Gama had landed there in 1498; how Britain had acquired the stinking swamp full of disease through Charles II's marriage to a Portuguese princess; how the original city rested on seven islands only joined by landfill and twenty miles of deep water anchorage to protect and secure it from storms. We approached the "Gateway to India" around 1 p.m. covered under a ghostly brown blanket of sky. Bombay is a coagulated bloodstream of humanity below assiduously carved Imperial palaces of buildings and cream-coloured façades of apartments that look as though they could collapse by their own misery. It is a dichotomy of the super rich and the incurable, unimaginable poor. Malabar Hill and Chowpatty Beach could easily be seen as we entered the magnificent harbour. We rounded the point and moved slowly to our berth that was in a remote part of the harbour where the normal gathering of officials and disgruntled dockhands awaited our docking. Among the officials was a grand fellow dressed in a Nehru style habit and wearing a shiny stove-pipe hat on his head. A small boy accompanied him holding a very large umbrella to shade his master from the sun. We later learned the official was the port medical officer.

The officer cadets were the last to disembark. The sense of having arrived was exhilarating. Alongside the dock was a train with a small engine, puffing importantly as if impatient to leave. This archaic model of a train was to take us to Kalyan, another staging center. As I made my way to the train, I noticed a young Englishman questioning others ahead of me who was pointing at me. When I came up to him, he stopped me and introduced himself as an employee of Grindley's Bank to whom I had been advised to write and make my number prior to leaving England.

He informed me that the bank had opened an account in my name and had taken the liberty of crediting my account with several hundred rupees to see me through until I could get myself organized. What a marvelous welcome. It was a nice gesture and excellent public relations. I banked with Grindley's throughout my stay in India and when I left, there were a few hundred rupees remaining in my account. Measure for measure.

Chapter 4

Kalyan Center and the Officers Training School, Bangalore, India

OUR initiation to India was quite different to what I had anticipated. There was no visit to Bombay to see normal Indian life, instead we entrained for the Kalyan Acclimatization Center about forty miles north-east of Bombay. The journey to Kalyan was particularly slow even by Indian standards; either the old steam engine was incapable of going faster or the engine driver was showing his displeasure at having to work during the siesta hours. Whatever the reason, our slow passage gave us plenty of opportunity to view the beauty of the natural scenery. Far less attractive was the extraordinary and sickening sight of hundreds of unfortunates suffering hideous diseases and deformities, such as elephantiasis, huge open and cancerous wounds, thyroid problems, faces and bodies caved in from some accident, armless and legless beings, who lined both sides of the railroad for several miles. They were also suffering from malnutrition and I concluded that they were derelicts, discarded by society. These poor souls all begged for bakhshish (alms), but I only had a few English coppers to offer and no food. As our first encounter with Indians, the sight was definitely off-putting and disturbed us to the extent that we fell silent until we had passed the last of these wretches. It was a rude awakening that I never forgot and throughout my stay in India, I was never able to look upon such people with indifference even though I realized that many millions suffered the same plight. I couldn't help reflecting on the comparison between my life and theirs. Why was I so lucky? It made me question God's compassion - perhaps it was justice. If one believed in reincarnation, as do all devout Hindus, could it be that these unfortunates were paying the price of a wicked previous life? If so, it was enough to make one follow a righteous path.

By mid-afternoon, we reached Kalyan; a functional, working town that a had an unkempt appearance draped in a constant thin film of dust. Every road was helmed in by shops, road stalls, buildings and apartments, reminding me of an endless regime of burnt out cigarette butts - and about as colourful. It was said that visitors staying in Kalyan would surely die of either malaria or cholera. Unless this was a test, it was a surprising destination to send new arrivals. The sun felt like a blowtorch while the heavy, almost suffocating, humidity clung like a ball and chain. Our reception and quarters were a delight at the Acclimatization Centre. The camp itself was quite small, covering about a square mile of flat, open land. There was orderliness wherever you looked and the place was spotlessly clean. The staff and servants were friendly and cheerful as well as helpful. Our quarters were spacious and comfortable, each room shared by four cadets. The beds were "charpoys," that is, four legged wooden frames with webbing of woven hemp to act as bed springs supporting a firm mattress. A mosquito net was suspended over each bed for protection against any potential disease-carrying pests and a ceiling fan helped circulate the warm air in a languid, hypnotic spin. The large windows had no glass but were protected from the sun by a roofed, wrap-around veranda. Beside each bed is a wardrobe, a desk and a chair. The Officers' Mess included several lounges, a dining room and a number of games rooms. The high ceilings and ceiling fans maintained a tolerable temperature. The Centre also had a large swimming pool and a number of sports fields.

TIME WILL TELL

Time has no feelings. Time is just a fleeting moment. Life is just a speck of time. It was a Kalyan that I first became acquainted with the pace at which things were done. In India, speed is not so important as it is in the West. An Indian would think: "By running, we may reach an unimportant destination a little earlier. We cannot reach the ultimate goal one second in advance." If I asked an Indian how far it was to some specific place, he would simply turn to the sun for an answer and respond: "When the sun is so high, you will be there." There is no way to hurry an Indian; the reason for hurrying is not understood. Other than small children playing, you rarely saw anyone in the act of running. As you became better acquainted with this perspective, so you revised your own judgment in completing any task. As a general rule, I multiplied the time I thought it would take me to do the job by three to arrive at the approximate time it would take an Indian to do the same job.

DAILY ROUTINES

It was also in Kalyan that I first met with the "Indian servant." Each room with its four cadets was assigned one servant. Our particular servant was a Muslim from the Punjab who was familiar with our needs and looked after us well. Despite our limited Urdu and his slight grasp of English, we were nevertheless able to communicate adequately. I discovered it is often the case with servants in the East to have a number of helpers, these being members of his family or friends. The helpers clean the room, do the dhobi (laundry), iron the clothes and do such other chores as requested by the Sah'b. The women, who did the laundry, would take the dirty clothes to the nearest creek or river, soak and soap the clothes and then slap each item against a rock, then rinse them and continue this process until the item was thoroughly clean. This routine got the dirt out; however, in so doing, it broke all the buttons on the shirts and smashed the brass buttons on the tunics. The solution to this problem was to buy shirts and tunics without buttons but with openings into which buttons placed on a separate cloth tape could be inserted later. So as to keep their shape, shirts, trousers and tunics were starched and then ironed. A man would iron the clothes and starch them by filling his mouth with starchy water and spray of mouthful of this mixture onto the cloth. The result was quite satisfactory though at times some residue of betel nut he had been chewing, would fly out and leave its distinctive stain.

At the Officers' Mess, uniformed servants who were not only smartly turned out, but were also efficient and courteous, served meals and drinks to the officers. It was the custom in Messes throughout India to sign chits rather than pay cash for such things as drinks and cigarettes; the account would be paid at the end of the month or prior to leaving the establishment. The camp was kept clean by the "Untouchables," members of the Dalit, the lowest of all castes. Some say these people were the original native Indians; however, they were shunned and dismissed by the other Indian classes for their lack of education, leaving them without opportunities and extremely poor. Few understood Urdu and intercommunication was rarely possible. They could be seen throughout the camp in their torn and bedraggled garments, sweeping the dust with their brooms made from twigs. Their most important task was that of cleaning the latrines that had no running water.

The daily routine was leisurely so formal parades were kept to a minimum. Following breakfast, we were given classroom instructions on hygiene, anti-malaria precautions and the dos-and-don'ts in India. Time was allotted for our continuing study of Urdu, a munchi (teacher) being available to help those in need of further assistance. During mid-morning and the afternoon, officers were required to participate in some form of sport, be it soccer, cross-country runs, volleyball, or basketball. It was only when we underwent our first game of soccer that we realized how weak we had become. Most of us were underweight as a result of our sea journey, but the sports program, that started with easy exercises and gradually built up to a full 1½ hour regime, together with the excellent meals served, soon had us all fit again. It was interesting to note that old Public School rivalries crept to the surface during many of the sports and was further encouraged by the staff. Though I felt less affected by the heat than others, I found playing in such conditions took me hours to recover.

During our first day at Kalyan, we were issued with khaki bush uniforms. These were made of lightweight cotton, resembling aertex shirts. What a pleasure it was to wear this material rather than our heavy battledress. The local darzi (tailor) soon had us looking smart. He was a delightful old rogue whose shop was the doorstep of the entrance to his house where he would work, squatting cross-legged behind his Singer sewing machine surrounded by piles of different material, balls of thread and clothing awaiting his attention. None of us had any civilian clothes and he came to our rescue, making us casual wear the pattern chosen from an English catalogue. The camp staff was all from the British Army. The Commandant was a jovial giant with a complexion well seasoned by sun and booze. He wore the biggest and most starched Bermuda shorts I have ever seen and resembled a man with a barrel around his middle. He explained that they provided air where it was most needed. The instructors were all Sergeants and it was they who were responsible for putting us through the acclimatization program.

During the week in which we remained at Kalyan, it was recommended that we make an effort to orient ourselves with Indian culture. Since the town itself was out-of-bounds, our only recourse was to use the many Indians within the camp to study the ways in which they lived and behaved. Very apparent was the caste system that prevented certain castes from addressing lower castes. With time, I came to appreciate that caste meant order and that the caste system undoubtedly made for an ordered society that, in theory, guaranteed peace between the different sections of the population. The objection to the system lies in the opportunities it grants for the upper castes while oppressing the lower ones, but it has stood the test of time. It isn't so very different to the class system in England, except in India, should you be rejected by your own caste, those in the lower castes won't tolerate you and you end up at the bottom of the heap.

I soon became accustomed to not shaking hands when meeting. It was not the Indian habit to do so. They prefer to salaam as a gesture of greeting. The salaam or "nameste" as it is called, is by pressing the palms of your hands together (in prayer fashion) and holding the hands up to the face or chest while bowing the head slightly. The nameste is usually accompanied by a few polite felicitations. By the end of the week, we were bored with the program and ever more impatient to be at the Officers Training School, and so when it came time to embark for Bangalore, there were no regrets.

JOURNEY TO BANGALORE

Bangalore was some six hundred miles to the south and situated in the centre of Mysore Province. The trip took us a day and a half and was tiring as the seats were wooden benches with no cushions and there were no sleeping births. That night, we slept where we could: on the luggage racks, on piled kitbags, and on the wooden benches. It was an uncomfortable night. On the journey, the train would stop at different railway stations making certain that it arrived at the bigger stations at around meal times. There were separate dining rooms for Europeans, Muslims and Hindus, the division being strictly adhered to. The conductor would hold the train until all the Europeans had finished their meal, even if this meant delaying the train. The meals were adequate but the sanitary conditions at the dining cars were shoddy. As we had been warned not to drink the water, we drank "chai" (tea) instead that was served scalding hot with or without Nestlés condensed milk, for no milk was safe to drink. To be on the safe side, you ordered eggs and bread for breakfast and chicken or curry for the other meals. You were never sure as to what you were about to eat when offered chicken. It could be any similar sized bird disguised as chicken.

The journey to Bangalore took us first south-eastwards to the city of Hyderabad and then southwards to Bangalore, hence we missed the magnificence of the Western Ghats that reached a height of 8,600 feet. We crossed the Deccan Plateau in Central India that is the most densely populated area in India maybe because of the less harsh climate where the plateau is 2,500 feet above sea level. The sub-continent is interlaced with rivers that flow East or West. During much of the year, the majority of waterways are dry and only the major rivers provide sufficient water for irrigation purposes. At the time, few dams had been built and irrigation for farmland was mainly accomplished through digging artesian wells. We occasionally saw examples of the local irrigation system; a bullock or donkey, usually blindfolded, would be seen plodding in ceaseless circles around a well, drawing water that steadily flowed along prepared channels, or wherever the stream existed. A boy would ladle the water into the irrigation ditch using his foot to manoeuvre the five-foot long ladle rather than using his hand.

There was a constant flow of traffic on the roadways while peasants worked the fields either side of the road. Since few tarmac roads existed, people used either dried-up riverbeds or dirt tracks that must have been used for centuries. The mode of travel identified the financial status of the individual; for example, the very poor walked, those that could afford it, rode a bicycle, a few men rode donkeys – a somewhat awkward mode of transportation; however, status is everything. The more affluent travelled in a box-like contraption with cushions inside on which to lie and with curtains to provide privacy and would be carried by two or four servants. It reminded me of the Romans. Anyone who drew attention to their status also drew young urchins who ran alongside the "chaise" making ribald comments until chased away or too tired to continue the nagging. I never saw a woman on the back of a donkey instead a woman walked either behind her man or on her own (or with a group of women). They seemed to be the workhorses in each family for it was they who carried the baggage and, as often as not, a small child astraddle on one hip. The baggage was carried balanced on the woman's head. Maybe this balancing act is the reason why Indian women have such a graceful bearing when walking. Also seen on these routes was the heavy wooden country carts pulled by one or more bullocks or cows. The solid wooden wheels creaked noisily and since the cart had no springs, the ride must have been hard and disagreeable. The wheels and axels were seldom greased, the tale being that should the bullocks pulling the cart stop the lack of noise would automatically wake up the driver. To keep the bullocks moving, the driver would occasionally ram his big toe up the beast's rear – it certainly got things moving.

At the time, the foundation of the Indian economy was agricultural from which seventy-five percent of the people drew their livelihood. Increasing numbers of peasants were moving to the cities seeking better opportunities as industries and commerce grew; nonetheless, the countryside was alive with humanity. Whether it was in the fields or mending roads, it was the women and children who were to be seen toiling from dawn to dusk. The women wore their saris drawn skin-tight between their legs and tucked up behind. The man in charge, if around, would be sitting in the shade, dozing. Occasionally, one would see a farmer lying on his charpoy, guarding his precious stand of barley or whatever, against fire, thieves, or wild animals. The villages appeared very poor, dirty and dried-up. There was a constant smell of human and animal excrement that permeated the air. This smell was attributed to the lack of toilet facilities and that cow dung was used as cooking fuel. What astonished me most was the obvious ease with which natives carried heavy loads. They all looked emaciated yet they worked long hours with hardly a pause, a task often requiring them to work bent over that must lead to permanent physical damage. Their stamina was extraordinary. And to think, all this work for a meager salary. The impression it left on me was how cheap a life can be.

During the early afternoon of the second day, the train pulled into Bangalore, the capital of Mysore. We were welcomed by a junior officer accompanied by several British Army non-commissioned officers. It was immediately obvious that the Officers Training School was going to be a differently run establishment to those we had recently been to in England. I was surprised at the apparent lack of huge throngs of people in the outskirts and suburbs of the city; on-the-other-hand, the downtown area was teeming with humanity. As we passed the market, I noted that the clock over the main building was out of order and some humourist, most likely a cadet, had hung across it's face a piece of cardboard inscribed upon it the word, "SICK."

I was taken aback to observe no main gate or quarter guard at the entrance to the Officers Training School (OTS). The campus was a few miles outside Bangalore and was like entering a university campus. The layout had been cleverly planned to combine functional needs with the enormous amount of space available producing a general effect of peacefulness – something uncommon in a military camp. Scattered throughout the area were small umbrella shaped trees that provided essential shade, and moreover, was pleasing to the eye. The large parade square was centre stage with the administration buildings and Messes surrounding it. Further back and separate to each other, were the different company lines. I could also see several sports fields and a large swimming pool in the distance. Having toured the campus, the buses took us to our accommodations for new cadet contingents. This was a small compound the size of a village with numerous bungalows. Each bungalow had three or four rooms and each room had been furnished as a bed-sitting room for two people. My room companion was the same person with whom I had shared a double-tiered bunk at the depot in Maidstone. Washing facilities and toilets were situated some fifty yards away and surrounded by a bamboo fence for privacy. From the giggles and whispers coming from the other side of the fence, it was obvious that several cheeky little Indian children found delight in peeking through it to view the antics of those engaged in their ablutions. The Indian adults, on-the-other-hand, respected our privacy and kept their distance.

An Indian servant attended each bungalow. Ours was a small, dark and sinful man, generally unkempt and what teeth he had left, protruded from his mouth at different angles. He was a cheerful but thoroughly irreparable rascal who always got the best of us when any bartering occurred. He catered to our needs without over exerting himself, most of the work being done by members of his large family. His main value lay in his understanding of camp rules and how we could circumvent these without being caught. We later learned that he had once been charged with murdering a man and that insufficient evidence had saved him from the noose. Having unpacked my few belongings,

I then spent several minutes inspecting the immediate area. I was conscious of the many Indians within the lines and was concerned at leaving my belongings unguarded, for the bungalow door had no lock. I mentioned this problem to the servant who assured me that nothing would be taken from the bungalow as the servants and the members of their families acted as guards for the whole area. During my whole stay at the OTS, I had nothing stolen thanks to the honesty of the servants.

There were columns of trees everywhere in the compound that helped shade us from the sun; however, these same trees also housed the ubiquitous tree rat that looked and moved like a squirrel. These rats would raid the bungalows looking for food and even found their way into the drawers of desks and cabinets. I once placed an unripe pineapple in a draw to ripen slowly only to find the rats had got to it leaving a filthy mess and smell. These inquisitive rodents were covered in fleas that were known to carry the dreaded bubonic plague. Consequently, enchanting as they might appear, the rats were anything but welcome and much time was wasted chasing them out of the bungalows. If and when a rat was cornered, you made sure to keep at arms' length. A ground hockey stick was a useful weapon with which to put down such vermin. Once a rat was killed, you immediately had the body burned ensuring this was carried out some distance from the bungalow. Other intruders were the lizards, different types of ants, and the occasional scorpion and snake. The little lizards would dart about the walls and ceiling, killing mosquitoes, not that this made much difference to the huge invasion of them. We once had the visit of a small furry creature the size of a small monkey with huge eyes and almost human hands and feet. It was quite tame and didn't mind being handled. It moved very slowly and could attach itself to the walls where it spent its time catching and eating insects. It was a beautiful animal and since it made no noise or mess, we didn't disturb it.

Each training company had its own Mess. These Messes were large white washed brick buildings with a tiled sloping roof and surrounded by a deep tropical veranda. The Messes were similar to the ones at Kalyan but even better furnished. Each Mess could accommodate about a hundred cadets. The officers and NCOs had their own respective Messes and so the cadets ran their own shop. The Messes were organized and run on similar lines to those in an Indian Army unit thereby conditioning us to the rules and regulations we were later to encounter. Cadets took turns at being the President and Secretary of the Mess and at chairing the different Mess Committees. Formal Mess Dinners were held once a month to which senior officers were invited to liven the occasion. Following the dinner, the normal Mess games were played requiring an abundant consumption of refreshments (whatever was available). Since alcohol was expensive and our pay relatively insignificant, most cadets refrained from drinking anything alcoholic except on special occasions. A Mess Havildar (Sergeant) kept a "bar record" on individual's intake and was reviewed by the Mess Committee each month to check on any cadet living beyond his means. In the Card Room, an open record book was kept in which was recorded each individual's gambling losses and gains during bridge and poker matches. Cadets never used cash in the Mess except to pay for their Mess bills. All barchits, purchases in camp and gambling debts and gains were accounted for on your monthly Mess bill that had to be paid within forty-eight hours of receipt.

At that time, each training company had a small number of Indian cadets who shared the facilities of the Mess with the British cadets. Unaccustomed as I was to the way the Indians ate their food (using no utensils), I was caught by surprise the first time I shared a table with some Sikh cadets. They ate with their fingers rather than with a knife and fork. There was nothing wrong with that, but the accompanying sucking noises distracted me from polite conversation. I was unwilling to follow the maxim: "When in Rome do as the Romans do," since the result seemed so unnecessarily messy, but some time later, I did eat curry enveloped in a chipatee and enjoyed the experience without making a mess of my clothes.

All the cadets with whom I had travelled from England were posted to "B" Company. To bring the Company up to strength, half a dozen Sikh cadets and thirty British cadets were also posted to the Company, the latter being cadets who had failed to qualify the year before due to reasons of health. This influx of new blood in our midst to some extent broke up the cohesion we had achieved in England. We requested our new Company Commander to keep us grouped in the same two platoons such as we had been in England. I believe he agreed to this because the majority of the new British cadets had changed their minds about joining the Indian Army and opted for the British Army. These other British cadets formed the third platoon while the six Sikhs were evenly distributed between our two platoons. During the months we were at the OTS, neither the members of the third platoon or the Sikh cadets made much of an effort to assimilate with our group. I suppose it was difficult for them to do so in that they had come from different training units and had not had the opportunity to get to know each other well; furthermore, they were not as fit as us nor as well trained. Nevertheless, relationships between the members of the three platoons were quite good and, generally speaking, it was a happy company.

Our Company Commander, Major Dottiwala, was a Parsee. He was a tall, well-built, good-looking man and sophisticated in his ways. He had been educated in England and had attended Sandhurst. He was an avid sportsman and ran his Company as he would have captained a cricket or rugby team; that is, he allowed the cadets enough leeway to exercise their imagination and energetic enthusiasm while treating with firmness those who abused his good heartedness. He also had a sense of humour that he often demonstrated even on formal occasions. For example, several weeks later, I was up before him on a charge for having ridden a bicycle at night without lights. I had run into a particularly unpleasant Staff Captain who had placed me on report. On the charge being read out, Major Dottiwala asked me the name of the Captain and on being informed, bellowed with laughter, explaining to me that I was the umpteenth cadet to be charged for that offence by that same officer. I was given a caution and told not to run into the fellow again.

When time or the occasion permitted, Major Dottiwala would recount stories about the Parsees. The Parsees fled Persia when the Arabs conquered that region in the 8th century. They brought to India their Zoroaster religion that describes earth, water, and fire as too sacred to be defiled. While explaining this religion, he told us of the manner in which Parsees deal with their dead. Instead of burying their dead, the bodies are place on platforms that are left on the flat roofs of temples, such as Bombay's famed Tower of Silence, where they are plucked and eventually consumed by vultures. As he jokingly remarked, this may seem reasonable to the Parsee; however, during flight, vultures have been known to drop pieces of human cadaver. On one occasion, a finger was dropped into someone's prize-winning geranium to the distress of some white memsah'bs, especially when such an incident occurred during a garden party.

In addition to the Company Commander were two young Captains, one of whom was the Second-in-Command and the other, the Training Officer. There were no Platoon Commanders, instead, officer cadets were assigned as Senior Under Officer and Junior Under Officer for a period of one week on a rotational basis. The senior appointment acted as the senior cadet and was in general charge of all cadets in the Company whereas the Junior Under Officers acted as temporary Platoon Commanders. These Under Officers were authorized to place a cadet on report for disobeying an order, but I don't recall such an action ever occurring. We did what we were told though the Sikh Cadets took unkindly to being ordered about by a "white" cadet. During field exercises other cadets were appointed as Second-in-Command and as Platoon Commanders for the duration of the exercise. In this way, all had the opportunity to exercise our command and leadership potential under the eagle eyes of our immediate superiors, instructors, or umpires.

The instructors, who were all from the British Army, taught us weapon handling and how to drive different types of wheeled vehicles. They also acted as safety officers during live field firing exercises. Unlike the conditions at Maidstone, fraternizing between officer cadets and NCOs was frowned upon. An NCO addresses an officer cadet as "Sir" even when delivering a well deserved blistering reproof as for example: "Sir. If you would be so kind as to point your bloody rifle down the bloody range, chances are that we shall all come out alive from this bloody exercise. Sir." Though the climate at Bangalore was hot, but not unpleasantly so, any forced exertion still resulted in copious perspiration. To save our more formal uniforms from endless washings, we were issued with several pairs of loose-fitting coveralls made of strong cotton material that had two deep pockets for carrying things. Under the coveralls, you wore underpants and a singlet and, on the outside, you wore a web-belt on which to hang equipment. When first issued, these coveralls were black in colour, but with time in the sun and countless washings, these would fade to off-white. So as not to appear a "new boy," you had your servant bleach the black overalls at the earliest opportunity. Thanks to these airy coveralls, the agony of being victim to prickly heat was reduced considerably. Prickly heat was a rash produced by sweat and could impair a man's performance should the rash develop into large and very uncomfortable boils. The sensation was like an itch that you could never reach.

A Bicycle Built for None

As a means of getting about the huge camp, each cadet was issued a bicycle with an oil-wick lamp. These bikes were anything but new and would be in constant need of repair. Each bike had a registration number painted on its crossbar; nevertheless, this didn't stop anyone from exchanging wheels with someone else's should he have a puncture or worse. The oil lamp was a farce. When travelling at night, any slight breeze would extinguish the light. You had to travel at a snails pace with your hand in front of the lamp to prevent it from blowing out. As you can imagine, it reduced visibility to nil. This fun also applied in rain resulting in a sodden wick that couldn't be relit. The answer was to find other means of transport at night or carry a torch. I came to the conclusion that the lit lamp was not so much for the benefit of the rider but as a warning to others to get out of the way of the bicycle's approach. When we were required to ride as a group, the formation taken up and the words of command were similar to those used by the old cavalry regiments, for example: "In file...Prepare to mount...Mount...Fooorward." Given the antiquity and unhappy conditions of most of the bicycles, any group activity was prone to disaster. Collisions would ensue as riders slammed into each other, back-ended each other, or ran off the road into a ditch.

The training area most frequented was on Agram Plain, several miles from the camp. Agram Plain was a huge, flat, cement-hard, red-sanded piece of land with hardly a tree or bush to be seen. It was the Devil's Anvil. There was no shade anywhere and those undergoing training on that plain, baked under the scorching sun. The annual monsoon rains over the years had carved deep nullahs (ruts or narrow channels) that interlaced the plain. These channels were a curse since they caused unevenness and could easily sprain or break someone's ankle. It was on this piece of ground that we were taught how to drive different types of vehicles. From ground view, you couldn't see the nullahs until you were almost on top of them.

For field exercises, we would go much further afield where the terrain was better suited for such purposes. The terrain normally chosen was one with hills and bush jungle, and for good measure, the occasional village. Surrounding each village would be some form of agricultural field. To compensate the villagers for any damage to their crops, each peasant was paid a day's wages, even when there were no crops to harvest. Each time we passed through a village, all its inhabitants would be outside waving small Union Jacks and praying for a day's wage. The children would follow us shouting their heads off for bakhshish or sweets. We tried to steer clear of all villages, most of them being very small, very poor and very primitive. It was the appalling stench that really drove us away. When required to move through a village, you did so as quickly as possible. I remember clearly one particular incident during an exercise that required my section to clear a village. As we were carrying out the operation, we came upon a beautiful young woman, one who had not been ravaged by small pox. As we came nearer, she beckoned us to her hut; her gestures leaving no doubt as to her intentions. In our confusion and regret at having to miss the anticipated pleasure of her company, we ignored several other huts that were occupied by the "Enemy." For this mistake, the exercise umpire pronounced us "dead." Had we accepted the young woman's invitation, we might have ended up as real casualties.

During the first four weeks at the OTS, the daily routine and training was not overly demanding. Reveillé was at 6 a.m., breakfast was from 6:45 a.m. to 7:30 a.m. and the first parade at 7:45 a.m. The training day, if not on a field exercise, ended at 5 p.m. We spent one hour each morning polishing up our Urdu and a further two hours was devoted to studying such matters as man-management, current affairs, Indian Army customs, solving administrative problems and learning the Acts of Military Discipline as they applied to the Indian Army. Most afternoons were taken up with practicing battle drills, learning advanced weapon handling or how to drive various vehicles. On Saturday mornings, the whole School would parade for the Commandant. We played sport on Saturday afternoons and Sunday was free.

LESSONS FROM MUNCHIS

Probably the most enjoyable training period was that concerned with learning Urdu. I grew up in a French- and English-speaking household. My parents (French mother and English father) each spoke over five languages and I developed an aptitude for languages. At the OTS, these language classes were divided into small groups of five or six cadets, each group having an Indian munchi (teacher). These delightful teachers were either Hindus or Muslim. The classes were held under the shade of a tree and the attitude of all concerned was very relaxed. We spent half the time on improving our proficiency in Urdu and the other half questioning the munchi about the state of affairs in India, the political situation, the way of life in an Indian family, and the reaction of Indians to partition and to Jai Hind ("long live India") that we interpreted as "Quit India." I believe the munchis enjoyed these sessions as much as we for it gave them the opportunity to sound-off and in doing so, they would embroider their answers with some hair-raising stories. They were as uncertain of the future as we were. Muslims, Hindus, Sikhs, Parsees, etc, had lived in relative harmony under British rule, but there was fear that this would not last once the British left, especially to the minority groups located in the large cities. They saw independence as a natural follow up to British rule but were uncertain as to its timing; they wanted no unnecessary delay, but neither did they wish a hasty political decision. They saw problems for any new Indian government in its being able to please all the different "peoples" of India. The Hindus were generally against partition whereas the Muslims could see no other way. None foresaw the horrendous slaughter that took place in 1947 involving the massacre of hundreds of thousands of Hindus and Muslims. Like any optimist, independence meant prosperity, but that the industrial revolution, that had already started, would cause considerable social unrest. Though they were all for independence, they emphasized that most Indians were not particularly concerned as to how India was governed. I took this to mean that the life of the average Indian, who was a poor peasant, would not be greatly affected no matter who governed and so their interest was naturally low and dubious.

The Indian is a polite individual and when discussing the British in India with the munchis, this trait was very apparent. In commenting on British politicians, they tried to disguise their contempt so as not to hurt our feelings. They openly admired the British Indian civil servant. "Let him take 12 annas in the rupee," said the munchi, "and leave me four and I shall we well content, but the British civil servant will not take even one anna and I too get nothing." It was the custom in India for the one at the top to get a large share of the extra profits resulting from any business transaction. This still applies today. Both the British and Indian businessman followed this practice but not the British Indian civil servant. The munchis praised them for their integrity and their devotion to their responsibilities. They expressed no fear of these officers since the latter were not politically inclined and, in general, were friendly towards Indians. They considered that the standard of conduct set by the Indian Civil Service and by the British Indian Army officers, would be the goal that their Indian counterparts would endeavour to attain.

Interestingly, our Parsee Company Commander supported much of what the munchis had said. He considered that one of the top priorities of a new Indian government should be to re-move the current denial of human dignity and aspirations of the less fortunate Indians, including the Untouchables. He felt very strongly about removing the power of the Princes, but could see no way of preventing or even diminishing the habit of nepotism, patronage, corruption, and graft practiced by most officials since, after all, this was a way of life in India. He was concerned how-ever at the unrest in the country that was fermenting at an alarm-ing rate due in part to the distribution of disinformation by par-ties interested in partition and by the lack of a clear government policy regarding the timing of independence. He was convinced that violence would erupt prior to such policy being established and that this violence would likely start in the Punjab – India's Middle-East. He cautioned us to be prepared for action in aid to the civil powers and wished us luck in such circumstances. On reflection, I'm surprised that we received no training in the roll of aid to the civil powers (i.e. in helping to suppress rioters.)

PIAT (PRACTICALLY ILL-ADVISED TECHNOLOGY)

The first four weeks of training took the form of on-the-job training. We continued weapon training from where we had left off at Maidstone and were introduced to new weapons. One of these was the PIAT, a form of bazooka that was considered far more lethal to our own men than to the enemy. It had to be cocked from the prone position and this took some strength when doing so lying down. Standing up under fire was discour-aged. When the weapon misfired, which was often, you had to use a bayonet to prod the live missile loose, hoping it wouldn't explode in the process - an absolutely unreliable device. The kick when firing the weapon was considerable and if the weapon was held incorrectly or loosely, the butt of the weapon would whack the soldier straight in the face causing much work for the medics and dental officer. Not surprisingly, there were few volunteers to be PIAT man in the section.

Whereas in England, after firing on a range, you simply tidied up the place and left. In India, all personnel were required to dig up the spent lead bullets and collect the empty brass casings. The retrieved lead was then weighed to ensure that it had all been dug up and collected. The reason for this monotonous routine was that the Indians would deviously wait for the soldiers to leave the range and collect the lead and brass casings and use it to make new ammunition, some of which might be directed at us. This necessary practice was executed throughout India and woe it be the officer-in-charge who returned a "short weight."

Vehicles

At home, I had learned to drive a two-stroke motorcycle with some confidence, but had yet to drive a car and so I was delighted to hear that we were to be taught to drive all types of wheeled- and track-vehicles. The 2½-ton truck is a magnificent form of transportation. It has excellent manoeuvrability and is easy to handle while sitting high up in the cabin thus giving exceptional observational advantage of traffic ahead. Driving the ¾-ton truck required your full concentration as it had enormous power and could suddenly use its own initiative. The Jeep was a toy and lots of fun to drive, but you had to watch taking a corner too sharply for it had a tendency to flip. The armoured tracked vehicles were quite a different story. To turn a tracked vehicle, you simply slowed down and eased, instead of spinning, around a corner. The danger of riding with a student driver was the probability of his jamming on the brakes when told to stop instead of first slowing down with the result that the vehicle would come to an abrupt stop while the passengers would continue the forward motion only to be stopped by some immovable solid object.

Driving a powerful motorcycle was the most exciting experience; a vicarious thrill. It was somewhat like riding a horse. You found yourself sitting upon a powerful object which, when in motion, gave you the feeling that if you didn't control it, you would be left behind. When it came my turn to drive one of these monsters, I lost all sense of caution and, feeling the exhilaration of speed, went tearing around the vast plain. In my excitement, I failed to see a deep nullah. I suddenly jammed on the brakes and managed to avoid flipping head-over-heels. On my way back to the instructor's class, I realized all was not as it should be. I had torn the rear tire to shreds. As punishment, I was to mend the tire. I spent a miserable lunch hour, out in the blazing sun, trying to patch the outer tire with an inadequate repair kit. Nothing would hold it together and I gave up. I was later made to pay for a new tire; even so, it was worth it.

That afternoon, another cadet provided us with a few interesting moments. When his turn came to drive the motorcycle, he clambered aboard without first taking the bike off its stand. He kicked the started violently, revved the throttle ready to shoot ahead and was stumped to remain stationary. A surreptitious shove in the back by a friend set things in motion but rather too rapidly. The machine roared off with the cadet grimly hanging on but unable to control its direction. It circumvented in every direction: at a group of cadets, at the instructor, at a group parading; everyone scattering in all directions. I was anticipating the rider to fly through buildings, coming out with an officer on the handlebars. The scene reminded me of a hilarious scene from the Keystone Cops. Luckily the engine stalled before any serious damage was done.

THE MULE: WHAT AN ASS

Members of the Indian Army have a special place in their hearts for the mule. During the Burmese campaign, the mule was used to carry all the heavy equipment, weapons and stores. Under fire, it remained surprisingly calm. It would cross obstacles such as rivers, jungle, thickets and climb steep hills and mountains without complaint. Each mule had a sepoy (soldier) skinner or handler who became the mule's best friend. The OTS had a mule park containing about twenty well-fed and well-cared for mules. Cadets were required to know how to handle these animals since each infantry unit had a mule transport sub-unit. We were taught how to clean and feed the animal and how to load it correctly. In the cleaning of the animal, no part was forgotten and this could be tricky as you got around to the rear end. The mules were accustomed to being handled by cadets and generally tolerated people, but they would occasionally amuse themselves with tricks of their own. Once when brushing a mule's flank, it leant against me, pressing me to the wall. When I pushed it off me, it stepped on my foot, looked round the nipped me on the arm. When cleaning a mule's backside, it was apt to get excited and would suddenly kick out with its rear legs. Since a mule's kick could easily cave in a man's chest, you made doubly sure to stand well back. I used a broom-stick.

TRAINING MANEOUVERS

For our battle drill training, much of the instruction and activity took place in the hills surrounding Bangalore. The valleys would be covered in gorse or spiky bush and as you moved away from the dry riverbeds to climb the hills, you would enter dense thickets and a jungle of trees, bush and undergrowth. The tops of the hills were usually bald with not a tree to provide any sort of shade from the burning sun. In the days of World War I and II, the infantry always tried to secure the highest ground during a battle and so, naturally, the objectives in most of our exercises would be on top of one of these ghastly hills. By the time you arrived at the objective, you were completely soaked in sweat, scarred by numerous scratches and utterly exhausted. A 'break' would be announced in the form of lunch. We would queue up and get a mess tin filled with hot tea and a hearty main course with the addition of sliced bread and dessert. But there was a catch to all this goodness. Flying overhead were hundreds of kitty hawks that would swoop down and carry off whatever they could grab from your mess tins as you moved away from the serving tables. Since your hands were full, you couldn't do much to protect your rations. I lost much of my lunch from these attacks. The next day at lunch, I brought a cloth and covered my food with it as it proved an effective deterrent.

During one of these lunch breaks on the crest of a hill, I noticed a small tunga (man-made lake), about three miles away in the direction we were to take. I wasn't the only one to see such an inviting temptation and it was agreed, by those I was with, that regardless of the battle drills that afternoon, we would go for a swim before nightfall. In due course we arrived at the water's edge to find a few Indian women washing their bullocks in the centre of the lake. The water stank and was more mud and floating flotsam than clear water, but this didn't prevent us from throwing ourselves in. The water felt so refreshing. I know I must have swallowed at least a couple of mouthfuls of this foul water while the numerous scratches on my body were exposed to it as well. Oddly enough, I suffered no ill effects from this experience possibly due to the many immunizations I had received. Let's just say, I was fortunate.

Prior to returning to our quarters following whatever form of training we had undergone, we were required to pass through the "assault course," often with battle order and rifle. The course was about one hundred yards long and consisted of various types of obstacles each one being a challenge to either your initiative or strength. The obstacles included: nine foot long pits, six foot deep that you had to jump across; long underground crawl tunnels that twisted in all directions and were only wide enough to hold a body in the prone position; a six foot smooth surfaced wall that had to be scaled; various barbed-wire fenced sections that you had to cross while thunderflashes exploded nearby; narrow logs over open (or water-filled) pits that you were required to run across; scaffolding to climb and narrow beams nine feet above ground to cross over; nets twenty feet high to climb, then cross over a thick branch and come down on the other side of the net; a 30 foot high wire to wrap yourself around to cross hand-over-hand over a pit; and finally, a booby-trapped demolished house to get through. With practice, most of us became quite expert at getting through the course and platoons would challenge each other to see who could complete it the fastest. I don't believe any of us actually enjoyed going through the course as several parts of it were quite dangerous and falls were a common occurrence. On top of everything else, I suffer from claustrophobia and vertigo, consequently I had trouble at the long underground tunnels and crossing the high-wire act without feeling dizzy or weak at the knees. Although I had my share of spills, I came away with only a bruised knee (and ego). Only the Sikhs had real trouble in completing the course. Though we showed them the tricks in getting over or through the more difficult obstacles, they never learned and became increasingly embarrassed at their own clumsiness and incapacity to accomplish what the "white" cadets could do.

Following the short initiation phase of our training, we were moved from the bungalow compound to the main accommodation area where each cadet was given a large, well furnished room. An Indian servant was assigned four pairs of cadets. The Sikh cadets also moved into the same building compound much to our annoyance for they rose very early in the morning to wash their hair, afterwards they would loudly sing their prayers, making sleep impossible. I was sure they sang that loudly simply to torment us. From here on, our training consisted mainly of tactical field exercises, some of which lasted several days. A new element was introduced to liven things up. The exercise enemy was a company of Sikhs who used live ammunition when firing with small arms weapons. They had been through the different exercises we were about to undertake and knew exactly where to fire without inflicting any injuries to the cadets (or so we were told). This live firing also added a sense of reality to the drills.

LIVING WITH PESTS

I had arrived at the OTS in December when the climate was pleasantly hot but this soon changed to a constant and uncomfortable humidity as April approached only to get hotter by the day until the onset of the monsoon in June. As each month passed, a new species of insect or reptile would appear. The mosquitoes were a perpetual irritant and present in the millions, covering everything in sight. In the evenings, when working or writing in my room, I would put on two pairs of socks, tuck the bottom of my trouser legs into the socks, put on a dressing gown and place a towel over my head as a means of protection against this flying petulance. As you can imagine, writing became a labour of love. When getting into bed, I would take a torch with me and, having secured the mosquito net, I would carry out a careful search for any insect that had managed to get inside the net or bed. I would try to make sure that no leg, foot, hand or arm was touching the net before falling asleep for fear of being bitten and contracting malaria.

The busy ants would eat or carry away any food that you might have left in the room. They could be seen trekking across the floor or walls in one huge and continuous procession. There was no way I could get rid of the ants and so you accepted them as fellow roommates. The flying ants would arrive in the thousands at the beginning of the monsoon. There were so many that the walls of the room and the mosquito net were black with them. Thankfully, this only lasted a few days after which they died. During the monsoon, you had to be ready for frogs in the showers and other dark humid areas, and the frogs brought in the snakes, most being poisonous, like the cobra. Scorpions were always about but not in large numbers. I once threw a boot at a large black scorpion and though I hit it, the creature seemed unfazed. As a precaution, when getting dressed you made certain to turn your boots upside down and shake them to regurgitate any unwanted tenants out. When about to pour water from your large earthenware jug, you first checked to see what visitors might be lurking inside. All this became second nature.

To relieve the strain of the training program, we played sport such as ground hockey and cricket. A large swimming pool was available and I recall swimming in it on Christmas Day. One would assume this as a luxury, but even the water was too warm and considerable sand that had drifted into the pool clung to your body causing itchiness in the heat. From time-to-time, we would have a game of ground hockey with an Indian Unit. Once I played against a team from a local Indian Army Women's Auxiliary unit. They were ferocious players, using their sticks to batter our legs. The umpire, a man, was too scared to call any foul shots or penalties for unsporting behaviour, consequently, the women easily won. I must admit, they knew how to play the game very well. It was while playing hockey that I got blood poisoning. I had slipped during a game and had scraped my finger on the ground. Thinking nothing of it, I continued to play and had a shower after the match. That night, a Saturday evening when all the facilities were closed on campus, my finger became swollen like a small potato, and progressed to my horror, to infect my hand and arm with the similar inflationary results, throbbing painfully. After searching for help in the middle of the night and disturbing a number of people who weren't especially sympathetic, I at last found the duty medical orderly sound asleep in someone else's room. He wasn't enthusiastic about treating me, but after some forced words, took me to the dispensary where he made several attempts at removing the poison by lancing my finger with a needle. After unsuccessful attempts making my finger look like a pin-cushion, I had had enough. He tried cold compresses, hot compresses and other equally useless ideas. Since he had exhausted all possible solutions, he told me to return in the morning. I asked to see the doctor but was told I was out of order. By the time I got back to my room, I was feeling definitely unwell and had become feverish. In an attempt to relieve the pain and swelling, I placed my arm up to the elbow in a large jug of cool water. I felt immediate relief as jets of puss and blood squirted from the pin-prick holes in my skin, slowly dancing and turning the water crimson. The relief was beyond imagination. I continued this treatment all night and by morning was feeling much better. I went to see the doctor who reprimanded my foolish actions informing me that I could have burst open my finger when I placed it in the cool water. His unsympathetic comments annoyed me and I retorted that I had looked for the duty doctor the night before and had he been on duty, it wouldn't have been an issue. Instead, I had little alternative but to act on my own – end of conversation. It took a week of medical care before I was able to return to normal duties. The doctor did tell me about an excellent ointment that seemed to cure most ailments called Zambuc. To this day, Zambuc, a bottle of antiseptic Dettol and aspirin is usually an ideal first aid kit.

Our life at the OTS was not totally devoted to work and sport. We were given ample time to relax in the evenings and on Sunday. At Christmas and New Year's Eve, we decorated the Mess with coloured streamers and arranged to have the appropriate meals served as if we were in England. Thanks to the rich mother of one of the cadets, we had plum pudding from Fortnums and Mason. With plenty of wine and spirits to drown any sorrow we might have felt at not being at home, we thoroughly enjoyed ourselves. The New Year's Eve festivities were somewhat more rowdy, as we visited other Messes and it became a rather drunken affair. The next day, we had to pay our respects to the Commandant and different staff personnel, this being accompanied by more drinks and very little to eat. Most of us spent the afternoon recovering in our rooms (or by the toilets).

Though we had been together as a group for a number of months, there were few long lasting friendships made. I'm not sure as to the reason why other than the fact that we were constantly on the go, and you rarely worked alongside the same individual for a long enough period to get to know him really well. We were all friendly towards each other and helped each other whenever possible. Those with the same sense of humour would gang together when going to town, but this was more for the sake of company than friendship. The fact that we were competing against each other may have been the cause, plus a certain arms length attitude generated each time we were appointed as a temporary commander. There were four or five cadets whom I liked but on leaving the OTS, I never thought to keep in touch with them. On being commissioned, I only once met a past acquaintance from OTS and that was in Bombay as I was about to leave India.

Bangalore Entertainment

The citizens of Bangalore treated us with tolerance and understanding, realizing that the School brought in considerable revenue to the city and its shopkeepers. Among the city's population were many Madrasis who I found to be the most pleasant of all the Indian peoples I encountered. They were jovial, polite, had a good sense of humour, and were pleasant to deal with. When buying any form of merchandise, negotiating the price was a must and normally both parties came away feeling satisfied. The city itself offered plenty of entertainment, most of which was inexpensive. The Gymkhana Club, a very swank club, was out of bounds to cadets – most of us couldn't have afforded to belong anyway.

There were several cinemas in town but only one cinema featured English films. Few Indians went to the English cinema, preferring their own brand of films that were ebullient musical romances. The English cinema was quite different to the others in that it had two-seater sofas covered in white cotton that provided ample space for yourself and a female companion. There were several intermissions during the program. Each intermission being announced by the tinkling of a bell a minute before the lights went on and the side doors opened to let in air. The theatre was held outdoors and could either be a pantomime depicting the story of some God or Goddess of which there are many, or a dance by a number of very graceful young men and women. In both cases, the audience would watch transfixed until the performance was over. Sometimes these performances would last for hours. I attended several of these types of shows and was fascinated by the different interpretations given to the same story.

As regards to restaurants, there were hundreds of them: Hindu, Muslim, Chinese, you name it, but many of these were out of bounds to us due to our colour and religion. There were several that catered to both whites and Indians and these were frequented. The restaurants were anything but clean. On picking up a fork you could usually tell what the previous patron had eaten and the tablecloth was always stained with all manner of food and other things. This, together with the hubbub of noise and the smell of curry and spices, gave character and colour to the place. I invariably ordered curry as being the safest thing to eat and by far the most appetizing. In Mysore, it was impossible to be served anything but hell-fire curry that invariably left you bathed in perspiration, different shades of purple and having gas or diarrhea for the next couple of days.

Long hair was taboo and most cadets had their hair cut every week. I went once to the School barber and came away almost bald. From there on, I had my hair cut in town and what an experience that was. Whether I asked for a short haircut or a trim, it mattered little to the barber for there was only one style available – the Army short cut. Actually it was neat and kept your head cool. The difference in having your hair cut in town was the face massage that left you feeling utterly refreshed and relaxed even if you did come away stinking of coconut oil. Should you also ask the barber for a shave, you immediately became his lifelong friend for he thoroughly enjoyed demonstrating his dexterity with the cutthroat razor. The barber would demonstrate, a theatrical performance, his skill and the sharpness of the blade by splitting a hair. He completed this after his third attempt. The barber covered my face with scalding hot towels that seemed to shrink my head to a red pulp. This torture lasted but a moment and on removing the towels, a scented soap was lathered over most of my face. The barber pinched my nose resulting in a nasal-sounding mating call. I tried breathing through my mouth but only swallowed a mouth full of shaving foam. After the scraping was over, a further face massage was administered that brought me back to normal except for a sensation of a sting here and there where the barber's razor nicked the skin. Before leaving, I tipped the barber outrageously simply for having come through the experience alive.

Every time I hear the tune *Rum and Coca Cola*, I am reminded of the main shopping street in Bangalore. One of the shops would constantly play the tune very loudly. Oddly enough, instead of getting on my nerves, it had the opposite effect. It not only blended in with the cacophonous noise of the downtown commotion, it seemed to reduce the jarring noise made by the people, traffic, and animals. When I think back to those times, I can still hear the old gramophone playing that familiar piece.

To get to town, you had several options: you could walk the several miles, ride in a tonga or rickshaw, or use a bicycle. Walking took time and brought on perspiration. Cycling should have been the fastest means of transportation but the bikes were unreliable, they didn't have lights, and there was also the concern of having the bicycle stolen. The small, light two-wheeled tonga pulled by a horse was a pleasant means of travel. It had bells attached to the canopy that tinkled and jingled as the vehicle moved and this, together with the not unpleasant smell of horse, old leather, burning oil and the driver's lunch, produced a feeling of well being in a somewhat romantic setting. The chances that you might catch a few fleas, for the passenger seat was used as the driver's sleeping quarters, did nothing to reduce the charm of the ride. The rickshaw provided an excellent way of seeing the passing scenery when downtown as it shielded you from the ever present and cloying beggars, and for the price of a few piase, afforded you a good view of one of the liveliest spectacles on earth – the bazaar where you could rub elbows in narrow lanes of shops, tea houses, and food vendors. Here, everything is accentuated: the colour, the noise and the flurry of activity. The rickshaw wallah (coolie), was normally wrapped in his own filth of stained rags and, when toiling as the locomotive, was usually asleep in the back of his rickshaw, the shafts on the ground.

From time-to-time, cadets would take the rickshaw wallah's place and race against each other insisting that the worried coolie sit in the back and watch the proceedings. The coolie was naturally concerned that damage would befall his precious vehicle, his only means of livelihood. I think that we all felt sorry for these coolies who were skeletal and seemed to suffer from some form of respiratory disease or other and, consequently, generally gave them a generous tip.

In India, as throughout the tropics, darkness of evening comes suddenly like a blanket being set. At one point, it is broad daylight and a few minutes later, the sun has died and you find yourself in total darkness. The evenings at Bangalore were always warm to hot depending on the season. As darkness descended, I began to feel hemmed in; the heat seemed to increase and my senses became more acute. The tinkling of the tonga's bells was a delightful background sound as it harmonized with the jingling of the metal rings heard on women's ankles and wrists; and the smell of cooking mixed with the smell of the myriad oil lamps, cooked up a soothing effect that dispelled any discomfort caused by the heat. Among the many traits that I came to admire of the Indians was their wisdom and understanding. I came across it so often that I no longer noticed it. Such understanding was not only adhere to adults, children also seemed to possess this maturity. As an example of this, I received a "Dear John" letter from a girlfriend in England that naturally bruised my pride and I must have looked dejected as I slowly walked away from the Camp Post Office deep in thought. I suddenly realized that a young Indian boy was holding my hand. When I looked down, he perkily inquired "Thik hai?" is everything all right? I assured him that everything was fine and thanked him for his solicitude by giving him a few annas. Taking the money, he salaamed and with a laugh, skipped away. I don't know where he came from but his kindness and understanding brightened my day.

While living a hand-to-mouth sort of existence while on exercises, I started to think about getting myself a suitable camp kit since it seemed that I would be spending a good deal of my service life outdoors. I was unsuccessful in finding what I wanted at the local sporting goods shops, and so I designed a kit that could be rolled up into a one-piece package. I took the design to a leather merchant in town and explained my needs. He checked the package, nodded and agreed to do the job at a reasonable price. The main part of the kit was a bed in the form of a large box-shaped contraption about 6'X3'X4', the base of which was thick leather with strong mosquito netting and the top, another but thinner sheet of leather held up by folding metal struts. Inside was a mattress and, lining one wall, were cotton pockets to hold personal belongings. From the Quartermaster's store, I bought a canvas bath, washbasin and chair, all of which could be folded and contained in the bedroll. It took a strong man to carry this kit and thankfully, I never had to do so myself. When I got to my regiment, I found the kit to be comfortable and very practical. During an exercise or operation that required sleeping in the open, I would, on awakening, wriggle about to warn such creatures as had harboured the night close by for warmth, the Master was getting up. Once the rustling had quieted down, it was safe to step out. I retained this kit throughout my service in the Indian and British armies and brought it home when I eventually left the army. For some reason or other, my mother gave the kit away which was a pity since I would gladly have used it when later serving with the Canadian Army.

About a month before our term at the OTS came to an end, each cadet was required to fill out a form identifying the Corps and regiment he wished to join. You were asked to name three regiments in order of preference. Should you pass the final exams with an overall rating of "A", you would likely be sent to a Headquarters. A "B" rating would almost certainly get you the regiment of your choice, whereas lower ratings would guarantee you nothing special. An "F" rating was a failure for which you would be returned to England "for disposal." I had already decided that the Gurkhas would best suit my purpose as some of the regiments might transfer to the British Army on the declaration of India's independence. My choice of regiment was the 7th Gurkha Rifles as 7 was supposedly my lucky number and, rather stupidly, I showed my second and third preferences as being the same regiment. Had I chosen three different regiments, I might have conceivably remained in the Gurkhas for many years.

The final written and practical examinations took place during early June. The written and language test plus the practical weapon and driving tests took three days. On the fourth day, you were advised as to whether you had passed all the tests. Of the forty-nine cadets who had come to India with me, fifteen failed the written, practical and language tests; these unfortunate fellows were returned to England. I found the written and practical tests quite easy but had some trouble with the language examination though I managed to scrape through. During one of the practical tests, I was required to assemble a mortar. I made a complete balls-up of it. Having put the weapons together, I forgot to lock it in place with the clamp provided. As I stepped away from what I had thought to be a good piece of work, I gave the mortar a tap as if to say "that wasn't difficult." To my embarrassment, the whole contraption fell apart to the ground. The instructor was very kind and only deducted a few points for my having forgotten the clamp.

THE EXERCISE TEST

The monsoon that had hit Bangalore the week before the field tests, was still in its fullness and the country was threaded with stray streams and emerging bodies of water. Only the locals knew where road tracks were and these seemed to alter from one week to the next, as sometimes the sun would dry up water routes while the rain produced new ones. Many of the smaller bridges had been swept away causing further confusion. All this made our problems, during the four-day field exercise, that much more difficult. The field exercise took place about fifty miles from Bangalore. The main part of the exercise took the form of a withdrawal while under constant pressure from the enemy. This meant preparing defensive and alternative defensive positions, carrying out counter attacks, establishing lay-back patrols and withdrawing when so ordered. A Sikh Company acted as the enemy and, to give the exercise some reality, live small arms ammunition was used by these Sikhs (preferably to shoot above us). On reaching the exercise area, we set up camp on a small hill. Tents had been left in place since the last group of cadets had passed through. As we unrolled the marquees, we found hundreds of small scorpions in the folds of the tents. There was a lot of stamping in our efforts to kill as many of these pests as possible, but many escaped. We were somewhat restless as we slept that night. We had our briefing by the Chief Umpire early the next morning. He explained how the exercise was to be conducted and how our performance would be marked. As during normal training, cadets were appointed to different command positions and these were rotated at least twice a day unless someone made a mess of things, at which time, he was pronounced a casualty and someone else took his place. You were marked on: your initiative, leadership, and command skills, problem solving skill, your cooperation with others, teamwork ability, your field craft and tactical skill, and on your staying power or stamina.

The first test consisted of preparing defensive positions. As we started to dig-in, the rain started and soon all the newly dug trenches were full of muddy water and the surrounding area became an oozy mess of steaming, stinking, slippery mud. We were taking a break to eat a cold and soggy lunch, when suddenly the "enemy attacked us." From that moment on, we had no respite; we ate and slept where and when we could. We withdrew in staggered formation with one group giving covering fire while another moved back to the alternative defensive position. Naturally, the trenches in this new position were also full of water. The steaming water and mud from the trenches made visibility almost impossible. We spent the first night in our wet dugouts and on patrol. What with constant enemy activities to keep us alert and the wetness of our surroundings, there was no sleep that night.

My first temporary command was as a platoon commander and my mission was to destroy a stong enemy outpost located in a village close by. I carried out a quick reconnaissance, made a plan and gave my orders to my section commanders. As we entered the village, the enemy opened fire. Amidst cheers from the villagers and encouragement from the umpires, we ran for the nearest cover. I remember running like a madman to a large hole in the middle of the village and jumped into it. Imagine my horror at seeing the two ends of a snake writhing on either side of my boot. Without a pause – I doubt that my right foot even touched the ground – I was out of that hole in a split second. The closest umpire noticing this abnormal behaviour immediately pronounced me "dead." Having explained to him that I could have been a real casualty and after his confirming that there was a snake in the pit, he agreed to let me continue the exercise. Sometime later, one of the cadets in my group was judged a casualty that was unable to walk. This meant we had to carry the fellow back to our lines. We made a stretcher using two rifles and a poncho that was the best we could do and since the casualty was tall, his feet dragged on the ground. He had been hoping for a rest, but in fact, had an uncomfortable ride as, quite often, he was rudely tipped off the crib accidentally-on-purpose whenever the stretcher bearers wanted a breather.

My next and last command was as the commander of the layback patrol. I was given four men and two wireless sets. We were to hide ourselves when the company withdrew and wait until the enemy had also passed us by and then, from behind the enemy line, report on their movement. We managed to escape detection and had much fun dashing about behind the enemy positions. After about six hours of this activity, and as darkness was about to envelope us, I was ordered to rejoin the company at a given position. I knew where the enemy was and had a rough idea as to where my company was located and decided that the safest route was to swing around both groups and come up behind the company. It was just as well that I chose this route because the company was forced to withdraw from its position once again and I luckily met the company halfway to its new position. Had I cut through the enemy lines, I would never have found the company, especially at night.

After a particularly exhausting day, our Parsee Company Commander, who was the Exercise Director, called a halt to the exercise. We were grateful for this show of humanity thinking that we would have time for a hot meal, a good wash and a few hours sleep. Our dear Company Commander had other ideas. The headman of one of the villages we had recently passed through had informed the Major that a black panther was in their area causing great consternation. Since the Major was passionately fond of shooting big game, he had decided to hunt the panther, using the cadets as beaters, hence the break in the exercise. We never did see or even hear the panther – hardly surprising in the dark – but we went through the motions of sweeping the area and returned to the campsite in time to have a quick hot supper. At least the Company Commander was happy and the panther hadn't been harmed, and we got a little rest, so, in all, it wasn't a complete waste of time. The exercise started up again as soon as we had finished our meal.

At the close of the exercise at the end of the fourth day, the Exercise Director and Chief Umpire debriefed us on how we had done. They seemed pleased enough that gave us much needed encouragement. We lost another three cadets during this test. One was a real casualty who had broken his hip and the other two just didn't have the stamina to finish the exercise. Following the briefing, we had an excellent hot meal accompanied by several bottles of cool beer. As a finale, we were faced with a "night forced march" of twenty-five miles, the route being along roads and cross-country. The goal was to reach Bangalore before 6 a.m. and then march directly to the OTS. If the group was late in arriving in town, it was made to march to attention through the town accompanied by the OTS band, making lots of noise thus announcing to all and sundry out failure to meet the deadline.

In a last desperate fling, the monsoon that had been rumbling in the distance, fell upon us with fury. The ground, already slippery with mud, soon became a quagmire making it difficult to trace the roadway. My poncho did nothing to keep me dry and I was soaked to the bone. Moreover, the heat generated under the poncho simply added to the heavy perspiration. Marching at a forced march pace, that is at five miles an hour, and in such cumbersome conditions, resulted in painful sores caused by the friction of equipment and wet clothing constantly rubbing against your wet skin. I placed a large towel round my neck and under my backpack and managed to get some relief.

To keep some form of control, we marched in platoon formations formed up in three ranks or columns of route. Every fifteen minutes those in the lead would fall-in at the back – it was the three fellows in the lead who controlled the pace of the march. Every so often, we would double-march to ease our leg muscles. I found that I could doze without difficulty while on the march. We would stop for five minutes on the hour to rest with our feet up; you left your equipment on as it was too tiring to take it off. Our march went well except for one particularly bad area where we had to climb a high bald hill, the surface of which had become as slippery as ice. Torrents of water were cascading down the hill as we tried to climb it, and occasionally, a man would slip and be carried down by the force of the water to the bottom of the hill. On his way down, he would bounce into others who either fell and followed him down or pushed him away. It was useless trying to help the individual in difficulty for you would simply find yourself in the same predicament. Though thoroughly exhausted, I couldn't help but chuckle on seeing someone else being trundled head over heels down the hill. We eventually arrived at Bangalore well before the appointed time and marched on to the OTS. Rather than give the command "Halt," to which we would have been incapable of complying having become marching robots, the officer-in-charge sensibly called out "Halt in your own time – Halt." On that command, we broke ranks and continued for a few paces until able to stop.

On being dismissed, I headed directly for my quarters. Discovery is a delightful process, but rediscovery is even better. Few can have enjoyed the luxury of a hot bath, clean clothes and a hearty breakfast more than us. Though the exercise we had been through was attended by anxiety, exhaustion and some minor suffering, we emerged from it with a feeling of pride and accomplishment. We were given the rest of the day to rest and clean up our equipment. I slept for about twelve hours and, on awakening, felt terrible as if I had been drugged. The feeling soon wore off and, apart from having caught a cold, felt fit enough. Surprisingly, it took me several months to rid myself of this cold.

GRADUATION

The Passing-Out Parade (graduation) took place a few days after our return from the field exercise test. All the cadets at the OTS were on parade with the two companies graduating in the front facing the saluting base. After the normal parade drills, the two companies marched past the saluting base in extended line and at the slow march, a particularly difficult execution. A friend of mine took a photograph of our company as it was passing the saluting base. Every man, foot and rifle were in exact line; it was quite extraordinary, not even the Guards could have done better. The visiting General presented the Sword of Honour to one of the original "Indian Army Contingent" cadets. Following the parade, we received our commission scrolls and were informed as to which regiment we were to join. Wonder of wonders, I had been accepted by the 7th Gurkha Rifles. I immediately went to the regimental tailor in town to purchase a uniform with all the necessary regalia.

We had organized a luncheon for the day following the graduation parade. It was amusing to see one's friends dressed in their regimental outfits and wearing one "pip" denoting the rank of Second Lieutenant. A number of guests had been invited, including our Company officers who we continued to call "Sir" out of habit. Our Parsee Company Commander had a few words to say that brought us down to earth. He underlined that our days as trainees were over; that the days during which we were constantly under someone else's care and protection, were a thing of the past. From now on, he said, we were on our own and accountable for all our actions. A sobering thought.

I was granted seven days leave plus travelling time to get to the 7th Gurkha Rifle Regimental Center. I had planned on spending part of my leave in Ceylon and part in Secunderabad where my father had some friends, but the monsoon discouraged me from following up this itinerary. I managed to persuade two other acquaintances to accompany me as far as Lahore. The three of us spent a couple of days in Bangalore before moving further afield. We decided that what we needed most was female company and therefore, made our way to the Gymkhana Club where, after careful scrutiny, we decided that one particular family suited our needs. The mother and father had, whom we assumed, two quite attractive daughters. It took little effort to get introduced and, as it turned out, we were lucky in our choice. Though the daughters were several years older, they were good company and, together with one of their female friends, willingly went along with our invitations to go swimming, dancing, picnicking and even sailing. The latter could hardly be called sailing. We borrowed three Irrawaddy canoes from an Indian unit situated close to a large man-made lake. These canoes had outriggers and carried a small sail. When caught by the wind, that followed all monsoons, the wind would inflate the sail and the canoe would hurtle across the lake. Since the wind always came from the same direction, it would drive the canoes to one end of the lake consisting of large boulders and rocks. The only way to stop was to lower the sail and jump overboard. We returned the canoes somewhat worse for wear.

On the way to our respective units, we decided to visit Madras, Hyderebad, Benares, and New Delhi, judging that the eighteen hundred mile journey would take us five days. From Lahore on I would continue on my own. Unlike our previous train journeys, we were to travel in comfort having reserved a first class compartment.

Chapter 5

To the Himalayas
1946

TRAVELLING long distances at that time was by way of the train. Compartments were divided into First-Class for Europeans and affluent Indians and Third-Class for everyone else. The "Mail" trains (Delhi to Calcutta or Bombay) were punctual, well maintained and comfortable and were the only ones with air-conditioning. As a First-Class passenger, you had or shared a compartment that was about the size of half the carriage. The compartment contained four bunks: the top two being retractable, a table plus an additional room, being a bathroom. Air conditioning was provided by means of vents and windows. All the windows had three means of protection: glass, slats and shutters to keep out the dust, the sun and the unwanted. At the rear of the coach was a separate space for the servants and the cooking necessities. All very civilized. On-the-other-hand, travelling Third-Class was hectic. Due to overcrowding, passengers had to squeeze into small wooden-seated carriages, often using the windows to enter the train rather than the doors. Passengers had to sleep upright as there was no room to lie down. Fruit skins littered the floor as well as blood red spit from "pan" (a mixture of betel, areca nut, and lime). The stench was overpowering, similar to an open sewer from animal feces and urine, rotting food, and unwashed humans in a breathless and confined space. Those unable to afford a train ticket would stowaway. They would travel on the roof of the coaches or hang on to the sides of the train. As the train slowed to a standstill, the stowaways would creep off the roof and jump onto the opposite line as not to be caught by the railway officials. When the train pulled out again, the stowaways attempted to climb back on. The stowaways had to take precautions against being brushed off the roof or swept off the side of the train from another train; a regular occurrence that drew little sympathy from the other passengers.

I was travelling with two companions on our way from Bangalore to Palampur, located in the foothills of the Himalayas. We shared a comfortable compartment and watched the train rattle through the suburbs of Bangalore. Within a short period of time, we were climbing through Eastern Ghats. This range of hills is not as impressive as the Western Ghats; nevertheless, on reaching the eastern side, we had a magnificent panoramic view of the plains reaching out to the Coromandel Coast, but the monsoon rains blotted out any further view, altering the landscape into a smeared watercolour painting.

The train stopped regularly at stations to refill the engine with water. Each stop took about an hour to complete the refilling process. These stoppages gave the passengers the chance to stretch their legs and the local merchants a chance to sell their wares. "Chai, chai" would cry the tea-vendors as they weaved about the platform with steaming pots of tea. "What you like? Nuts, roast gram, bananas, oranges, betel-nut, sweets?" urged the vendors. "Very good price." All these goods were waved under my nose in keen competition. Every vendor fought like demons for my patronage. If I hesitated for a second, I found myself landed with nuts instead of fruit or vice versa. Each station platform was cluttered with humanity either sitting *en famille* on top of their few belongings or asleep, wrapped up in cotton shawls. At meal times, you ate at the station restaurant following which you could take a stroll up and down the platform. It was during one such stroll that, on reaching the end of the platform, my companions and I noticed a body lying between the rails. We advanced to take a closer look and found the remains of an old man whose legs and one arm had been severed as a result of falling under the wheels of a train. The man was barely alive. On locating the stationmaster, we reported our find. The official, showing no emotion or interest, shrugged and stated: "He is lying there since one hour time." When we asked him what he intended to do about the matter, he replied: "What is there to do, Sah'b? It is in God's hands." Life is cheap in India.

Branson Square

When we arrived at Madras, the "Gateway to Southern India," I mentioned to my companions that I was interested in seeing Branson Square, named after a relation of mine, James
Charles Branson, a successful barrister-at-law. My companions
were willing to accompany me and so we hired a tonga and asked
to be taken to what I imagined was going to be a magnificent
square. The driver, a Madrasi the colour of polished mahogany,
looked puzzled and had to ask directions from the other drivers
who seemed equally nonplussed. I mentioned that I thought it
was near the harbour and for the driver ask directions once
there. We passed down wide avenues lined with trees and soon
got to the harbour that had literally been torn from the surf-
beaten shore on which generations of British had landed in
Masulipatam craft, or on occasion, did not land and were
drowned in the attempt. At last we came to Branson Square. It
turned out to be a disappointingly small and grubby place surrounded by dilapidated grey buildings with windows like hollow
eye-sockets. The others had a good laugh at my embarrassment,
but I was able to overcome this with the knowledge that a relative had been sufficiently appreciated to warrant the naming of a
square in his honour. It might have been a beautiful square in his
time.

The Nizam

We still had a few hours to waste before our train continued
its journey and so we decided to stroll about the center of the
city that was of interest, as it had been a key British settlement in
the early days of the Raj. Our interest quickly lagged when besieged by beggars, the sick, the disfigured, and the lame pleading
for alms. I could never accustom myself to being touched by
such people and always shrank away in horror; at the same time,
I couldn't ignore their plight and misery, and thus a feeling of
guilt would overcome me, leaving me uncertain as to how I
should behave towards these retched souls. Once back on the

train, we continued our journey until we reached Hyderabad, the large Muslim city and capital of the state of Telangana. The Nizam was understood to be by far the best ruler of any state of India and one of the most forward thinking. In many respects, the city reflected this with electricity throughout much of the town, clean streets, and an air of prosperity that was lacking in most other cities. The Nizam had his own army that was well equipped and, as we passing the palace, neatly turned out.

While at Hyderabad, we noticed that the citizens were differently dressed to the natives of Madras. The Muslims appeared more colourful in their dress, especially their headdress. I was to learn that the Indians dress according to rigid social divisions that may change from state to state. The dress code matters much more in India than it does in the West. Clothes spoke a language that was understood by all. For the uninitiated, such as ourselves, it was at first very confusing and we had to beware of not offending anyone by inadvertently addressing the individual without due regard to their status. From Hyderabad, we travelled to Benares, crossing the Deccan and the Satpura Range that is a low mountainous region covered in scrub, much of it being wasteland. In the countryside, you could see peasants trudging to the nearest town to sell their wares. They might have to travel many miles just to sell a few tomatoes and chilies. It seemed that the trouble of getting to town bore little relation to the profit to be made from the sale. On-the-other-hand, the journey cost nothing and the handful of chapattis they ate on the way was most likely made of wheat from their own fields. I later learned that the bania or shopkeeper had a monopoly on trade and exploited the poor peasant, making a profit as high as two hundred percent. There was always the possibility of making a bargain by side-stepping the bania back home, but this was tantamount to cutting one's own throat. Bullock carts were a constant sight. In the rural areas you would be lucky to see one car to a hundred carts and, as the greater part of India is agriculture, there are bullocks aplenty – fifty million at the time. Indians discuss the merits of the different breeds of bullocks the way we discuss the different models of cars.

GANGA-MA

Hindus revere the river Ganges so much that they have at least a hundred different names for it: The Destroyer of Poverty, The Mother of all that Lives and Moves, and Ganga-Ma (Mother Ganges) to name a few. Hindus believe that they must make at least one pilgrimage to the Ganges in their lifetime. When they grow old, or if they fall ill, they believe that if they can reach Benares, then they are certain to end up in paradise when they die. The people bathe here to wash away all sins and corruptions. There is an uncanny and unusual quality about the Ganges that seem less toxic than from the waters of the Juma or Hooghly rivers that are more heavily polluted. If you drink from these rivers, you will be in a critical, if not fatal, state within days. For some reason, the Ganges is different. Thousands of tons of filth and sewage pour into it every day. You'll see people defecating and urinating its banks as the bloated and putrefying bodies of drowned dogs, cats and even humans float past yet, every morning at dawn, thousands of believers are there on those same banks drinking the water, washing themselves, and cleaning their teeth in it. These believers have true faith; they believe because they want to believe.

There are numerous ghats at Benares, one for each week of the year and some more holy than others. Here, corpses wrapped in white sheets, feet protruding at unnatural angles, lie in a row while boys toil to arrange pyramids of sandalwood and old men manoeuvre the still. The concealed bodies are leveraged onto pyres, a funeral pile for burning corpses. Mourners chant and wail as the old man touches the pyres with a burning splint. There is a sudden flare and a roar as the petrol on the wood ignites. Other men rake mounds of hot ash and move unburned portions of corpses over the burning embers. Sometimes a body sits upright as though still alive, when the sudden fierce heat tightens the dead stomach muscles. Boys beat the corpse down flat with poles. Though our short visit to Benares was intensely interesting, I was glad to leave as I found the whole atmosphere morbid and weird. The pungent smell of burnt cadavers permeated our clothes and we brought this terrible odour into our train coach. Once the train was in motion, we hung our outer clothes out of the window to air and this was sufficient to brings things to normal.

Our reason for wanting to see Old Delhi was mainly to visit the Red Fort at sundown as we had heard that it was a magnificent spectacle. We arrived at the city during mid-afternoon and headed immediately for its center. Once you move off the main boulevards, you begin to see the real Indian side of the city. Vendors set up shops on the pavement where they hawk an incredible variety of wares and services. There are men who, for a price, will clean your ears with a sliver of bamboo dipped in sweet oil or cut your toenails; others will write a letter on a typewriter for the illiterate or cut your hair. There is the inevitable Indian sitting cross-legged with his Singer sewing machine in front of him and a stack of material to mend. There are also young Sikhs ready to tell your fortune and display numerous letters of recommendation, none of which a banker would approve. At one stage, we were so pestered by one of these fortune-tellers that I eventually gave in. To increase my interest, the fortune-teller starts by telling you the major events of your past. In my case, the young lad was astonishingly accurate, including some quite abnormal events. What he foretold was also correct, even to my spending time in the Middle East prior to returning to England.

Traffic congestion had to compete for space with oxen- and human-drawn carts, the ubiquitous "holy" cow and thousands of cyclists and pedestrians, all rubbing elbows together. The scene was thick with noise, dust and smell that never seemed to dissipate until sundown. We entered one house at the invitation of the owner who warned us to tread carefully because the floor was not safe. There were enormous rats meandering through the place that, at first, I mistook for cats. The owner had let rooms as offices, and in one room was a lawyer with his clerks, surrounded by bundles of deeds tied up with string and turning yellow with age. I asked him how long did he retain such documents and was informed that he had yet to destroy any. He guaranteed that he could find any document in a matter of minutes. I didn't doubt him.

We spent the rest of the afternoon sightseeing and ended up at a large park where we rested awhile. We soon realized that something unusual was happening and that the place was starting to get crowded. An old Indian gentleman spotted us and politely suggested that we make ourselves scarce for there was to be a demonstration that afternoon against something the government had or had not done. At that time, it was possible for a trained agitator to gather a large crowd numbering in the thousands and bring the people to an agitated and rebellious fervour within a short period of time. We withdrew from the park without drawing undue attention. On the way to the Red Fort, we passed the 17th century domed Jami Masjid, the world's greatest mosque. I could but wonder at the history associated with the mosque and felt rather ignorant at not knowing more about the city, its people, buildings and overall historic significance. As we arrived at the Red Fort, the sun was setting and we witnessed the most splendid sight; the red sandstone was illuminated in a burning bronze-red glow from the sinking sun. While admiring the extraordinary scene, I tried to imagine what secrets had been dreamed up behind those immense, sun-drenched walls.

It was getting late, so we returned to the station where our coolie was waiting for us with all our luggage that had been entrusted to him – something that you would never dream of doing in the Middle East. He had been guarding our things for several hours. We had simply taken his number shown on a brass plate attached to his pugri (turban), told him when we would be back and what train we would be taking. He had moved the baggage and placed it at the door to our reserve compartment. Given the very little that was paid the coolie, it always amazed me that such people didn't steal the baggage and then disappear, yet I had nothing stolen when travelling in India.

On reaching Lahore, I bade farewell to my companions. They were going East and I, to the North. With several hours to spare, I took my soiled clothes to a local laundry and had them washed, starched and pressed for I was certain not to have the time for such a necessity prior to reaching my destination. The journey from Lahore to Pathankot was particularly interesting as I was entering the Punjab – the agricultural garden of India – and thus much more fertile than the countryside I had previously passed through. The track skirted the Sind Desert and finally entered the wild mountainous land of the Himalayan foothills. Once well into the foothills, I had to change trains owing to the narrower gauge of the mountain line. At frequent points, the slow moving mountain train had to stop to take on water. I got off for a better view of the exceptional panoramic vista. There, several thousand feet below was a river flowing strongly but looking like a silver thread while across the valley, the scene was shrouded in mist from a cascading waterfall. It is sights like this that fill me with awe.

While the train made its tortuous way through the mountain ranges, tea was served on a continuous basis. Young boys balancing tea trays with all the trappings, would walk beside the puffing train as it laboured up the mountain; the boys' paces often being faster than that of the train. They would cry out "Chai, chai" and, if interested, I would get a cup of piping hot tea with lemon, sugar and biscuits for a mere bagatelle. The slow pace of the train produced no breeze and the temperature inside the compartment was decidedly hot; any exertion, however slight, instantly resulted in floods of perspiration. I decided to walk beside the train and found it much more entertaining and cooler. Several passengers joined me and as we strolled up the mountain, conversed in attempted languages.

On reading numerous books about India, I rarely came across any comment honouring the men who designed, planned and built the miracle of the railway system that linked the different Indian states. The enormous distance that had to be crossed in Northern India alone were immeasurable engineering achievements. I must admit that on sighting a railway bridge that had to be crossed, it being several thousand feet above a river, I would not be thinking about the engineering feat but rather of the chances of the train crossing the gap safely. Towards 7 p.m., the train pulled into Pathankot, a fair sized mountain town. Progress from thereon was to be by ¾-ton truck. I was glad to find a Gurkha driver and a rifleman awaiting my arrival; however, on my arrival the clouds opened up and unleashed a fierce, torrential thunderstorm. For the most part, we drove to the Regimental Centre in silence. These Northern roads seem almost porous and aren't equipped to uphold monsoon rains, especially in the mountains. It is common for landslides to occur and chunks of roads are often swept away in flash floods as though the soil is made from chocolate sauce. These dangers didn't seem to worry the driver who drove like Sterling Moss at top speed all the way. We drove in a series of convulsive spurts and stops, plunging down the snake-like circuitous road only to dart around hairpin bends, often on the wrong side of the road. Through all these difficulties, the driver kept his composure admirably while I hung on grimly, my feet making dents in the floorboard. The constant turns and switch-backs made me feel car sick and it was such a relief to see the lights of Palampur and my Regimental destination. One journey was over and a new one was to begin.

Chapter 6

The 7th Gurkha Rifle Regiment

I arrived at the Officer's Mess in a sorry state. My uniform was creased and wet from the rain and I badly needed a bath. On entering the Mess, I was met by the Mess Havildar (Sergeant) who, on inspecting me, escorted me to a guest room where I was able to wash while my uniform was being cleaned and pressed. As I entered the dining room, where some thirty officers were dining, the Adjutant noticed me and beckoned me over. He introduced me to the others at his table. On learning that I had not dined, a place was set for me and I was made welcome with no further fuss. Had this been ten to twenty years earlier, my superiors would have ignored me. I was asked the usual questions posed to a newcomer: what schools I had attended; was I the first in the family to come to India; what sports was I keen on; etc. My answers didn't raise any eyebrows, but the fact that I played rugby drew a cheer for a match had been set up between the 7th and another Gurkha unit that weekend and reinforcements for our regimental team were needed. I was immediately recruited.

During the ensuing conversation, I gathered that of those at the table, about twenty percent were members of the staff, about thirty percent were unit officers about to go on long-leave (or a long course in England), and the remainder were waiting to return to England to either join the British Army or be demobilized. I was told that the number of battalions in each Gurkha regiment had been reduced from ten to three and that all the "hostilities only" officers (i.e. the non-regular officers), were being sent home to England, hence the large contingent of officers at the Centre. It was the custom for an officer about to go on long-leave (anything over three months), or on a long course, to first visit the Regimental Center for a few days so as to get reacquainted with some of his brother officers and to bring himself up-to-date with regimental plans for the future. All newly commissioned officers had to undergo indoctrination training and vetting at the Centre before being posted to a battalion. All these extra officers helped to enrich the quality of Mess life in this remote part of the world.

My first impression was that I was with a group of professional soldiers who seemed well pleased with military life. The majority of the officers present were under thirty years of age and all appeared friendly enough, yet there was something that set them apart from the civilian and non-combatant military person. These young officers exuded self-confidence and were completely at ease. The Mess was comfortably furnished and had all sorts of regimental mementos hanging on the walls. It looked like a regimental mess should look – displaying an air of establishment. The servants were mainly Pathans with a few Gurkha orderlies to serve drinks and all of them were immaculately turned out. I was wondering where I would be sleeping that night and on making inquiries, was assured that everything was in hand and that one of the officers would see me to my quarters. The Adjutant suggested meeting after breakfast tomorrow morning to receive information as to my duties. I was warned that due to the overflow of officers, I would have to put up with being billeted in temporary quarters that had little or no creature comforts.

Later that evening, I was shown to my billet. I would never have found it on my own. Outside, it was pitch black and still raining. Given my sense of lack of direction, I couldn't tell east from west. The temporary quarters were some distance from the Mess and this was made all the greater by the destruction of a number of bridges due to the torrential rains. My escort and I made our way, with the help of his torch, down slippery paths, across a swaying rope bridge and up steep passageways between huge boulders to eventually arrive at the accommodation compound. After I settled in, I said: "That's fine, I can see Kashmir from here." We had a good laugh and then he left me to fend for myself. My luggage had been already deposited and I unpacked and made the place ship-shape. The room was nondescript, decorated with functional furnishings. I went to bed covered in layers of blankets to fight off the cold air. The next morning, at what seemed like the crack of dawn, a Gurkha servant woke me up. He presented me the "chota hazri," a customary early breakfast consisting of a cup of hot, sweet tea plus a few biscuits. It was still cool and I welcomed the warm bath being prepared by the servant. I had my own canvas-folding bath that was part of my camp kit. The hot water was being poured from a Heath Robinson contraption in a tent close by. The toilet was a primitive wooden outbox placed in a separate hut known affectionately as "the Thunderbox;" its contents that the Americans called "digestive ash," was emptied by a sweeper. I was surprised to find mould on my boots, and the brass of my webbing had turned green. I realized that living literally in the clouds, all manner of dress and equipment would suffer from the damp and humid conditions. The servant soon had the boots and brass shining to perfection and I was ready to face a new day and a new way of life.

The servant offered to show me the way back to the Mess that I gladly accepted. As I left the billet, I saw that there was numerous other huts spaced haphazardly, scattered throughout; amongst the boulders, the forest, and on dirt ground. All the huts were made of wood similar to a log cabin with a sloping tin roof and a small veranda on one side. The windows were glassed in. The general size was about 18 feet by 24 feet. On our way to the Mess, we passed a hamlet that I had not noticed the night before. It consisted of less than a dozen hovels made of stone and mud with grass or tinned roofs and all set close together. There was an air of neglect about the place; maybe due to the climatic conditions. Small, unwashed and cheerless children stool in doorways to inspect us as we passed. Breakfast was legendary in the Indian Army and was considered one of the two major meals of the day. I was offered a choice of haddock, duck, kidneys, eggs, toast and marmalade, and even porridge. Other than the occasional "Good morning," as an officer entered the dining room, there was almost total silence broken only by the shuffle of a newspaper page being turned or by an order being given to a servant. Sometimes an officer would exclaim over something he had read in the newspaper. The newspapers were airmail editions of the more conservative English syndicates and these were displayed on a table in the Mess Hall. They were exactly one week old. I was shown to a seat by the head servant and asked what I wished to have for breakfast and which newspaper I wanted to read. The next morning as I sat at the same seat, I immediately noticed the Daily Telegraph opened at the section I had been reading the morning before as it was propped up on a reading stand for my convenience. The breakfast was identical to what I had previously ordered and the way I wanted it (without the edges on my toast). The table had no mats or linen other than the napkins. You ate off fine china or silver plates. A Pathan servant, in full Mess uniform, stood to attention behind each chair, whether it was occupied or not. Pathans are members of the Pashto-speaking tribes from the North-West Frontier region and, ironically, were enemies of the British and Indian Armies for many years. They are a tall, fierce-looking group of individuals with dark complexions, cruel faces emphasized by their piercing eyes. Though at first disconcerting, I eventually became accustomed to having these men stare unblinkingly at me as I ate. I can just imagine what thoughts passed through their minds as they stared at the "Britishers" at the trough.

As directed earlier, I reported to the Adjutant after breakfast. His office was in the Headquarters Building that was made of brick with a tiled roof and enclosed by a wide tropical veranda. The Adjutant was a Captain in his late twenties, fastidiously turned out and looked very self-assured. He explained the duties I would have to perform while at the Centre. These responsibilities were: taking my turn as Duty Officer, assisting with the training of the recruits, and helping others with the program for the "Boy's Company." I was also to learn Gurkhali. He was emphatic that I become proficient in this language in order to obtain the Gurkhas' trust and acceptance. I was also expected to read and know the history of the Regiment and its traditions.

The number of surplus officers as a result of the reduction in the number of battalions had given me quite a shock and I was puzzled as to why I had been accepted in the Regiment when so many battle experienced officers were being sent home. I expressed my thoughts to the Adjutant who agreed with my views. He informed me that most of the officers on their way home were aware it was only a matter of time before all "hostilities only" officers would have to face the same situation and they had opted to leave now rather than later. The Duty Officer, who had been asked to give me a guided tour of the Centre, also provided a running commentary on the history of the Regiment and on its traditions. The Regiment began operations in 1902 at Thayetmyo in Burma. Its "home" had been in Quetta, Baluchistan but was moved from location to location as dictated by the exigencies brought about during World War II. The Regimental Centre at Palampur was located in a fold of the Himalayan foothills, some eight to nine thousand feet above sea level. The area was devoid of beauty replaced by thick shrubs, prickly thickets, dried patches of grass, grit and emaciated trees. The mountains were the dominant factor and, when not covered in mist or cloud, were a formidable sight. There was something slightly disproportionate about the unmanageable vastness of the mountain range; something both majestic yet sinister, even seen from a distance.

Due to the remoteness of the Centre, it had to be as self-sufficient as reasonably possible. Much of the food came from Lahore and Pathankot with some fresh vegetables being grown on the base; the local villages having only enough for their own needs. The men's barracks, the stores and offices were brick buildings and these were placed close together in a compound of their own. The hospital, if it can be described as that, was in a small house and the medical services were the responsibility of an Indian doctor in the Indian Medical Corps. The hospital was more of a first aid station rather than a fully functional hospital. Anyone seriously ill was immediately sent to the military hospital at Lahore. Medical treatment was quite primitive as exemplified by the joke: "All pains below the umbilicus are treated with a strong purgative; all disturbances above, with a cough mixture; and lesions on the rest of the body, with turpentine liniment." In front of the Headquarters building was the Parade Square, a piece of ground that had previously been rough and craggy terrain. It was on this hard and stony piece of ground that sporting events took place. Somewhat removed from the main elements of the camp were the Officers' lines that consisted of a dozen or more well built and fully furnished bungalows. At the opposite corner of the camp was the transport park that included the stables for the beautifully kept cavalry horses. They were treated better than the natives.

The Adjutant had noticed my non-regulation uniform and had told me to see the Quartermaster (QM) and tailor and get myself properly fitted out. Following the tour of the Centre, I paid the QM and tailor a visit and within no time was correctly attired. I was also issued a pistol and a kukri. The kukri is a broad-bladed peculiarly curved knife, weighing about three pounds and about eighteen inches long. Only the Gurkhas carry this knife that they use for slicing, opening, dissecting, gauging, maiming, and butchering anything in their path, including tree cutting, vegetable peeling, can opening, meat slicing, protection and attack for hand-to-hand combat. The knife could easily slice a head off. I was asked to select a topi, a stiff bush hat with a wide brim. The clerks gave me one to try on but I found it too small, it sat and wobbled on the top of my head. I returned it and asked for a size similar to that my head size. With a laugh, the clerks handed me the larger sized topi. I didn't understand the humour for the hat felt just right. I smiled satisfactorily, but this made the clerks laugh even more. I was then shown how the topi was worn on top of the head and kept in place by a leather strap placed under the chin. At first it felt awkward and ridiculous, but I soon got accustomed to wearing it at a jaunty angle. I had to change the strap often as it deteriorated quickly from the perspiration that would inevitably collect around the chin area. The unit tailor had at least made me one regulation uniform to wear and this was made of green, light woven cotton. The buttons and insignia were black as in all Rifle Regiments.

Later that afternoon, I was introduced to the Commandant and his wife. He was a tall, borad and jovial officer who had served in both World Wars and with some distinction. She was petite and round and sympathetic. She had suffered a terrible misfortune as a result of a riding accident; her horse had thrown her and she had fallen down the side of a mountain. Her face was badly scared as was her right arm and hand. She was the only white woman living on the base. They were both delightful people and made me feel at ease. During our conversation, I naturally brought up the subject concerning the future of the Gurkha regiments and the possibility of my obtaining a regular commission in the 7th Gurkha Rifles. As the Commandant of the Regiment, he was privy to some of the ongoing discussions being held in Delhi regarding the future of the Gurkhas, mentioning that there was considerable political confusion; nothing new there. As he put it, it was a question of how many, if any, Gurkha regiments would Britain retain and this question had been put aside for the moment as the Gurkha situation had of necessity to be subservient to the larger problem of Independence and Partition. He understood that Lord Wavell was being pressed by London to withdraw the British Army units sooner than he thought advisable. Wavell feared that to withdraw too quickly would only surmount to increased tension and turmoil, particularly as many of the Indian Army units couldn't be trusted to maintain law and order. Moreover, such Gurkha units that were chosen to join the British Army would have to be withdrawn together with the latter thus diminishing further the number of units that could be trusted to keep the peace. As to the possibility of obtaining a regular commission, there could be no thoughts on the matter until the question regarding the Gurkhas had been settled. I left the Commandant's house with mixed feelings. I was terribly pleased at having attained one of my goals, that of being in a Gurkha regiment; on-the-other-hand, I was concerned that the Gurkha regiments might be disbanded or taken over by the Indian Army before I had the opportunity to serve with an operational battalion.

GURKHALI

The lingua franca of Nepal is Nepalese or Gurkhali as it was known in the army. There are many tribal languages and dialects throughout Nepal and some Gurkha recruits were ignorant of Gurkhali as spoken in the Regiment. The language I was to learn was the language of the soldiers and little different to that used by the peasants, except that it was mixed with common English military terms. To assist me in my efforts to learn the language, I was fortunate to find a Captain, who was waiting to return to England, who was willing to be my tutor. I spent an hour with him each day and a further hour was devoted to evening home-work. When speaking to the majority of Gurkhas, you had to use Gurkahli. Armed with basic Urdu, but for a few smattering of Gurkahli, I found myself mentally arm wrestling in painful conversation with the Gurkha Commissioned Officers (GCOs) let alone floundering in understanding the riflemen who would use slang or a number of colloquial expressions. However, the GCOs, with their infinite wisdom and dry sense of humour, would correct my grammar and vocabulary, and at the same time, initiate me into the intricacies of the Gurkhali tongue.

GCOs

The organization of a Gurkha Battalion was different to that of one in the British Army. There were far fewer British officers in the Gurkha Battalion, for GCOs did much of the work that commissioned officers did in the British units. The GCOs had at least fifteen years experience and were selected from the cream of the Havildars (Sergeants). Their intelligence, experience and ac-cumulated wisdom more than made up for the lack of formal education. There is no equivalent to these officers outside the Indian Army. The GCOs formed the connecting link between the non-commissioned officer and the British officer. They ranked just below the most junior British officer. The GCOs were skillful in tactfully correcting the faults of junior British officers without destroying their confidence. The British officers were strongly advised to listen to their GCOs when in doubt.

The Subedar-Major was the most senior rank among GCOs and only one was appointed in each battalion. He commanded nothing and everything. His duties were vague and large, permitting him such scope as he desired. In other words, he had carte blanche. He was the official guardian of the Gurkha's rights ensuring the men's dignity and religious susceptibilities were not offended. He was held in awe by the Gurkhas other ranks and could, whenever he wished, strongly influence their minds; a dangerous man in times of trouble. Each Rifle Company in a Gurkha battalion was commanded by a British officer, be he a Second Lieutenant, Lieutenant, Captain or Major. To assist the Company Commander were four GCOs: a Subedar (a Gurkha Captain) as the Second-in-Command, and three Jeadars (Gurkha Lieutenants) as Platoon Commanders. A Rifle Company consisted of about one hundred and twenty men divided into a Company Headquarters and three of four platoons. Battalion Headquarters included the command and administrative elements (i.e. the Commanding Officer, the Battalion Second-in-Command, the Adjutant, and Gurkha administrative officers). The Quartermaster was a British officer attached to the battalion.

Most Gurkha regiments recruited their men from four tribes: the Magars, Gurungs, Limbus and Rais. The 7th Gurkha Rifles recruited mainly from the area around Kiranti with its recruiting station at Darjeeling. Quite often, the headman of one or more villages was an ex-Gurkha GCO who would entice the young and able to join his old regiment. Those in charge of recruiting were quite particular about whom they selected. Priority was normally given to the sons of father who had served with the regiment, consequently, some Gurkha families military history extended back to well over a hundred years. A high physical standard had to be met and a number of men were not accepted as small pox, diphtheria, cholera and, most common of all, tuberculosis. Others had heart murmurs, enlarged thyroids or were colour blind. To not be accepted was heartbreaking for the young aspirant and very difficult for them to accept. It was considered a ignominious but often no fault of their own. Gurkhas, by some outsiders, have been branded as mercenaries. In a way they are, but unlike the modern mercenary such as the white mercenary, fighting for an African or South American employer, the Gurkha was not only attracted by the money, but also by the aspect of soldiering that was considered the "manly thing to do." He also wanted to leave the confined and restricted life of the village and to see the world beyond the mountains.

The training of recruits took place at the respective Regimental Centres where they underwent basic training. It must be remembered that in the 1940s, rural India was relatively philistine. There were no such things as wheeled transport, electricity, windowpanes, hospitals, telephones and telegraph, and most tools were unknown to the majority of Nepalese. The people were empiric as hygiene, as we know it, was unknown and the men had to be instructed to use a toilet. They also had to get used to wearing boots and not go barefooted. In other words, the recruit was being transplanted from the dark ages to the 20th century – a traumatic experience, but one the Gurkha quickly learned to adapt to. In addition to making the recruit aware of modern day living, he was taught drill, basic fieldcraft, battle drills, discipline, Gurkhali, accountability for personal cleanliness and order, rifle and equipment, the history and traditions of the Regiment and the organization of the different units and sub-units. Though recruits normally joined a regiment when they were seventeen years old, some managed to get in under that age barrier. There was also a Boy's Company established at each Regimental Centre. This Company was composed of the young sons of serving soldiers who wished to join the regiment on reaching the required age. These youngsters were taught to write and read and learn elementary mathematics and Gurkhali. They were clothed and fed, taught how to swim and play different sports and underwent teamwork activities. It was an excellent program and everyone benefitted by it. The Regiment had some partly trained potential recruits and the boys were kept out of mischief.

The British officers in Gurkha regiments felt themselves alienated even from fellow officers in the Indian Army, for the

Gurkhas were not Indians and therefore the regiments weren't exactly part of the Indian Army. Not only were you geographically distant from most of the other Gurkha units, even in the battalion lines, your Company was some distance from the next Company. Within the Company you were the only white person and the language spoken for much of the day was Gurkhali. As a result, the officers regarded the Officers' Mess as their "home," a refuge where they could be themselves by themselves, speak their own language and abide by their own customs.

SEX AND THE ARMY

Life was rendered smooth for the British officer by a full complement of servants, mostly Gurkhas. Each officer had a Gurkha orderly who had all domestic arrangements entirely under his control. The orderlies' sole occupation was to care for the needs of their assigned officer. The orderly belonged to the officer but the officer also belonged to the orderly who came to know all his officer's little idiosyncrasies better than any wife. British wives often felt alienated and were often ignored by the servants.

As a British officer in a Gurkha unit, I was expected to conform to traditions established during Queen Victoria's reign. Luckily, much of the trappings of bygone days had disappeared; nevertheless, even in the closing chapter of the British in India, conformity with the manners of behaviour of those early days was still insisted upon. This was irritating since the behaviour was so hypocritical and, given the political climate, so unnecessary and imbecile. Though there was dalliance whenever possible with the opposite sex, most of the officers were bachelors and for good reason: the climate, the costs involved, the loneliness when the husband is away, a woman lived in very much a man's world, and the dearth of other female company, particularly the company of white women, didn't provide a very inviting or prosperous environment. Given that so many officers were single, sex complicated their lives. Many British (and Commonwealth) young women, eager to meet eligible officers, would flock to the hill stations located in the British Quarter of the major cities. These young women were made welcome but they and their mothers were watched with a good deal of suspicion. The girls were known as the "Fishing Fleet." Some officers managed to have sex with these young women without being caught, but living in such close proximity there was bound to be gossip and, more often than not, if this liaison became serious, the officer would be sent to another unit. Unions outside one's own race were frowned upon and often resulted in a broken career. Some officers availed themselves of Indian maidens as mistresses and, as long as this was done discreetly, were accepted by the white males, though the white Memsahibs, with unmarried daughters, took offence to such behaviour. The British officer was viewed as a role model and was expected to be better than his men in all things. Of course this was quite impossible, but one tried and that seemed to satisfy all concerned. As long as the officer was physically tough, courageous, cheerful, debonair, smart and never jeopardize his men to save himself, the Commanding Officer would find little to complain about.

THE GURKHA

In the hope of learning something about the Gurkha prior to my being posted to a battalion, I took the opportunity of questioning the officers at the Centre who had served with "Johnny Gurkha" in battle. I thought that most of the officers would think along the same lines and was taken aback by their various views. One and all considered it a privilege to have served with the Gurkhas in wartime and all praised the Gurkha as the fiercest and finest fighter in the Indian Army. On-the-other-hand, some considered the Gurkha as a man still in his childhood; a cheerful and unconcerned individual who was apt to take orders literally rather than think them out and use more common sense. Others thought him as being the ideal soldier with unstinting loyalty to his officers. The controversial view of the Gurkha as a "savage" had only been partly tamed. Over a period of time, I came to my own conclusions. It would be incorrect to assess the strengths and weaknesses of the Gurkha without first understanding the background and environment that he was molded. The history of Nepal, until quite recently, has been a long, sad tale of brutality, greed, cruelty, betrayal, treachery, rebellion, and assassination. Public affairs were conducted with the aid of intrigues, torture, bribery, intimidation and other unsavoury techniques. Plots and conspiracy were part of everyday life.

Nepal consists of the Alpine region that includes the main Himalayan range, hills and mountains in the grasslands that reach 9,000 feet to 16,000 feet and can escalate to the highest peak of Mt. Everest, at 29,029 feet. The valleys at the foot of the hill country and low-lying land, jungle and swamp at about sea level. On one side of Nepal lies China – "The Dragon" – and on the other side, lies India – "The Tiger." The tiny kingdom of Nepal, barely five hundred miles long by as little as fifty-six miles across, can be likened to a mountain fortress. There are very few roads – about one hundred and fifty miles of all weather roads – and pack animals form the major mode of transportation. The land is inhospitable and very rugged. Previously, Nepal had been divided into small principalities on the lines of English or Scottish counties; however, the ruler of Gorkha, one of three states in Nepal, became alarmed at British influence and power throughout much of India and was determined that this power should not extend to Nepal. He seized control of the other states and proclaimed himself King of Nepal. The British, in turn, became concerned with the growth of this kingdom that extended from Kashmir to Sikkim. A border dispute between Britain and Nepal ensued into a two-year war that the British won. The war left each side with an increased respect for the other. A Treaty was mutually signed. One of the provisions was that the British would have the right to recruit Nepalese subjects into the Indian Army.

From the moment of his birth, a Nepalese peasant feared for his life and lived amid varying elements of peril. Disabling and killing diseases and maiming injuries were a normal occurrence. The hillsman was either a shepherd or a cultivator eking out a meager existence from the uncooperative soil on terraced hills eight to ten thousand feet above sea level. The recruitment of some of these natives was of considerable benefit to the Nepalese in that it provided a source of constant revenue in the form of subsidies from the government and money sent back to their families. The Gurkha is a small man, being only 5'4" in height. He has comparatively fair clear skin, Mongolian features with almond shaped eyes and little facial or body hair. He has extremely strong legs, abnormally developed thighs and calves from carrying heavy loads up and down mountains since early childhood. On arrival at the Centre, a recruit was likely to be a scrawny being having been brought up in privation in a hard and hungry land, but he soon filled-out when properly fed. Having got to know him quite well, I would judge the trained Gurkha rifleman as very brave, a stickler for regulations, and physically tough. He was adaptable, instinctively excellent in fieldcraft, intensely proud of his military record and unswervingly loyal. He was always cheerful and had a sense of humour that was earthy and often macabre or ridiculous. He had a quick and dangerous temper that disappeared as quickly as it erupted. He was highly disciplined and obedient without being servile, maybe because he loved soldiering. He could stand just about anything but abuse. He was honest and had natural integrity; an inborn frankness. If he were caught in the wrong, he wouldn't deny his guilt or blame others. One could say that the Regiment was bigger than the man and to most Gurkhas, service meant "to serve the Regiment, do the job well and not let the uniform down." The Gurkha was rarely astonished by anything new to him; he looked at the world around him with a practical, objective and unromantic eye and, more often than not, was amused by what he saw. In some ways, he was like a bright schoolboy: inquisitive, full of initiative, energetic and explorative. He seemed able to enjoy every minute of the day.

Give the life the Gurkha led in his homeland and the way he was treated there, it is no wonder that he was so loyal to the British officer who treated him like a human being, firmly but with kindness. The Regiment provided the necessary family environment. It is interesting to note that the fierce Pathan warrior (the

Mahsud) had this to say about the Gurkha: "the Mahsud respected only the Prophet and the Gurkha with his kukri."

It was not long before my turn came to be the Duty Officer. I had studied the verbal orders and drill for Mounting-the-Guard and was thankful that the orders were to be given in English rather than in Gurkhali. This ceremony, that was viewed as a test, was taken seriously by the men on parade for the two soldiers who performed the best would be chosen as the Commander's runners. This was regarded as an honour and far less irksome than being on guard duty. The Adjutant insisted that the Duty Officer give his orders a good fifty paces from the guard that resulted in the Duty Officer having to bellow his orders to be heard over a gusty wind. I was quite hoarse by the time I had completed this rather long and tedious task. One thing that intrigued me as I was inspecting the men was the fact that several of them were actually shivering. I mentioned this fact later on to the Adjutant who wasn't at all surprised, explaining that the men knew I was newly commissioned and were nervous that I would make some error resulting in confusion in the ranks. He slyly remarked that, no matter what orders I gave, the men would likely have carried out the correct drill. Trying to be clever, I addressed a member of the guard during the parade, acting as if I were a visiting General, in what I hoped was passable Gurkhali. The poor young chap almost had a fit. I learned later that the officer was not supposed to speak directly to a man, but if something was seen to be wrong, to address the matter to the Sergeant of the Guard. The Adjutant, who had been watching the proceedings from afar, guessed at what had happened and later gave me a ticking-off for being such an idiot.

As Duty Officer, I also had to visit the hospital and the sick. When sick, the Gurkha is very sick and looks the picture of woe. It is very difficult to get a sick Gurkha to report to the doctor or medical staff and even harder to get him to agree to enter a hospital. Most of the patients were suffering from tuberculosis and when asked how they felt, would rarely answer or simply close their eyes. In the evening, I would inspect the defaulters, those men who had been charged with some offence and had been given certain punishments. For this inspection, the men were lined up on the parade ground in front of the Adjutant's office. I was astonished at seeing the sheepish grin on the men's faces as if they were ashamed at having done something wrong. The last duty of the day was to check the guard. When on guard-duty, the Gurkha prefers to roam his area of responsibility rather than stand in one spot like a sentry outside Buckingham Palace. This habit of moving about made the job of the Duty Officer all the more tiresome. Being evening, it was pitch black and even with the help of a torch, it took time to find the guards who, I'm sure, were playing cat and mouse with me. Having learned my lesson, I decided that in future, I would have the Duty Sergeant accompany me on my rounds. It was amazing how quickly the Sergeant was able to find the sentries.

WATCH MY FLANK

In earlier days when Indian Army forces were required to quell riots in the region of the North-West Frontier, the protection of a column of marching troops against attack from bandits hidden in the crags of the mountainside was the responsibility of the flank guard. Guerilla tribesmen, armed with ancient but effective long barreled rifles, would shoot at the marching column down in the valley, sometimes as far off as a mile, and inflict casualties among the tightly packed troops. By the time the troops had taken up a defensive position, the guerillas had long disappeared. It was up to the flank guard to spot and deal with these snipers before they could do any serious damage. It would also help avoid such vulnerable predicaments, but circumstances sometimes prevent this from happening, so flank guards were established on the mountainside to scrutinize any potential danger above. A number of outposts or *sangars* were built, each containing three or four men. The men of the flank guard, laden down with equipment, ammunition, rations and weapons, would climb the mountainside and establish these outposts well ahead of the marching column. Once the column had passed an outpost, the men would descend the mountain, pass the column and once again take up a new position ahead of the column. This leapfrogging procedure would continue until the column reached its destination. The most dangerous moment for the men in the outposts was when they had to leave the sangar. Pathan bandits would sometimes crawl unseen towards the outpost and lie in wait and as the men left the protection of the sangar, the bandits would attack. Moving up and down the mountainsides was tiring and so, as an incentive to keep the flank guard moving, the men received a financial bonus for every mile covered in one day that exceeded twenty road miles.

The Centre was not in the North-West Frontier region; nevertheless, it was considered appropriate that recruits and the new officers be taught the art of "picketing," (i.e. learning the intricacies of establishing mountain flank guards). This involved the strategy of ascending and descending mountains and building sangars (round pits made of stone and rocks about two or three feet high.) I was amazed at how fast a fully laden Gurkha could move on the wild and rugged mountainside. In climbing the valley walls, I was able to keep up with the men, but then I had no heavy load to carry. In the descent, things were different. I would go ahead on the pretext of reconnoitering the route and when about halfway down, would signal for the others to follow. Follow be damned! Whereas I would carefully choose my steps and route, the Gurkhas would stampede past me. All I saw was a mass of equipment with two feet sticking out from under, bouncing from one rocky outcrop to another with the agility of a mountain goat. Since we were in the mountains, our Training Officer, an avid mountaineer, decided that we should undergo mountain warfare training as a follow-up to our training in Picketing. As the Centre was not equipped for this type of training and no one could imagine any reason for our being called upon for such an operation, the project was squashed; however, the Staff agreed to mountain climbing as an alternative.

Not Having a Heart for Heights

A suitable slab of mountain was selected. Though we were assured that it was chosen with "beginners" in mind, most of us were aghast at its steepness and height. To get to the site, the climb was a trial. There were no roads leading to it and the paths were precipitous and treacherously slippery. The only officer at the Centre who had any experience in mountain climbing was the Training Officer, so naturally he was assigned as the instructor. He forgot to tell us that he suffered from a weak heart and must have thought himself capable of climbing a beginner's slope. On arrival at the climbing site, we spent about half-an-hour learning how to hitch ourselves to ropes, how to use crampons and spikes, what knots to use and what holds to look for on the face of the mountain. Following this crash course, we started our first climb. We had been divided into several groups, each consisting of four men. I was number three in the group led by the instructor as the first group to climb. As mentioned previously, I suffer from vertigo and all I can remember of the climb is clinging convulsively from one grip to the next. Whether I looked up or down, everything seemed to be swaying. I had been warned not to look down and made sure to follow this advice. About twenty minutes after starting this terrifying experience, there was a cry from our leader. His heart had started to give him trouble and he thought it best to return to base. Unfortunately, he began to feel faint and obviously needed support in getting down. Without his supervision, we had to improvise a secure technique in getting him down. We hitched him to a spike while we discussed how to go about the job. It was agreed that the easiest way to lower the man, now almost unconscious, was by means of a pulley system with two men acting as guides to ease the victim around sharp outcrops. In this way, we got him down to the ground where he came to and, after a short rest, was able to walk. I've never been happier to touch terra firma and was relieved to hear a few days later that the mountain climbing lessons would be postponed until further notice.

The first lesson in supervising either the Gurkhas or the Boy's Company was the inspection of their morning kit. It must be remembered that the majority of recruits only owned what few rags they stood in. To be the owner of such riches as the issued kit was a blessing from the Gods and, as can be expected, every item was cared for with minute attention. From time to time a fault was found, such as when a cork had been left in a water bottle or a pair of shining boots weren't in line; all trivial affairs but noted nonetheless and the offender placed on charge. The hillsmen rarely wore boots or shoes and never wore socks, so it was a new experience for the recruits to have to get used to such items. The young lads soon became accustomed to wearing boots but they couldn't abide wearing the thick woolen socks and often decided to do without. Consequently, periodic checks were made at which times the man had to remove his boots to reveal whether or not he was correctly dressed.

To create team spirit, a sports program was organized. The men were taught how to play soccer, volleyball and basketball. They were also taught how to swim and box as a means of instilling self-discipline. It was difficult at first to keep the men from grouping together when chasing after the soccer ball, but eventually they got the hang of the game. Swimming in very cold water was not new to them for all had bathed in rock pools and rivers and seemed immune to the cold. With patience, most of the men were able to do a sort of breaststroke after several weeks of effort. Boxing was not one of their favourite pastimes and when hit on the nose, they were apt to lose their temper and revert to kicking their opponent.

The Boy's Company program was somewhat akin to Cub or Boy Scout training. The sport's program was organized to teach team spirit and self-discipline as in the recruit's program. Camping was a favourite event due to the ample kit and good meals provided. First aid was also taught much to the delight of the youngsters who shouted with glee whenever a volunteer had been so wrapped up in bandages that he couldn't move. The boys were lively, energetic and enthusiastic and sometimes I had difficulty keeping up with them. They obviously appreciated being in the Company and only the very sick would miss the morning parade. The boys were clothed and fed by the Centre and several whose parents lived some distance away, were also housed in one of the barrack blocks. Though they were young, some as young as six years of age, they were taught how to use a man-size kukri. To watch a six year old wielding an eighteen-inch kukri with adroit dexterity was a fascinating and sobering sight.

HORSING AROUND

Horseback riding at the Centre was encouraged by the Commandant. Given that each officer who went riding had to share a horse with another officer, yet had to pay the full cost of the horse's care, one can see the Commandant's intention. On-the-one-hand, the half dozen or so charges needed exercising if they were to remain in good condition and this meant having a good supply of eager riders. For those without previous experiences, lessons in all matters concerning the horse were organized. These lessons started at the unearthly hour of 5:30 a.m. and went on for about two hours. Due to the altitude, the time of day and the coolness in the air, the horses were normally restless and nervous. Our first lesson consisted of cleaning the animal and inspecting it for any signs of sores or ill health. Given that I had done this sort of thing with mules in Bangalore, I quickly proceeded to the next stage that entailed saddling, usually with a horse that had other ideas. By the time I had finished these exercises, both the horse and I were apt to be short tempered. I was eventually allowed to ride the beast. Once up in the saddle I was surprised at how high off the ground it seemed and how very small the English saddle is once covered by my rear end (and I don't have a large bottom.) It was while practicing the trot that I discovered I had very little padding on my rear and that it was more comfortable to squat in the stirrups; however, this was discouraged and would be slapped with the instructor's whip on my posterior each time I broke the rules. In either case, I had a sore backside. I also had to learn to dismount in various ways, including doing a back somersault. This odd method often ended up with the rider falling on his head or back, especially when the horse decided to side step. I'm certain the instructor had Cossack blood.

After a week of basic horsemanship, we were told that we were ready to try the canter and gallop. For this, we had to first traverse some treacherous paths to get to a small grassy plain where it was safe to gallop. On the first day, we walked the horses along the narrow mountain trails mainly to give the riders a chance to look over the route. It was on one of these trails that the Commandant's wife had been thrown from her horse; a fact that didn't escape any of us. The following day, we were made to ride along the narrow passage. The instructor advised us to give the horse its "head" when moving along the trails as it knew the way and would follow the horse ahead. On reaching the dreaded narrow ledge, I loosened my grip on the reins and, sure enough, the horse became less restless and moved along at a steady pace. Meanwhile, I hung grimly to the pommel of the saddle wondering why I had volunteered for this exquisite torture. At last we reached the plain and both riders and horses moved about at random, riding themselves of nervous tension. The canter and gallop made all the previous training worthwhile. It was exhilarating and huge fun even though I fell off the horse a couple of times. There was the time when my horse was moving at a good pace and I was in a standing crouch position when either I, or the horse, decided to turn sharp left. The horse went left and I went straight. The horse was friendly enough to come back to me.

It was while returning from a ride on the plain one day that we noticed a pretty young white woman talking animatedly with a group of officers outside the Adjutant's office. The other riders decided that a gallop in passing the group would draw attention to themselves. My horse was ready whereas I wasn't. The horse took chase and I was hurled backwards in the saddle, feet out of the stirrups and jolting up and down like a ping-pong ball in a blender. I frantically grabbed the reigns too hard and the horse, having had enough of this foolishness, came to an abrupt stop while I continued forward. I was later told that I gracefully flew through the air to land on my feet still holding the reigns. From then on this form of dismount was referred to as "Branson's Choice," not to be confused with Hobson's choice.

SPORTS AND ENTERTAINMENT

Other than riding, my passion for exercise found its outlet in a number of sports. There was soccer, rugby and hiking. Playing soccer with Gurkhas could be frantic and was often painful. The terrain was hard ground covered with sharp stones. Instead of the allowed tackle by feet, the Gurkha would jab his elbow into his opponent wherever it had the most effect – ribs, face, stomach, groin, leaving his nemesis squirming on the ground much to the delight of cheering spectators. When this happened to me, I retaliated and brought down my opponent with a quick chop to the kidney, again delighting the spectators with encouraging cries of "Shabash!" (well done).

Since one spent a good deal of the time falling to the ground when playing rugby, it was agreed that the game be played on the more forgiving grass rather than on the gritty parade ground. Who needs enemies when you have Gurkha rugby players? Where such areas were available the height of the grass stood some twelve inches high. Running through the high grass was similar to running through beach waves and was exhausting. Due to this natural obstacle, we often lost sight of the ball and would take a break with a beer as a pick-me-up. As the game proceeded and the players grew more weary, the stops for the lost ball became increasingly frequent and the players more and more belligerent. It was during a tête-à-tête with a member of the opposing team that I realized I knew the man from my school days at Bedford School – what a small world.

Before dinner I would sometimes take a walk along the mountain trails hoping to discover an interesting vista, a dramatic sunset, but with little success. Occasionally I would meet a native coming from the opposite direction. We would salaam to each other and stop to chat; neither would understand what the other was saying but both of us would feel pleased at the courtesy shown. It was a bit dicey when meeting an individual sporting a rifle and bandolier. I would offer the ritual salaam and as I continued my walk, would keep a sharp lookout to ensure the other's mood had not become hostile for Dacoit bandits were said to be in the district.

Due to the Centre's location there were no evening attractions that drew one away from the camp, thus the Mess became the focal point for one's evening entertainment. Thanks to the large number of officers, Mess life was both interesting and agreeable. After dinner, bridge and billiards were the preferred pastimes. For a poor player, bridge could be costly and since I was not a good player, I stayed away from the card table as much as possible, but sometimes I had to play to be sociable. There was always a group of officers sitting around the fireplace with drink in hand, recounting war stories. I would listen, entranced as they spoke about the good and bad times and of some of the amusing incidents that had taken place. I remember one story about a padre. Somewhere in Burma, one of the Gurkha units was holding a defensive position. One day an army chaplain visited the unit to see the officers and men. During his short stay, he found that he had to go to the bathroom and having been given directions, was left on his own. The bathroom was a large pit with a couple of poles across it on which to sit. While the padre was sitting on the crossbeams, he happened to look up and came face-to-face with a large serpent dangling from a branch directly above him. The shock was so great that he fell backwards into the deep pit. His cries for help were heard by a number of men who pulled him out of the mess with the help of a rope. Instead of being furious, the good padre jokingly remarked: "I had to go number one but I ended up doing number two." His visit was shortened since we couldn't get rid of the terrible stench that clung to him. Shortly after his return to Brigade Headquarters, the Brigadier sent a message to the unit Commanding Officer that went somewhat along the following lines:

"Clerics unholy fall from space,

"In particular ungainly grace,

"Has cost him loss of face among the lads at the Base."

MESS DINNER

About once a month a formal Mess Dinner was held. On such occasions, the officers wore Mess Dress or their best uniform. Candles only were used to light the dining room that simply increased the heat and stuffiness of the room due to a lack of air-conditioning. The long, highly polished dining room table, laden with regimental silver, gold and crystal, was an imposing sight as was the retinue of servants in all their finery. At one end of the table sat the Mess President and at the other end sat a junior officer who acted as the Vice President. When possible, a guest was invited as well as the Commandant, the latter not being a member of the Mess. The service was excellent, everyone at the table being served at precisely the same moment. When the guest of honour or senior officer had finished what had been placed before him, his plate and those of all the other officers were removed no matter whether the other officers had finished or not. Once the meal was finished, the table was cleared of all plates, dishes and utensils and a port decanter was placed in front of the President and the Vice President. Once the port had gone round the table and everyone had been served, the President would rise and say: "Mr. Vice, the King Emperor," following which all would rise and the Vice would say: "Gentlemen, the King Emperor," and all would repeat: "The King Emperor." From that moment on, smoking was permitted and the port decanter would circle the table with hardly a pause. Eventually the guest or senior officer would leave the table and withdraw to the ante-room followed by those wishing to do likewise. There was always a number of older Captains and Majors who would remain at the table to exchange stories and they would all move up the table to sit close to the President, leaving the Vice in isolation at his end of the table. Since neither the President nor the Vice were permitted to leave until all the other officers had let, Mr.

Vice sometimes had to sit alone with his port decanter far into the night.

Strong drink and wine was expensive at this time, consequently, I drank my tipple in moderation, but before leaving the Mess, I would fortify myself with a brandy to keep me warm during the night. I found that the drink also helped me overcome my fear at getting lost when returning to my billet. I had no troubled crossing the rope bridge but sometimes became confused as to which path to take thereafter. As I stumbled in the dark, suddenly a voice barked out. A Gurkha sentry demanded the code word to pass. I gave what I thought was the correct answer after which the sentry would patiently tell me how to correctly pronounce my part of the exchange. It sounded like "groundrun" but had a few "tch" thrown in. The sentry would then take me by the arm and conduct me personally to my quarters. Such service was not to be rejected.

An officer passing through the Centre had brought with him an 8mm copy of the film, *The Seventh Veil* directed by Compton Bennett with James Mason (not to be confused with Swedish classic, *The Seventh Seal* made in 1957 by Ingmar Bergman). The film was shown to the officers and it was suggested that it be shown to the Gurkhas, especially as the majority had never been to a cinema. For a screen, the side tarpaulin of a 2 ½-ton truck was used and the audience sat in the open and cool night air. Though the dialogue was in English and the theme somewhat dull, the Gurkhas nonetheless were enthralled by the spectacle and, at the end of each reel, insisted on seeing it again. I found the expression on the men's faces more entertaining than the film.

Life at the Centre was in fact very pleasant, even for a newly commissioned subaltern. The more senior officers didn't expect wonders from the newcomers and treated them well as long as they maintained the regimental customs and didn't break too many taboos. When you stepped out of line, you were dealt with severely. An incident occurred when a newly commissioned officer decided to take a bath and ordered his servant to prepare the necessary arrangements. This, the servant did, and then left the room. When the officer stepped into the tub, he found the water insufficiently hot and yelled for the servant to bring more hot water. The servant, having filled a can with hot water, left it at the doorway without entering the room – it was improper for a Gurkha to look at a nude officer. The young officer got annoyed and chased after the servant without bothering to cover himself, yelling insulting remarks. The servant reported the incident to his superior who, in turn, reported it to the Subedar Major, who then informed the Commandant. Within a week, the young officer was on his way back to England.

LESSONS FROM LAHORE

About ten days after my arrival, the Adjutant asked me whether I should like a weekend pass in Lahore. I should have known better than to accept, but I was keen to again visit this major Muslim city. As he gave me the pass, he mentioned as an afterthought that seeing how I was going to the city, would I mind returning a broken-down truck to the vehicle depot. Having arranged to get the vehicle onto a railway flatbed and provided the necessary guards, I lost no time in getting to Lahore. The temperature rose steadily the nearer I got to the city. On my arrival, the temperature was 127 degrees Fahrenheit in the shade. Hundreds of Indians had died from heat exhaustion and their bodies had been wrapped in shawls and placed all over the place, including on the streets. Though I was wearing my uniform, the sun's rays still managed to burn through the cloth forcing me to seek relief by taking shelter every hundred yards. On reaching the hotel, the receptionist expressed surprise at my being there, explaining that the railways, telegraph and telephone services, banks and the postal office had all gone on strike in sympathy with some local political cause. Every morning I would check in at the Railway Transport Office in the hope of locating the train with the flatbed and truck. During one of these checks, in the middle of the week, the Gurkha Naik (Corporal), who had been in charge of the guard on the flatbed, came up to me and cheerfully told me that the flatbed had been left at the siding about fifty miles up the line. He had left the rifleman to guard the useless truck and had walked to Lahore following the tracks – a two-day march with hardly a *sou* in his pocket. A truly remarkable feat considering the wilting conditions. I arranged for him to be paid, fed and quartered him and made arrangements to us to meet each morning at an appointed hour to see where matters stood.

I was staying in a first-class hotel that unfortunately was not air-conditioned. To stay cool, I spent a good part of the day sitting in a bath filled with lukewarm water and sipping orange juice. About halfway through the week, I ran out of money. The hotel staff became suspicious since I was no longer taking my meals there and was unable to confirm my departure date. Since the banks were still on strike and the local military were not prepared to help, being themselves short of cash, I decided to see whether the regimental tailor could lend me enough money to see me though the week. I was given a lecture by the owner about the dangers of borrowing money in India, but I pointed out that I was ordering a couple of uniforms and that the loan cold be added to my bill. We finally agreed to a small loan at a reasonable rate of interest.

THE GOVERNOR'S RESIDENCE

On getting back to the hotel, I went to the bar to have a drink and got into conversation with a middle-aged Englishman who, as a civil servant, worked at the Governor's residence. During our conversation, I mentioned my predicament in which I found myself. He explained that he had been unexpectedly summoned out of town for a few days and, with all the white civil servants having moved to the hill station for the hot season, there would be no one left in charge of the residence. In a joking manner, he asked me whether I would be interested in sitting in for him during his absence. I thought it an amusing proposition and told him I was willing, provided that should the flatbed arrive in town, I would be required to immediately return to my unit. I was given to understand that I would have no administrative duties but that my presence was all that was required. We then went to the Residence where I was introduced to the security guard and to the Anglo-Indian civil servants who had remained in town to carry out routine administration. The few days spent at the Residence were most enjoyable. The house itself was relatively cool indoors and the garden afforded considerable shade. There was also a large swimming pool, refreshingly cool, clean and inviting. I made full use of it as did the Anglo-Indians. Each evening, a generous buffet was served and I gladly accepted the invitation to attend. I found the Anglo-Indians pleasant company. They certainly worked harder than the average Indian and seemed better educated. Much of the conversation centred on the conditions that would likely apply to them after Independence. Most realized the difficulties they were to face in the near future. As one individual put it, "Under the British, everyone knew where they stood, but under an Indian government, prejudice against certain tribes or groups was a certainty and the Anglo-Indians always called Britain "home," even though the majority had never been out of India." I was filled with empathy for them and was sorry when the time came to hand over my charge to the Englishman on his return, but he kindly invited me to continue to use the pool and to participate in the evening entertainment until I left the city.

It was during an evening cocktail party at the Residence that I was invited to a party to be held at the prestigious Prince's Hotel. Though the individual who kindly offered the invitation was a swarthy, fat and unprepossessing Indian, I accepted mainly in order to see this grandiose hotel, and I wasn't disappointed. The hotel was immense. The halls and rooms were all exquisitely large with high ceilings and the furniture, expensive and ornate. A pleasant temperature seemed to infiltrate throughout the building yet there was no visible air conditioning. On entering the suite where our party was being held, I realized that it was an informal affair. Most of the guests were Indian with a sprinkling of Indian military personnel and two British officers. Everyone was exceedingly polite, almost solicitously so, avoiding the topic of Independence and its associated problems. I was surprised at seeing Hindus drinking hard liquor as I had been told that Hindus and Muslims never touched alcohol. The party continued for about a couple of hours after which many of the guests departed. As I was in the process of thanking my host, he asked me to stay a while as he had arranged some further entertainment for some of the guests. We moved into a more comfortable room that had a number of couches spread about the interior. In the centre of the room was a low table where there were a number of plates with all types of appetizing foods and more drinks. We were invited to sit and shortly thereafter, a number of "Nautch" girls came into the room and entertained us with some intricate and suggestive dances. Nautch girls are the equivalent of the Japanese Geisha girls. These Nautch girls are highly respected by both male and female Indians. They have learned how to please a man, how to speak well and how to make a man feel at ease. My female partner was a graceful young girl whose only blemish that I could detect was the dreadful pockmarks that covered her face, presumably were the result of small pox. She had a composure that was old for her years and when she sat down, she arranged her body and legs in a very gentile manner. Speaking in English, she opened the conversation by asking about my background and I then asked her about the training of Nautch girls, but she skillfully evaded answering the question, when suddenly, I was rudely interrupted by the fat host who shouted across the room, "Kiss the girl!" I looked around and was stunned to see the other guests in the initial stages of making love to their willing partners. I felt suddenly uncomfortable and gauche. I was out of my depth once again. This sexual orgy in public was something I had never come across and I was acutely embarrassed. My partner was bright enough to guess my awkwardness and with a smile, suggested that I leave quietly. I took her advice and left immediately. By the time I got to the front door, I was cursing myself for being so naïve. As I walked out of the hotel, my annoyance was increased by what felt like a furnace blast of heat that rocked me back on my heels. It was still the afternoon and after the darkness inside the hotel, the sun's reflection off the sun-bleached buildings was blinding. I eventually made my way back to my own hotel.

A few days later the strikes ended and the Naik and I were able to return to the Centre. I was shocked to discover that the truck and guard had both disappeared without a trace. I reported the dilemma to the Adjutant who was surprised by the strikes. During those days it was often quicker to pass a message by train than by telegraph or telephone this is because rioters would normally cut telegraph lines as a protest. I was astonished when the Commandant ordered that I be the President and sole member of the Board of Inquiry into the loss of the vehicle and rifleman that had been in my charge. As I considered the situation, I realized that the Commandant had placed me in a Catch-22 position. Though there were circumstances beyond my control, the fact that the man and truck were under my charge automatically made me responsible for their loss, but not necessarily guilty of negligence. In preparing the report, I was aware that I couldn't lie and realized how heedless it would be to fabricate false incidents, so I stated everything that happened in connection with the subject matter. On reading my report, the Commandant fined me one thousand rupees for the loss of the useless vehicle and 600 rupees for the loss of the rifleman, presumed dead; so little value for the life of an Indian solider. The Commandant explained to me that this was a lesson in responsibility but he generously offered to pay the fines from regimental funds. I wondered what the Gurkhas might think about me being associated with this fiasco, but it was never brought up. All night I thought about the missing vehicle and soldier. What could have happened? Where did the train go? If it reached its intended destination, why wasn't the vehicle on the train? How did someone take it off the flatbed? Where was the soldier? If he died, how did it happen? Was it exposure? Was he killed? What happened to his body? I felt wretched, filled with guilt and a sense of incompetence. As an officer, even a non-commissioned one, I was accountable. It was something I would never forget.

DAM IT

The monsoon was still raging in the foothills and threatened the local villages as the river levels rose, overlapping the banks and becoming new estuaries. The Commandant received a number of requests from several village elders to help divert the water as it was jeopardizing the village huts. Four officers and about sixty men were assigned to the task, I being one of them. We first reconnoitered the area to determine the best places to build the dams. Prior to the construction of the dams, it was essential to establish a "life-line" across the rapid current to protect the men working in the water. The men were split up into a number of sections and directed to either side of the main river. A thin line was shot across the river and attached to a strong cable that was then hauled across the river by hand. At first, all went well, but there was a snag when the cable became entangled with some object underwater. Several ways were tried to disengage the cable but without success; it required someone to do it by hand. One of the other officers volunteered and started to move down the line. About halfway, he lost his footing as well as his hold on the cable and was carried downstream at a frenzied pace. The Gurkhas found this intensely amusing while the remaining officers became increasingly concerned about old Jock whose progress down river was marked only by the sight of his topi that was fast disappearing, bobbing endlessly from one rapid to the next. He somehow struggled to shore about a half mile down river and slowly made his way back to us to a chorus of cheers. Not surprising, some of the spring had evidently gone out of him.

Once the cable had been fixed, the building of the dam was essentially an easy task. Small boulders were used as a backstop to the larger boulders that formed the key elements to the dam. To move a large boulder that was already in the water required a slight shove and the momentum of the water then swept it forward. In spite of our precautions, one man had a leg crushed when a rolling boulder pinned him to the partly constructed dam. He was obviously in great pain but managed to hide it and even managed a smile as he was carried back to the Centre. It took a couple of days to construct four dams, each one being of a different size depending on its location. Having finished the dams, four officers visited the villages that had asked for help. They were in a sorry state. Several of the rice terraces had been destroyed and many of the houses had been swept away. The latter was no tragedy for it was easy to rebuild the homes, but their few belongings had also been lost. On returning to the Centre, we asked the officers and men to donate any useful items of clothing or equipment they no longer needed. The Quartermaster also provided a number of useful items such as buckets, axes, pans and bedding. We returned to the villages with a sizeable assortment of goods. The locals grabbed our arms and hands to shake them, nodding their heads.

Sometime later I visited the rifleman who had had his leg crushed and found him in remarkably good form considering the pain he must have endured and the fact that his military career had come to an end. Though he would receive a pension, it would be miserably small and of little compensation.

After three or four weeks at the Centre, the Adjutant informed me that I had been posted to the 2nd Battalion (2/7 GR) together with John Mellor, a South African. The battalion was located close to the city of Ahmadabad, the third largest city in India with a population of around three million, mostly Muslims. Ahmadabad is two hundred and seventy miles due north of Bombay and is the capital of the state of Gujerat. I was disappointed at not being posted to the 1st Battalion in Rangoon, but that unit was already at full strength. I would like to see Burma, and Rangoon in particular, for I imagined the country to be quite different from India and even more interesting. A couple of days after receiving our posting instructions, John and I set out for Ahmadabad. Our journey was to be by way of Lahore and New Delhi where we would change trains. On arrival at Lahore railway station, we left our luggage with a scarlet-uniformed coolie, or rather one of these stalwarts grabbed some of our baggage as we descended the train thereby claiming us for himself. Since we had several hours to waste before our connecting train departed, we decided to have a good meal in town. We informed our coolie of the time and destination of our next rain, took his badge number and left him in charge of our belongings. Most coolies cannot read or write and many can't tell the time either, but they know the approximate time a train leaves by the actions of the platform staff. By the time John and I returned, the station platform was peppered with sleeping human forms wrapped up in their all-enveloping saris or cotton cloth. It was a stew of hot and sweaty passengers mingled with the unclean and homeless. We soon found our coolie standing outside our reserved compartment, arguing like a kettle boiling, with an irate platform official. It seemed that two nuns had bought tickets for the journey but had forgotten to make reservations. The official suggested that John and I share the compartment with the nuns, but I would have none of it and told the official to find other accommodations for either the nuns or ourselves. While the official looked for something suitable, we talked to the middle-aged nuns who were members of some religious order and who were trying to get to a Catholic mission somewhere in East India. They were pleasant enough though not sufficiently so to allow us the use of our reserved compartment. Some ten minutes later, the harassed official returned to inform us that there was room for two people in a large compartment if we didn't mind sharing it with two Hindus. John and I didn't mind in the least and thought it preferable to sharing a compartment with two nuns. When we got to the carriage, we met our travelling companions: a respectable man of about fifty years of age and a pretty young woman. He introduced himself and his daughter and made us welcome. From the obsequious behaviour of the official, it was apparent that the man was a person of some importance. He informed us that he was a senior official of the railway company we were using – most fortuitous. At every stop the compartment was cleaned out and baskets of fruit brought on board. Some of his servants were travelling on the same train and, at the appropriate hours, hot meals cooked by the servants were served in the compartment. Our host, for so he turned out to be, invited us to share the meals that were delicious. Both he and his daughter spoke excellent English and he enlivened the journey by providing a running commentary on those areas through which we were passing.

As we passed several rural villages, he gave us an insight into the life of an Indian labourer. The labour force for much of India's industrial base is drawn from rural districts, particularly from the poor and over-populated territories. The migrant spends just so much time in the factory as will allow him to return to his village, look after his land and enjoy a spell of idleness until his funds run dry. It is the responsibility of the Sirdar (jobber) to recruit the labour. The individual native is always in the grip of the moneylender at home and is under the thrall of the jobber in his work. The factory worker had to work up to ten hours a day in a steamy atmosphere accompanied by physical strain. After work, he likely had to share a single room in the slums with ten or more people. Given this situation, the industrial proletariat was meat for the intriguer, whether the latter was a communist or revolutionary. One can understand the peasant's wish to return to his village as soon as the occasion permitted.

Though seventy percent of the population lived in rural areas, one rarely saw masses of natives in any one place; they seemed to be on the move or working in the fields, spread evenly wherever there was agricultural land. The degree of poverty was staggering. We asked our travelling companions for their views on the future of the desperately poor. Our host painted a grim picture of feudal India as it had been, ruled by invaders, warriors, and Princes for several thousands of years during which a large segment of the population was denied dignity and aspirations, yet they survived. Once independence was established, he foresaw a rapid increase of industrial plants throughout India that would result in an improved way of life for many of the poor, but not for the majority. Being Hindu, he believed such a change would help overcome some of the anguish of being among the downtrodden since their faith ordains that a Hindu is born, dies, following a rebirth into, hopefully, a better existence on earth.

The railway compartment was large but left little room to stretch. At every stop, we would get off and wander around people or stepping over mountains of luggage; not an easy task since the average railway station was heaving with humanity. There was a constant swirl of life and a cacophony of noise, colours and smells. It was a microcosm of the country: everything was on view – eating, sleeping, washing, caring for children and conducting business. There were little islands of people patiently squatting on their belongings. The stark contrast of Indian society was appealing in this apparent chaos. Though crowded, no one seemed to be in any particular hurry or annoyed because of lack of space, delays, or weather so thick with humidity, it felt indigestible. On the contrary, many were smiling, laughing or chatting away merrily, that is, until the train arrived, then bedlam occurred as fifty people strove to fit into a space that could not accommodate more than thirty at the most. The trains were mysterious relics. Rusting, rolling behemoths of black metal and steam; a incongruous blend of grandeur and no-frills practicality.

NEW DELHI

At New Delhi we again changed trains for passage to Ahmadabad. Rather than eat breakfast at the station's restaurant, we decided to go into town and find an Officer's Club where we could have a bath and an English type meal. We hired a tonga and told the driver to take us to the nearest Officer's Club and shortly thereafter, he deposited us at a grand looking building. When we entered, the Hall Porter was not at his desk, instead was an Indian clerk and we explained to him our needs. We were shown to a large room and while we were bathing, our uniforms were cleaned and pressed. We met no Club members on our way in nor on our way to the dining room and so it was with surprise and consternation that we noted nothing but senior officers eating breakfast. A number of haughty looks were directed at us but we felt that it was too late to withdraw and sat at a table close to the door. It was not long before one of these elderly officers came over to our table, introduced himself very politely as General Bernard and asked us whether we were on a visit to the city. We invited him for coffee, which he accepted between chortles of laughter, explaining that we had entered a very senior British Officer's Club. We apologized, saying that we had seen no signs to that effect and that on entering the Club, the Hall Porter had been absent from his post. On giving the General further details about ourselves and where we were going. He reassured us not to worry and to finish our breakfast. He would explain to the others that we were his guests. We much appreciated his thoughtfulness and having finished breakfast, wasted no time in leaving the Club.

AHMADABAD

Our journey from New Delhi to Ahmadabad was uneventful. We pulled into our destination in the middle of the night and were met by a Gurkha driver and rifleman who soon had our baggage stowed away in a unit vehicle. The driver dropped us off at the Officer's Mess where the Mess Havildar took charge and showed us to guest rooms where we were to stay until we could make arrangements for renting suitable accommodations. As it was close to 3 a.m., I didn't bother to wash, but went straight to bed. I fell asleep feeling very pleased to have arrived at an operational unit and looked forward to the morning. I was awakened four hours later; a luxury as the officers normally got up at 5:30 a.m. Later, when John and I entered the dining room, it was to find most of the unit officers already at breakfast. Introductions were made and one or two officers pulled our legs at our having slept in. The 2nd Battalion had but seven regimental British officers plus an English Quartermaster and an Indian doctor. The Commanding Officer was not a member of the Mess and the GCOs had their own separate Mess. Each officer was unlike any of his brother officers in looks, character and background. The Adjutant was a small, thin and tough Australian. The Second-in-Command and two of the Company Commanders were English probably from the middle- or upper-class by their clipped manner, accent and tone of speech. One of the other two Company

Commanders was a tall, lanky, good-natured Scot, and the other, a short, squat Welshman. The Quartermaster was a Cockney and full of mischief. Add to this mixture John, a South African, and myself with an English-French background, and you had the makings of a Commonwealth Association.

After breakfast, John and I reported to the Adjutant who gave us a lecture, as Adjutants are wont to do, on what was expected of us as officers. We had to be punctual, remain with our men throughout the training hours, and become proficient in Gurkhali. It seemed like déjà vu. We felt like schoolboys on their first day at school. Following this embarrassing briefing, we were introduced to the Commanding Officer (CO). He was also an Australian; small, thin and stern – I rarely saw him smile. He explained that the battalion had but recently returned from Greece and was now getting reacquainted with peacetime soldiering. I was beginning to wonder if I was ever to see any action. Only about twenty percent of the riflemen were new and hadn't seen action. He went on to tell us that we would each be taking over a Company from officers who would soon be returning to England. He allowed us a few days for the handover. I was to have "D" Company. The present mission of the battalion was to keep the peace in and around Ahmadabad.

I was later escorted to "D" Company lines that seemed to be far removed from Battalion Headquarters. On reaching the Company lines, I was astonished at the size of the Company sector. It must have covered up to thirty-five acres and included the offices, barrack rooms, stores and sports fields as well as an outside kitchen and a vegetable garden. The officer I was to replace was Captain Smith, a fair haired, slight and cheerful Englishman. I quickly discovered what a remarkable man he was. Though young, he was in poor health and, I believe, had been wounded in Burma. His wartime exploits had earned him a Military Cross and a Mention-in-Dispatches. The men of the Company worshipped him and he loved the men with whom he was always joking. I had hoped the men had hated him for these were huge boots to fill. He had a high-pitched voice similar to a woman's and, on hearing him speak when he was out of view, I mistook it for an English girl. Together, we went over the administrative routine that seemed simple enough and then discussed the problems concerning peacetime training. Here were men, most of whom had been in action for the past three or four years and who had become experienced and hardened fighting soldiers. Now that the war was over, what type of training would they need and how could their interest be maintained? He admitted that he had never served as a peacetime soldier and hadn't an answer to the problem, so it was up to me to see that the men retained their high standard of efficiency. As regards to my being wet behind the ears, he told me not to worry, all I had to do was adopt a paternal style of leadership, earn the trust and respect of the GCOs and men, show good will, humour, fairness and an understanding of "Kaida" – the way of doing things in a Gurkha regiment – and all would be well. A tall order that was going to take time and, as far as I could see, time was not on my side.

An incident that occurred in Burma typifies Captain Smith. He and his Subedar were sitting on a rock during a lull in battle when he spotted a live Japanese grenade lying on the ground just behind the Subedar. He realized that the grenade should have exploded and that it might possibly be a dud. He turned to the Subedar and in a joking manner said: "Don't look now but I think that you're sitting on a grenade," and invited the Subedar to retreat from the impending danger. After some time, the grenade still hadn't exploded, he remarked: "Typical, another cheap Japanese product." When Captain Smith left for England, a few days later, he was taken to the railway station in a jeep pulled by a number of riflemen and accompanied by the remainder of the Company who cheered him all the way. I felt less than adequate taking over from such a man. The Subedar must have realized my concern and put me more at ease by recounting how very awkward Captain Smith had been when, as a subaltern, he had joined the Company. I thanked the Subedar and promised him that I would do my best.

Without Captain Smith's guidance, I suddenly found myself very much alone. Maybe this was just as well. The key to the whole business was language. I had to learn to speak Gurkhali well and I had to do so quickly. I also had to show that I could command and be a Sah'b in the eyes of the GCOs. I considered the primary task to be the production of a suitable training program as none appeared to exist. To start with, I discussed the matter with the Subedar who felt that the pre-war training was out-of-date. I suggested competitive field training, drills in aid to civil power, better and more innovative field-firing exercises, a current affairs program, sports, and field trips to industrial plants. The Subedar did not voice his relief, nor did he show it, but I got the impression that he was secretly pleased with my suggestions.

My Subedar, whose name was Indradhoj Lumtar, was very tall for a Gurkha, being over six foot. He and the Company Babu (Clerk) were the only two who spoke and understood English. The Babu had the rank of Corporal and was much better educated than the riflemen and, consequently, had the respect of these simple hillsmen. The Gurkha calls himself by his given name followed by the name of his tribe or clan. There are a limited number of first names and most common being Bahadur (Brave), Man (Spirit), Dil (Heart), or Bhakta (Loyal); hence, a man often acquired the name of his regimental number as a nickname. For example, Rifleman Bahadur Rai would be called, Rai 32. In my Company, the majority of the men's names were Bahadur, Thapa, and Gurung, and so it was necessary to use their regimental numbers to differentiate between them and to prevent a score of men coming to you each time you called a name out.

I intended to give a brief talk to the men of the Company during my first official parade as Company Commander. With the help of the Subedar, I prepared a short speech in Gurkhali that introduced myself, informed the men about the training program and asked the men to call out their names when I inspected them during the next several days so I might familiarize them. Using a crib, I managed to pass the message and felt relieved to have done so. While I was talking, I could feel the men quietly observing and noting my every action and could almost hear their inner thoughts like, "Hello, what have we got here?"

ACCOMMODATIONS

For quarters, I went to see the local contractor who showed me a number of bungalows in the Officer's Lines. Having agreed on one, I then had to furnish it. Given the current political situation, there was no point in buying any furniture, so I rented all that I was told I needed and, twenty-four hours later, moved into the building. The bungalows followed a broadly common pattern – a high plinth that raised the floor a few feet above the ground; a living/dining room arrangement; a bedroom, and a bathroom. There was a wide, wraparound veranda while each room was equipped with large, electric ceiling fans that helped keep the interior cool, and when set at top speed, the force of the breeze kept the mosquitoes at ground level. This allowed you to sleep without a mosquito net that was a blessing for inside one of these nets, the heat was stifling. Occasionally, the fan would cut a large beetle in half and scatter the bloody remains out like a machine gun on the furniture, food and on anyone below. Water, rarely abundant, was often contaminated, and since the local filtration system was no guarantee or immunity from bacteria, you didn't drink any; instead there was bottled water. The water pressure in the pipes was low so that when you took a shower, the result was less than satisfactory in being bathed or refreshed from the humidity. During the day, the shower water was hot as the pipes bringing the water from the main source were laid close to the surface of the ground. By and large, the bungalow was attractive, comfortable and certainly adequate.

As regards to servants, I asked the Subedar to find me a reliable man. Rather than return to their respective villages, those men who had been wounded in battle were given the option of remaining with the battalion as servants and in administrative roles. Many preferred this alternative than to go back home. Those selected as officers' servants were delighted and viewed the position as one of honour and not a form of servility. The man chosen by the Subedar to be my servant was a Gurkha of about twenty-eight, who was badly crippled as a result of being too near a bursting mortar bomb. The right side of his face and body was terribly scarred and he had some difficulty using his right arm. This was the 'sound' man I had asked for. I was assured that he would make an excellent servant and, having been recommended, I accepted his service, though I was dubious at best. Those thoughts were soon discarded and, as it turned out, the Subedar was correct in his judgment. When the man reported to me, we discussed his duties that included arranging for and organizing the other servants I would need. His quarters was one of the smaller buildings used as domestic quarters behind the bungalow. By the time we selected the remaining servants, the domestic quarters were crowded with wives and children. This new 'family' of mine provided me with a personal valet, house cleaners, a cook, and the others to do the laundry and ironing – all at a hefty price as I had to pay for the extra help.

Since I was expected to entertain others to dinner, I had to purchase some silver cutlery and china. I made a point of only buying the minimum and whatever extra was required, my servant would borrow from another officer's servant. It was quite common when dining out at a brother officer's bungalow to see some of your own silver and china on his table. Sometimes, some of your servants would also have been roped into helping one another. The first time I entertained 'at home,' I decided to accompany my servant to the market to see what was available. The bargaining that took place between my servant and the merchants seemed never-ending as each individual manoeuvred in a thousand subtle ways to avoid any demeaning loss of face.

The Officer's Lines were shaded by a number of large trees that were inhabited by a plethora of monkeys. These primates, when fully grown, must have measured about three feet tall. They had a long tail used solely for balance. The monkeys moved about in troupes bounding or scurrying along the branches of the trees or sat on the ground grooming each other. They kept very much to themselves and caused no trouble other than their annoying manner of communication that seemed to consist of an incessant discord of piercing screams that, thankfully, ceased at nightfall. The monkeys, as well as many other animals in the region, were considered as religious beings and were not to be harmed. Our Welsh Company Commander, Taffy, owned a Dalmatian that spent much of its time chasing any monkey on the ground till it reached safety in the trees. When the dog caught a monkey, the other monkeys would scream fiercely and come to the victim's rescue, attacking the dog, biting it with their long yellow fangs. The dog never learned his lesson and had several wounds to bear witness to his foolish antics.

DAILY ROUTINE

The normal daily routine consisted of about fifteen percent administration and eighty-five percent training. At 5:30 a.m., I would be awakened by my servant peering down at me, holding my chota hazri. To be awoken at that hour by a badly disfigured individual with a ghastly expression, that I later recognized as an attempted smile, took some getting used to. I would watch him from my bed as he struggled to place the teacup handle just right so that all I had to do was stretch my arm and my fingers would fall onto the handle. Since I didn't enjoy tea in bed, I soon changed the ritual to our mutual satisfaction. Having washed and shaved, the norm was for the four Company Commanders, and any other officer who wanted to join-in, to gather at one of the Company Lines and take on that Company at basketball or volleyball. It was still cool at that time of day and I would play wearing a sweater. The game would last a half hour. Afterwards, I would return to my quarters for a shower and get dressed into the uniform for that morning's activities. I would then go to the Company Officer and attend to administrative details, instructing the Subedar and clerk as to what had to be done, how and in what priority. This would take up to an hour by which time the sun was up and the early morning coolness had evaporated into an expanding haze of heat.

Having dealt with the administrative matters, I, together with the Subedar and the three Jemadar Platoon Commanders, would inspect the Company Lines, the barrack rooms with the men standing by their beds, and the kitchen. The riflemen could expect to be placed on a charge for the smallest infractions such as: torn, damaged or dirty clothing, dust on a locker, poorly displayed equipment, and other oversights. Though this seems petty, it is all part of self-discipline in hygiene, orderliness, and responsibilities. Bearing in mind the officious subalterns at the Maidstone Depot, I left the matter of finding fault to the Jemadars and Havildars. The Company Lines were always spotless as was the kitchen; the latter being a small, round gallery built of clay that was demolished every month and a new one constructed nearby. The barrack rooms were routinely washed down and were always clean and well aired. It was a must to inspect the vegetable garden each morning, the main reason being to check on the growth of some form of vegetable that was to be exhibited at a forthcoming gala. There was a simple yet very effective irrigation system whereby waste-water from the ablutions would flow down a channel to the garden and, by means of directional viaducts, enable each part to be watered several times.

At 8:30 a.m., the officers had breakfast. Since I was up since 5:30 a.m., I was generally hungry by breakfast and enjoyed a substantial English type meal. After breakfast, I returned to my Company for the morning Company Parade where the day's program was announced. The training, if held in camp, would continue till 12:30 p.m. I would go home for a shower, change my clothes and attend lunch. Because of the immense heat, a siesta period of about an hour-and-a-half after lunch was permitted. I found it impossible to sleep or rest during this time of day, and instead, played tennis at the Gymkhana Club or soccer with the Gurkhas. I would drag the protesting tennis pro from his officer at the Club and have him play for an hour. I would follow whatever game I had played with a swim to cool down. The unit had a medium-sized indoor pool, the water being delightfully cool. I was informed that one of the departing Majors would sometimes take his Indian mistress to the pool to conduct his private affairs, so I normally made some noise entering the building to give him (or anyone else) fair warning. At 3:30 p.m., the training program continued until 5 p.m. at which time, I would return to the

Company Office to deal with disciplinary or personal matters and to attend to other administrative requirements.

I was always astonished at the Gurkha's stoicism when faced with a disciplinary charge. The individual would be marched in, the charge would be read out by the Subedar followed by comments by the individual's Platoon Commander and, during this commentary, the man on charge would continue to grin stupidly. Rarely, if ever, did the accused man offer an excuse in his defence. The grin would be plastered on even when the verdict was a severe punishment. I sometimes wondered if they understood the predicament they were in. Leniency in awarding punishment was not practiced. Strict discipline had to be maintained. Moreover, the individual never expected other than the maximum punishment that correlated with the misdemeanor or crime.

From 5:30 p.m. to 8:30 p.m., I either socialized at the Gymkhana Club or did whatever I desired. Officers rarely attended the dinner at the Mess unless it was an official Dinner Night. The Duty Officer and the Indian doctor were the only regular diners while the others were either being entertained or were hosting some do or other. I would then practice (have lessons) my Gurkhali for an hour, read and go to bed around 11:30 p.m. What an exhausting day! And here I was to train soldiers to prepare for civil unrest.

When training outside the camp, whether at the rifle ranges or on a field training exercise, you remained with your men and continued training day and night if necessary. You took your meals with the men and slept outdoors depending on the type of training being undertaken. Such training would occur about once a week and, though more interesting than routine camp training, it was tiring due to the ever present heat. Special parades were held during the week. The Adjutant's Parade was held at 8 a.m. on Wednesdays. The purpose of the parade was to train the British officers in the correct drill movements for official parades since the majority of officers had forgotten these during the war years. None of the officers enjoyed these parades, especially those who were tall and who had to keep up with a drum beating at the rifle regimental pace – one hundred and forty paces a minute. There were no Gurkha troops on parade and the officers had to maintain the correct distance one from the other as if leading a company of men. On the given commands, each officer in turn had to bellow out the correct order while executing intricate drills. It was far more difficult to perform the drills correctly without the men behind you than with them there. Many errors were made, much to the amusement of the Gurkhas, who were watching the circus act from a safe distance. I once got into trouble by appearing late for one of these parades. I had been held up by the Commanding Officer and turned up as the officers were patrolling up and down the parade ground prior to being ordered "On Parade." You were always required to be punctual which meant being at the correct place five minutes before the appointed time. The Adjutant explained that it would have been much better had I not turned up at all. The Gurkhas had witnessed my mistake and this had set a bad example. For my sins, I was required to be the Duty Officer for one week.

The Commanding Officer's Parade was a formal and very serious affair. The Battalion had to be on parade, including the lame and "walking sick." Those incapable of drilling, formed up on one side of the parade ground. The parade included an inspection of each company by the CO accompanied by the Subedar-Major, the Adjutant, and the Battalion Second-in-Command. The CO would purposely ask the Company Commander awkward questions about certain idiosyncrasies about his men to see how well he knew them – all one hundred and twenty of them. He would ask: "What recent trades training has this rifleman had in the past three months?" "How many riflemen are first class marksmen on the light machine gun?" "What is the ratio of married men to bachelors?" And, "Why is rifleman Thapa Sing's wife not with him?" You lost a few pounds of sweat on each of these occasions. The men relished these parades for they could show off their expertise in drill that was far superior to that of the officers. Even when you made a fool of yourself, the GCOs, and especially the Subedars, treated their young officers as if they were gods. When the parade was over, my Subedar would tactfully tell me what errors I had made and what I should have done. He advised me to follow Captain Smith's example of always answering the CO's questions even if it meant making up a plausible answer. He and the men would back me up no matter what I said. Following the inspection, the battalion executed a march to the accompaniment of the unit's pipes and drums band, the salute being taken by the CO. Rifle regiments do not have brass bands nor the normal Regimental Colours. The band consists of pipers and drummers and the bandsmen are dressed the same as in a Scottish unit, in kilts, even during the hottest weather. The regimental honours are shown on the drums.

On one of these Commanding Officer's Parades, the Battalion's Second-in-Command reported two senior Jemadars absent when he handed the parade over to the CO. They had received permission to be absent by the Quartermaster, their superior officer, but the Adjutant had not been advised and, anyway, the Quartermaster didn't have the authority to give such leave of absence. The Commanding Officer refused to take over the parade and instead ordered an immediate open court-martial. The battalion was then reformed into a square and the two Jemadars were marched under escort to the center of the square where the charge ws read to them by the Subedar-Major. Being found guilty, they were both demoted on the spot to Havildar-Major (Sergeant Major), the Subedar-Major performing the solemn duty of removing the Gurkha officer insignia. I was really shocked on this occasion partly at the speed with which the disciplinary action had taken place, but mostly at the severity of the punishment. It was overwhelming. I looked at the riflemen on parade expecting to see an expression of anger on their faces and was surprised to note no apparent hostility towards the CO or any others in authority, considering the Adjutant wasn't punished for his error. Given the turbulent times in which we were living, and the fact that there were a few troublemakers among the more senior GCOs, the CO's actions were correct. For a while, the troublemakers kept a low profile. This episode made me acutely aware of the harsh discipline that prevailed and of the formidable power of a Commanding Officer.

At 11 a.m. each Friday, the Commanding Officer held his weekly "Officers' Meeting" which all British officers were required to attend. These meetings followed a set pattern. The CO would review the previous week's program and express his satisfaction or displeasure on the praised or condemned officer, who had to give good reason for his blunder or his initiative. The following week's program was then covered. Each Company Commander explained his sub-unit's program and how it was to be implemented. General matters were also discussed such as forthcoming festivals, visits, new doctrines and policies.

NATURE'S WRATH

Due to the distances involved, I used a bicycle to get from my bungalow to the Officer's Mess and the Company Lines. Though there were roads, it was quicker to ride cross-country and this I did for a while. Much to my annoyance, the grass thereabouts contained minute but very sharp spikes that played havoc with the bike's tires, consequently, my bicycle was in constant need of repairs. Due to these spikes, it was almost impossible to sit on the ground or go barefoot without suffering a nasty sting. Even "Johnny" Gurkha (so called from the time the Gurkhas had served with the "John Company," better known as the East India Company), with his leather thick soles, wore boots rather than risk going barefoot. The grass also contained microbes that would infiltrate under your toenails and from there, slowly eat away the toe. To prevent this happening, you wore thick woolen socks when wearing sandals. Nothing is really safe here.

ON TARGET

Weapon firing on the range was hot work and often boring. The Company would spend several days each month firing different types of weapons to bring the men up to the required standards. Meals would be brought to us from the camp and, at night, all personnel would bivouac at the range. I was very glad to have my specially made camp kit with me for such times.

During firing practices, a red flag was hoisted over the butts and sentries were posted to warn and keep the locals clear of the area, but there was always the odd person who would disregard all warnings and enter the danger zone. While watching a rifle firing practice, I was appalled to see the men on the firing point switch targets from the recommended six foot square target to a group of women carrying water jars on their heads and who seemed oblivious to the danger. I immediately ordered a "cease fire" until the women had been chased away. Whether the Gurkhas would have tried to hit the water jars, I cannot say, but since they weren't particularly good shots, the chances of casualties among the women would have been probable. Some good resulted from this incident. I had always found range work dull and had often thought of ways to make the practices more interesting to improve the men's firing skills. Seeing as how the Gurkhas' attention had been drawn to a moving target, I decided to try using moving targets as an alternative to firing at fixed frames. At the end of the practice, I gathered the men to explain my idea. The butt party, stationed in a deep trench, looked after the targets and would use special targets that resembled troops in different firing positions. On the orders of the officer in charge of the practice, some of the butt party would raise a number of these special targets and run to either left or right for about ten seconds and then lower them to simulate men moving in the open when under fire. While this was going on, the men on the firing point, grouped in sections of ten and under the command of a Section Commander, would await the order to fire and thereafter try to hit as many moving targets as possible. When a target was hit, it was immediately lowered. The men on the firing point would start the practice at 400 yards and slowly advance under orders to 100 yards. This new procedure certainly created considerable interest and competitions between sections and platoons soon took place. It was not long before the other companies followed suit. Whether this new procedure improved the shooting skills of the men is questionable, but it did make firing much more fun and a little more realistic for all concerned.

One morning, when the men were firing the Bren light machine gun from the hip while advancing in line, an accident occurred that could have resulted in carnage. As one group was advancing, the people at each end of the line moved too rapidly and were in front of those firing in the centre. The NCO in charge of the group yelled at the men to fall back, but one man in the centre of the line, while firing his weapon, turned his head to find out what all the fuss was about and in so doing also turned his body with the result that several men to his left were shot down. I, who had been standing behind the group during its advance, shouted: "Karna" (cease fire) and for the men to place their weapons on the ground. I then dashed forward to see what could be done for the wounded men. Two men had been hit in the legs and another had a slight flesh wound. The first aid man bandaged the wounded while I phoned the Adjutant to report the accident. He told me to carry on and that he would send an ambulance to pick up the injured. I immediately started an inquiry into the accident and when that was completed, we continued with the practice. The reaction from the Gurkhas was "Je hola hola" (the equivalent of whatever will be, will be.) The exercise resumed as if nothing had happened. During the evening break, a Jemadar who had served with the fool who had caused the accident, remarked that this was the first time that particular rifleman had ever hit a live target and for the rest of the evening, rifleman Gurung, as he was called, had to put up with a great deal of rubbing from the others.

Night firing, particularly with all types of machine guns using tracers, was more enjoyable for the men. The lines of tracer bullets as they criss-crossed the range, provided a spectacular show. For a finale, an old oil drum filled with rubbish and rags, soaked in gasoline, was used as a target and the gun crew who was first to set it ablaze, received a bottle of raksi (rum) as a reward.

On another occasion, when in the middle of firing practice, we were buzzed by a Lysander aircraft, a motion that the pilot wanted to land. Some bright spark built the airstrip in the middle of the firing range (or vice versa). I informed the Adjutant that we probably had a VIP visitor. Since he hadn't heard of any VIP arrival, to delay the landing for half-an-hour while this visit was confirmed. I had the men brought back to the firing point where they cleared their weapons, and after these had been inspected, I fired a green flare to signal the aircraft to land. As I got to the plane, who should appear but General Slim, wearing a green bush uniform. After the usual courtesies, he remarked on our stalling activities, grinning as he did so. He correctly presumed that the unit hadn't received warning of his visit and so agreed to my request that he spend a few minutes talking to the men while waiting for transport to Battalion Headquarters. He had served as a young officer with the 6th Gurkhas and had also commanded the 2/7th Gurkhas, and therefore, was familiar with Gurkhali. He asked several riflemen to take off their boots and let out a roar of laughter when he noticed that one of the men was not wearing socks. He admitted that he had trouble as a young Gurkha officer in getting the men to wear socks. Within a short space of time, his transport arrived and I didn't see him again until his departure the following morning.

LESSONS ABOUT RIOTS

Being stuck on the range, I missed General Slim's talk to the officers. I later received a run down on the major points. The powers that be had agreed that the bulk of the Gurkha regiments would remain as part of the Indian Army and a few would be transferred to the British Army. Which ones would be transferred had yet to be decided. The Gurkhas would be asked to choose which army they wish to serve; however, the officers were not to get involved in this decision for obvious reasons. Elsewhere, disorder was on the increase especially in the Punjab and in the Calcutta area. With regard to the Battalion, it was to stand ready to come to the aid of civil power. At an Officer's Meeting, the Commanding Officer raised the matter about our readiness should we be called upon. None of the officers had the remotest idea of the procedures to be followed in aid to civil power operations and none of the men had yet been called out on any such operation. A crash course was to be started as soon as possible, including a course on civil power operations. I was the only officer available and so, a few days later, I set off for Jodhpur in the Punjab where the course was held and conducted by British Army personnel. The course covered in great detail all the standard procedures concerning the different operations we might be called upon to perform, for example, guarding essential government buildings and utilities; carrying out patrols and raids; accomplishing rescue missions; establishing road blocks on major routes; and containing mob action when the police had lost all control. By far the most dangerous was controlling a frenzied crowd. Film footage of actual crowd riots and how to quell them accompanied the lessons. We were also shown how an able agent, with little help, could incite a crowd to violence in a matter of minutes. A mob, whipped into agitation, was like a sponge that soaked up more and more people creating ever increasing confusion, fear, hate, irrational behaviour, and violence. Once the crowd was in full cry, it was almost impossible to make oneself heard and maintain control. The crowd could number anywhere from a few thousand people to tens of thousands.

The major portion of the course and the most interesting aspect covered was the manner in which to control a seething mass of screaming humanity who had lost sense of reason. The form was to channel the people down a wide road or avenue to a selected spot where they could be stopped while, simultaneously, preventing more people joining by way of side streets. The latter operation was the least difficult and could be handled by establishing roadblocks as necessary. The main concern was how to stop the forward movement of the large crowd. When confronted by a well disciplined military force that appears ready for action, those in the front ranks of the crowd are apt to lose their nerve and the majority would like to stop; however, those behind, unable to see what is going on ahead, press forward so that those in front cannot stop even when they so wish. Given this likely scenario, the Force Commander has to allow adequate space in which to slow down and eventually stop the mob before it could reach his force.

To block the forward momentum of a lava flow of angry protesters, the military is formed into a square. The side facing the mob can have two or three ranks of riflemen, each armed with a rifle and fixed bayonet. The front rank kneeling while the other two stand. As the front row fire, the other two lines are rearming their rifles. Once the front row has fired, they retreat to the back line while the second line takes the front position like an assembly-line loop. This group forms the main barrier and was remarkably affective for the British during the Battle of Waterloo in 1815 against the French and at Rorke's Drift in South Africa against the Zulu warriors in 1879. A single line of riflemen line each side of the square standing with their backs to the houses but facing the opposition – their job being to cover the windows and roofs of the houses on the other side of the street. The rear of the force is protected by yet another single rank of riflemen facing outwards. The force carries no automatic weapons to prevent excess bloodshed should panic set in. None of the GCOs or NCOs wear any visible rank insignia and each soldier is referred to by number to avoid identification later by members in the crowd. No one may start shooting without the express permission of the Force Commander. In the centre of the square stands the Force Commander with the local magistrate beside him. Only the magistrate may authorize the military to open fire on the crowd and, naturally, he is loath to sign the order to fire fearing for his own safety from local retaliation following the riot. The Force Commander has therefore to use all his ingenuity and guile to obtain such a signature at a time when seconds count. To assist the Commander, he has two orderlies close by to carry messages within the group, there is also a recorder who keeps a log of all the orders given and actions taken. Two banner carriers holding aloft a large cloth banner stretched across the road warning the crowd not to advance beyond a certain point, stand close to the front of the square. To draw the crowd's attention, a bugler is present and, when so directed, blows his bugle as loudly as possible in the hope of quieting the crowd sufficiently for the Force Commander to be heard with the use of a bullhorn. In addition, there is a special squad, armed with clubs and shields, who are either used as a reserve force or to collect the body of a civilian in the crowd who has been shot by the military as proof that the person shot was in fact the person identified to be shot. When time permits, the military force erects a concertina barrier some two or three hundred yards in front of its line. On paper or in the classroom, all this sounds quite straight forward, but in reality the unexpected happens to upset all your plans and you therefore have to be prepared to alter such plans at a moment's notice. An operation of this sort of challenge tests your initiative, courage and calmness under duress.

On my return to the battalion, I briefed the Commanding Officer on the training that had practiced successfully and some of the problems we might likely encounter. A special meeting was held that all British and Gurkha officers needed to attend. As I was the only one who was supplied with this new knowledge, I had to brief the assembly on the types of military responses the battalion might be called upon to perform. I was also directed to prepare the necessary training program. I was assigned one Jemadar from each rifle company to assist with the design and development of the program. During the course at Jodhpur, I had met several British officers whose units had recently experienced action in aid to civil power. With the Commanding Officer's permission, I got in touch with one of those units and broached the subject of assistance in training our officers and men in ACP operations. In response, we were promised a Captain for one week who would bring a record of their action during their most recent exploit and a pamphlet the unit had put together on the procedures they had found the most effective in controlling rioters. With this additional help, an effective training program was soon produced that the Jeadars translated into Gurkhali.

As there were no tall buildings or wide streets in camp similar to those in the city, it was decided to build a mock city area something like a Hollywood film set. The end product was sufficient for our needs but quite flimsy. The battalion used the area to train in all the different phases of ACP. One rifle company would undertake the duties of the military force while the other companies acted as the resisting crowd. Later during a practice, those simulating the rioters got carried away in throwing bricks and bottles and caused a few minor injuries amongst the 'military force.' In the ensuing melee, one of the props, a rather large and heavy wall, collapsed and fell on some of the 'rioters' causing further casualties. A Gurkha was heard to remark that this was an excellent way to deal with rioters. Within a few weeks, all ranks became acquainted with the correct procedures. When not on aid to civil power training, Companies continued the normal field training. To train battle experienced soldiers field training from someone who had no experience of the real thing was terribly embarrassing, and I had to rely on my Subedar for suggestions on how to maintain the men's interest. He told me that Gurkhas loved soldiering and, no matter the type of exercise being conducted, they would enjoy it and do it well. During a battalion exercise when my company was leading the advance, we were fired upon by an 'enemy' group located in two small villages. After giving my orders for the attack, I was amazed at the speed and expertise with which the men completed the task. With a shout of "Ayo Gurkha," that is the Gurkha's war cry meaning "the Gurkhas are coming!," the men dashed forward at the double and I found myself having difficulty keeping up.

Whenever on manoeuvres and we passed a village, the children and idlers would congregate to look at us, to beg for bakshish and to listen to us talk, for few Indians had actually met Gurkhas. On one occasion, I stopped to ask a man for directions, and instead of answering, he asked me a question. This kept the conversation going but proved frustrating in getting a quick answer. I soon learned that this ritual was common all over India. Another observation is that the unit of linear measurement often fluctuates according to the time of day and the season of the year. I was introduced to the 'handkerchief mile' while on a routine march with my Company. A wet handkerchief is tied to a stick and allowed to flutter while the men continue to march at the rifleman's pace. When the handkerchief is dry, a mile has presumably been covered. I suppose that without a map, such a measuring technique might have its use, but I could think of several more accurate ways of obtaining the same result. I asked the Gurkhas why they didn't simply count the number of steps it took to cover a mile and use that as a guide, but they didn't like the distraction. For my part, I continued to use the map.

The Gurkhas are a very superstitious lot and revert to their folklore whenever faced with sickness, injury or ill-fortune and even about travelling a long distance, as I was soon to find out. A few of my men were due for long leave and I had intended to send them off on a Saturday afternoon. My Subedar reminded me that the Gurkhas considered it inauspicious to depart for a journey on a Saturday or to arrive back on a Tuesday. I therefore sent some off on the Monday, but one had no choice but to leave on the Saturday. We got around this by giving him a letter to mail at a station about one hundred miles away but in the direction he would have to take to get home. This part of the journey could then be considered as being "on duty." The Gurkha has two mannerisms that, at first, I found confusing. When answering a question in the affirmative, he would shake his head from side to side. The other peculiarity is when a Gurkha is asked for directions, he would point with his chin rather than use his arm or hand. The chin would only provide a very general direction, but while in this grotesque position, he was incapable of speech and couldn't answer, but time is of no matter in India.

It was the custom when meeting a holder of the Victoria Cross, for the officer and not the private or other ranker, to salute first. We had one rifleman in the Battalion who had been awarded the VC while serving with the 8th Army. Our hero, being a well-disciplined soldier, would salute according to the regulations, that is, so many paces in front of the oncoming officer. As an officer, you had to arrange to salute the man before he came to the salute yet not so far distant that it looked stupid. To get around this, I would salute him when still some distance and then, placing my hands together, would offer the Gurkha salaam – "Ramro chha" – to which he would answer in like manner.

I remained a "griffin," (newcomer) until my men in my Company accepted me. Without my knowing, the Subedar provided a routine report on my behaviour and attitude to the Subedar-Major, who in turn, gave his opinion to the Commanding Officer. Once those concerned were satisfied, I would meet their criteria and a promotion would be recommended, such as to Lieutenant. One morning, as I entered the Company Office, the clerk, in his usual way, greeted me with: "Good morning, Mr. Branson." He was immediately corrected by my Subedar for not having addressed me correctly and by my new rank, Lieutenant Sah'b. What a feeling! I was taken completely aback as I had not been informed of the promotion by the Adjutant. My Subedar then helped to put on my new shoulder rank insignia. During that day, several of the men congratulated me on the promotion. I had the feeling that this accolade was being given as a token of welcome to their family group – the Battalion. On entering the dining room for breakfast, my brother officers made the usual complimentary remarks and jokes. It was while having breakfast that I first learned from the other officers that I had been under assessment since my arrival at this unit, as was the custom.

On returning to my bungalow that night, I was annoyed to find the fan switched off and incense sticks burning on the table, but when I noticed a tray on the table with a bouquet of flowers interwoven into the shape of a miniature garden and alongside it some money, I realized the offering was something to do with being accepted by the men. I had no idea as to how I was suppose to act or reciprocate, if at all, so I checked with one of the officers close by. He informed me that this offering was a custom similar to Nazrana – the offering of presents or coins on ceremonial occasions as a token of respect or allegiance. I was advised to leave the incense burning all night and to leave the flowers as they were but remove the money and, in the morning, I should hand my servant a sum of money in return as a token of my appreciation for services rendered. That night, I hardly slept due to having to sleep under a mosquito net. By mid-morning, the fan was back on and things returned to normal.

Rum for Dinner

Now that I was a full-fledged member of the Battalion, I was invited to dine out by each of my platoons in turn. The purpose of these get-togethers was to help me get to know my men and vice versa. On each occasion, the "dinner" was held in the platoon lines under trees decorated with coloured ribbons and hanging oil lamps. We sat on long wooden benches close to tables laden with bowls of all sorts of spices. Bottles of rum were placed in front of each man. The meal consisted of rum with a curry to act as blotting paper. Though the men's meal was prepared in a single large cauldron, an individual dish had been prepared for me and this had been discreetly placed in the cauldron to pretend it was the same food as that served to the men – a sensitive touch. During the meal, I was asked all about myself, my background and what I had done in the past, and in return, I asked several of the men similar questions as best I could using much the same phrases as those spoken by the men. Whenever I made a mistake, the men would unabashedly correct my grammar or vocabulary. When I, or someone else, made a joke, I was slapped on the back and none too gently, for the Gurkha is not gentle by nature. My glass of rum was constantly topped up and I was encouraged to drink deep and often. When in Rome... The Gurkha likes his rum, but I believe he enjoys gambling even more. After the meal, a number of games were played and, in particular, the game of Ludo. I was forced into playing numerous games of this children's pastime and never seemed to win. The victor of each game received a bottle of rum that I was expected to pay for. I spent the first such evening signing chits and as I became increasingly tight, I must have signed chits for anything placed in front of me. Whoever was in charge of the party made sure that I didn't become completely inebriated before I had spent the required amount of time with the men. I remember getting up from my chair and wondering what the table was doing in mid-air. I awoke the next morning in my bed with a cracking headache and my servant handing me a cup of hot tea laced with, of all things, rum, but this managed to magically clear my head. My servants had been alerted to carry me back to my bungalow last night. I was very relieved when my Subedar told me that these dinners would occur at infrequent intervals.

At these platoon parties, the Gurkhas would compete in a game special to the unit. It entailed cutting a bamboo cane with a khukri into as many bits as possible. A three-foot cane was thrust into the ground, leaving about two-feet upright. On the word 'Go' the player would cleanly slice the cane into smaller and smaller pieces. The more expert would try starting at the bottom and work up as the cane was in the air. I was invited to try and as my luck would have it, only managed to split the cane in one place and nearly took my foot off due to my clumsiness, but the Gurkhas politely applauded my futile effort.

Some time later, I was called upon to be the President and sole member of a Board of Inquiry into the loss of some equipment that had been held by an Indian Ordnance unit close by. The clerks, whose responsibility it was to safeguard the equipment were Muslims and Hindus, accused each other of incompetence. Each side was ready to bring forth an unending number of witnesses to attest to their honesty and to provide the necessary alibis. They were all well schooled in the art of deceit. Trying to decide which of the two false accounts was the less untrue and trying to dispense justice fearlessly to protect the weak against the less weak, the incoherent against the plausible, while surrounded by lies and flattery was a Herculean task. I mistrusted all the witnesses and, rather than permit a possible injustice, I took an example from the Bible. Putting on Solomon's cloak, I summarily found both groups guilty of negligence. I ordered that both parties pay an equal share to compensate for the lost equipment. Since each group had saved 'face,' each was satisfied with the findings of the court.

Life in the Indian Army could be expensive even during the time I was there and, if not well off, you had to be careful to live within your means. Fortunately, the pay of an officer in the Indian Army was considerably more generous than the equivalent rank pay in the British Army. Furthermore, most regimental British officers were assigned non-regimental duties concerned with the local government for which they were paid handsomely. For example, our Quartermaster received thousands of extra rupees in his capacity as the Chairman of the Hydro Commission and as a Director on the Board of Waterways. It is interesting to note that he sent most of this extra money to his wife in London to be distributed among the poor in the London slums – his childhood home. To entice officers to attend courses, they received a refund of two and a half times the cost of their travel expenses. Those due for long leave, which could be as long as six months, chose to attend a course in England and thereby had their passage paid and, in addition, received some extra spending money.

Other than being appointed the Company Commander of 'D' Company, I was also assigned the duties of Unit Cypher Officer, Unit Sports Officer, and Mess Secretary. I was also appointed to a non-regimental job of Anti-Malaria Officer for the North Bombay district, for which I received a monthly fee that easily covered the costs I incurred in game hunting and other more leisurely pastimes. As Cypher Officer, I was called upon to encode and decipher the odd confidential and secret messages going to or coming from higher headquarters. This job was anything but demanding and had one advantage, it kept me abreast of what was happening in general, both politically and militarily. I thoroughly enjoyed being the Unit Sports Officer. Other than organizing sports for the men, I also ran a program for the Gurkha children and organized several meets that the local schools were invited to participate in. The two groups of kids got along famously and friendships was started that helped to cement relationships between the locals and the Unit. I introduced the men to swimming and boxing. All enjoyed swimming but were not keen on boxing, preferring the Indonesian kick-boxing style to the Western fisticuffs. The children were keen pupils and bravely undertook whatever you asked of them. Most children are eager to do well. I recall a certain training lesson in diving. One very young boy insisted on looking where he was diving rather than tucking his chin into his chest. Instead of springing off a ledge, he would bend his legs and simply fall forward with his head unprotected, arms by his side and eyes glued to the approaching water. After each belly flop and his face becoming more and more red, I told the boy to dive in backwards. He peered up at me with a quizzical expression, so I demonstrated by flopping backwards into the water. The young boy did as he was told and I pointed out to him that he had dived without the need to look at the water. From then on he gained more confidence.

PETTY OFFICERS

I didn't enjoy being the Mess Secretary as it took up too much of my time and I didn't like working for the Battalion Second-in-Command who was the permanent Mess President. The man was a terrible snob who refused to recognize junior officers. I found he had a weak character for he would delegate to me not only matters concerning the Mess, but other jobs that resulted in my becoming his private secretary. At first, I accepted these extra duties, but when it came to disciplining other officers for misbehaviour in the Mess, I refused under the excuse that I was the most junior officer and therefore, unauthorized to deal with such matters. It wasn't long before a more pliable participant replaced me. I recall one occasion when the Quartermaster went out of his way to annoy the President. As the QM entered the dining room, he pretended to have a sneezing fit and instead of using a handkerchief to blow his nose, used the nearest curtain. The President turned purple but said nothing at the time. Later, he told me to put the QM in his place. It was then that I told him that it was not my place to do so.

MALARIA: THE STING OF DEATH

Prior to taking on the position of Anti-Malaria Officer, I was sent on the appropriate course that I combined with a short leave in Bombay. The course was held in a large hospital in Poona, which is quite close to the city. The course consisted of briefings on the causes of malaria; what preventative measures were recommended; and how to diagnose variances in the number of people contacting the disease. I always wondered why the public wasn't better educated regarding the prevention of fatal diseases and about proper hygiene. The instructors were all Indian doctors. In their view, malaria was a Godsend in that it kept the population growth at bay, killing off millions of unfortunates. We were shown a film on what it was like to contract the disease. The film came from reminiscences of those who had lived through a severe period of it. We also visited malaria patients at the hospital and were shown how to recognize inherent malaria. All these depressing scenes made me all the more convinced to take preventative measures against contracting this frightening affliction. To this day, I can't sleep in a room where there is a mosquito flying about. I have to find it and kill it. Towards the end of the course, we were sent to a small Indian village to collect speciments of the female anopheles mosquito that we later viewed under the microscope. Holding in our sweaty hands the test tubes in which we had to collect the specimens. We entered a number of huts, each one reeking of a pungent odour. The interior was very dark and it was extremely difficult in catching mosquitoes, little lone seeing them. On-the-other-hand, the mosquitoes had no trouble in finding us and, since we were wearing short sleeve shirts and shorts, we naturally were vulnerable targets. Whose bright idea was this? On our return to the classroom, I asked the instructors why we had not been made to take adequate anti-mosquito precautions? They laughed and one of them replied: "Do you know of any nurse that has succumbed to a disease from which her patient was suffering?" It was an incredulous statement. I mentioned diphtheria and he simply added: "O ye of little faith."

As District Anti-Malaria Officer, I was required to visit the schools in a number of towns in the area. The schools having been alerted of my visit would have the children already lined up for my inspection. As I approached, the children would bare their midriff so that I could feel the area around the bile duct. Depending on the hardness of the area, I was supposed to tell the degree of damage cause by malaria. I had little faith in this form of diagnosis but it was what I had been taught to do on the course and, moreover, the school officials and children expected it of me. I recorded the results of my findings and diligently forwarded these to the appropriate health department where, I'm sure, it was filed away with the thousands of other similar reports, never to see the light of day.

Child mortality was very high with five out of ten never reaching the age of ten. I discussed this with our unit doctor who explained that the main problem was one of cross stress, by which the body was unable to ward off anti-bodies due to inherent malaria, dysentery, malnutrition and poor hygiene practices. When visiting the schools on my regular rounds, I couldn't help but realize that about fifty percent of the smiling and seemingly happy children would die within a few years. Since most of the children were Muslims, death was regarded very much in the same way as in the Christian faith unlike the Hindu's belief in the cycle of rebirth.

Officers, who should have known better by refusing to take their Mepacrine tablets (anti-malaria pills), only made my job as Unit Anti-Malaria Officer even more exacerbating. I had the Mess cook crush the tablets and insert the powdered medication into the curry, but the officers would have none of it. Mad. These tablets, if taken over an extended period, turned one's skin yellow. The tablets didn't prevent you catching malaria, but helped to control the effects of the disease. I had been told that Scotch whiskey was almost as effective as the pills and so I gave the officers the option of either for breakfast, lunch and dinner. Those who chose the whiskey were charged for it and given the staggering price of whiskey, much more expensive than in England, many of the officers begrudgingly chose the tablets.

It was essential to keep fit to maintain good health. I tried to spend about three hours each day doing some form of physical exertion. Other than the morning volleyball game and the afternoon tennis or soccer game, I would sometimes also play a game of squash. The floor of the squash court was made of bamboo that, when damp, was as slippery as ice, adding a new dimension to the game. Most officers played some form of sport after working hours that resulted in their remaining overheated for most of the evening. We all drank copious quantities of orange-pani (orange juice and water) in an effort to keep cool, but all that did was make us sweat more. To prevent getting prickly heat, I showered and changed clothes several times a day and ensured the dhobi-wallah starched only those parts of my clothes that required creases. I rarely had to tell my servant what clothes I needed for the 'bush telephone' had already warned him.

SOCIAL CLIMBING

One's social life during the mid-1940s was quite different to pre-war days enjoyed by Indian Army officers. For one thing, we no longer had the afternoons off and were limited to visiting the country due mainly to the prevailing unrest throughout India. With the coming of Independence, many British families had returned to the United Kingdom with the result that "club life" was far less lively than before. Another factor was the rising cost of living. There were fewer officers with large private incomes and they had to live less extravagantly than had been the custom. There were very few officers who owned their own horses or who could afford to play polo. Some old social trends remained, such as not permitting women in the Mess. Mess life hadn't changed much, only the doctor and Duty Officer frequented the Mess in the evening except on the occasion of a Burra Khana (Official Mess Dinner).

The Battalion was located a few miles outside Ahmadabad and in the British cantonment. The centre of social life in the cantonment was the Gymkhana Club. As the wives and families of members had the right of user, it became the gathering place of the British clans. In the mid-1940s, Indians were granted membership. This changed the ambience from one of stiff manners to a more relaxed and friendly atmosphere, though the gossip continued as ever before. Since the club was within easy walking distance from the unit lines and the fact that a sprinkling of females were always present, most officers drifted over there for a drink or two and a game of billiards before dinner. If you weren't entertaining others or being entertained, you would often dine at the club with some of the other members and their families.

Gymkhana clubs were to be found in all the major cities throughout India. They were massive structures surrounded by enormous grounds, most of which were used for sport such as polo, cricket, golf, and rugby. Close to the club terrace would be a large swimming pool and a neighbouring tennis court. The Almadabad Club was no exception. The dining room could accommodate two hundred people at one sitting. A large covered veranda on the second floor overlooked the sports fields and it was there that most members congregated before and after dinner. There would be about a dozen people at the club during weekdays, while on weekends, the number would be ten-fold, socializing till the early morning hours. In earlier times, a newcomer was supposed to serve a probationary period before being accepted as a member to ensure he was "a good fit." Fortunately, by the time I arrived, the rules had changed, though some of the old members still held the view that newcomers should be seen but not heard. Cocktail parties were held once every two weeks and on special occasions, such as New Year's Day. Unlike many cocktail parties, these were well worth attending, given that much of the conversation focused on current affairs. Many of the businessmen, both British and Indian, had communication tentacles that stretched across the country and were thus able to analyze the overall situation that existed at a specific time. Since the information the unit was receiving through official channels was limited, and often confusing, this additional news proved valuable to our Commanding Officer.

Most of the wives I met at the club were quite charming, but had very little of interest (as far as I was concerned) to say, making conversation awkward. Some of the older wives insisted on wearing their husband's rank and were troublemakers with their gossip and incessant interference in other people's affairs. The younger women, including the married ones, were starving for attention and affection. I was willing to provide both but was cautious about the latter and was warned that carnal knowledge could come back to haunt me. Socially, it was an artificial society. Even though it was still carefree, to assume nothing had changed since the height of the British Raj was totally illogical. The fact that you had to follow protocol (curfews, restricted access to certain sections of the city, and a bevy of other stipulations) gave support to this illusion. Nevertheless, the presence and exemplary behaviour of the Indians at the club did help to bring the haughty British down a peg or two.

BE A SPORT

When not otherwise occupied, I would sometimes play cricket for the club team. As an opening batter, I was able to enjoy both batting at an early stage of the game and, once called 'out,' could enjoy the company of those watching the game with a cool drink in my hand. Once padded up, batting could be a trial due to the immense heat, but I rarely lasted more than a few overs and thus was soon in the shade of the veranda. Standing in mid-field for half a day was the worst part of the game, but it had to be endured like so many other things in India.

I tried golf but found it of little fun as there was no so-called fairway but hard grit and the greens pitted and poorly manicured. Furthermore, monkeys were everywhere causing additional hazards, usually stealing the balls, thinking they were eggs. In spite of these inconveniences, two elderly club members would go out and play one round each weekend. They would set off with but one set of clubs and a bottle of whisky. Their round of golf ended well short of the 18th hold. It was understood that a driver with a jeep would look for them around 3 p.m. and bring them back to the club, whereupon they would promptly order another round of whiskeys.

Shooting wild game was the favourite weekend pastime. The Commanding Officer would invite one or several wealthy mill owners in the district to join our hunting party. In almost every case, the man would accept the invitation and would reciprocate by inviting the officers to stay the weekend at his palatial home. Our group would normally consist of three or four officers who would descend on the chosen family a little before lunchtime on the Saturday and spend the afternoon playing tennis or going for a swim. After dinner, there would be dancing to records and games of bridge or poker. All this was made the more agreeable should the host have daughters or have invited other young people for the evening. Young white women were a rarity in India, consequently, their looks hardly mattered for the occasion was anything but permanent.

For the actual shoot, we always brought along a dozen or so Gurkhas to act as beaters. A non-commissioned officer (NCO) would plan the operation as though engaged in a battle. It was amusing to hear the NCO calling for a "left flank attack" or an "advance in extended line" as he directed his beaters. From time to time, the Gurkhas were invited to have a shot and, at the end of the day's shoot, the game was shared among all the participants. Being Hindu, the Gurkhas would chop off the heads of the game supposedly before the bird died, but whether it was dead or alive didn't really matter. Most times we shot duck and snipe; the former being a staple breakfast dish – a duck per officer. Since I was a poor shot, I missed most of the birds that came my way. To pull my leg, the other officers insisted that since I rarely, if ever, hit the target, my share of the trophy was the bird's bill. As I was having no luck in shooting down the small, fast moving ducks I decided to try my hand at pegging a crocodile. I was lucky and killed one. I brought back the skinned belly and hung it with the rest of the game outside the Mess kitchen. Within a very short space of time there emerged an odious stench. The culprit was the skinned belly. I volunteered to remove my "trophy" on condition that I would be served duck at breakfast. I had my revenge.

Shooting crocodile is quite a sport, if I may use the term. The idea is to shoot the crocodile just behind its head to paralyze it. You then approach the beast and immobilize each leg by clamping it down with a rope attached to a peg driven into the ground. This is followed by pegging the tail, and finally, give it a coup-de-grace. All this you have to do on your own. For much of the time, crocodiles remain on river embankments facing the water as a quick escape or a swift entry. When disturbed, they dig their claws into the earth and slide down the muddy slipway into the murky water. You have to be sure to paralyze the reptile before it can slither into the water. Since accuracy was not my forte, I had to get pretty close to the target to ensure some degree of success. After firing, I was never sure whether I had hit the animal, let alone paralyzed it, and this made the sport that much more exciting. The crocodile is a wily creature and would sometimes "act possum" on the surface of the water with a wishful, perhaps slightly covetous look and, if not paralyzed, would lash out with its tail or leap out of the water, its cavernous mouth gaping wide displaying its rows of white, daggers of teeth. When engaged in this sport, I would invite a number of my men and have them take turns at pegging a crocodile. Its tail is as lethal as its mouth. The men found the exercise huge fun, more so when the crocodile hadn't been paralyzed and came charging.

On one of these expeditions, I had managed to peg down a crocodile and one of the Gurkhas offered to take my picture in the classical pose with one foot on the trophy. As the photograph was being taken, the crocodile gave a tremendous reflect death spasm. I was photographed in a most undignified position – flying upside down through the air. You can imagine my surprise and terror. On collecting my wits, I carefully approached the now immobile body of the crocodile and gave it a few prods here and there to assume myself that it really was dead. Meanwhile, the Gurkhas were having fits of laughter. It does one good to occasionally be ridiculed. It is a useful reminder to not take oneself too seriously, but the Gurkhas' sense of humour was always ready to ensure that one didn't.

OFFICERS MESS ETIQUETTE

The Officers Mess was comfortably furnished and had all the amenities you could wish for, but there was too few officers to create any sort of congenial atmosphere. Breakfast was a silent affair with next to no conversation whereas lunch was a cheerful event. You normally had a drink and maybe a game of billiards followed by a curry lunch. I've always found that a curry, especially a hot one, encourages conversation. Anyway, during the meal, there was considerable chatter. Maybe this was due to the fact that officers saw little of each other during the working hours. It was at the Mess that you got to know your brother officers since the four Company Commanders shared a good sense of humour and were loquacious companions. The clown in the group was John, the South African. He was full of energy but could be a loose cannon and I was constantly on guard wondering what he was going to do next.

A Burra Khana (Mess Dinner) was held once a month where the Commanding Officer was invited to partake. Only candles lit the dining room that meant the fans had to be turned off. A punkah, trailing a tasseled cloth fringe suspended from a long pole, swung slowly to and fro above the heads of those dining in a feeble attempt to dispel the heat and humidity in the room. An occasional shout from the Mess Havildar would keep the punkah wallah from falling asleep on the job, but to little purpose. The body heat generated by a room packed with men, all in full dress, together with the heat of the food and the outside temperature, produced a suffocating atmosphere. In an effort to lessen the effects of body heat, the seating was arranged that your neighbour was at least two arms length from where the next man was sitting. I had difficulty seeing the individual sitting across from me as down the centre of the table were a number of tall silver sculptures, each depicting the action of those Gurkhas in the Regiment who had won the Victoria Cross. We ate off silver or gold plates and drank from crystal glasses. It was the custom on joining the Battalion for each officer to buy and present to the Mess a complete set of service ware for one person. Over the years, a considerable inventory was accumulated that permitted the unit to 'put on the Ritz' on special occasions. On the silver side plate, the donor's signature was engraved. Tablecloths were never used, but the table was highly polished reflecting the image of the candles, the sculptures and those seated round the table. These dinners were long drawn out affairs and it was regarded as very rude to leave the table before the Commanding Officer and guests had moved to the ante-room, thus you took the precaution of having an empty bladder before proceeding to the dining room. After the King Emperor's health had been drunk, the pipers of the unit band would enter the dining room and slowly march around the table playing doleful Scottish tunes, all the while perspiring terribly for they wore kilts with all the trappings. Eventually, the President of the Mess would offer each piper a full glass of rum that was eagerly downed at incredible speed. When the pipers had left, the chef was then brought in and congratulated on his efforts; however bad, and given a drink of his choice and a cigar. Some nights he should have been given arsenic. He remained a few minutes to chat and amidst applause, left the room. Following the dinner, the officers would retire to the ante-room where drinks were served. Later in the evening, and usually after the guest had left, the officers would participate in a number of games, most of which were pretty rough. Many non-military persons have considered such games juvenile, but in fact, these allowed the officers to let off steam in the only place in which they could do so and was thus encouraged by Commanding Officers. Damage to dress and furniture was a common occurrence. All damage to Mess property was charged equally to all the officers regardless as to whether you were present or not or whether you had been the main cause of the damage.

Throughout the year, the unit would receive invitations to attend a number of social functions given by senior Indian officials or wealthy mill owners. The officers would attend on a rotational basis. There were also several Gurkha festivals and battalion concerts and ceremonies to brighten our lives. One weekend, I was invited by a local mill owner to visit his enterprise. He was very proud of his organization or "village" as he called it and he had just cause as the plant equipment was the very latest and far more advanced than that to be found in the Lancashire mills. He had also spent a considerable sum of money in the building of good housing, a hospital, schools and a recreational centre for the employees. This had paid dividends in that the workers were satisfied with their lot and this had resulted in a significant increase in production. Years before, this mill owner had visited a number of mills in the United States and had been converted to their way of operation. He couldn't understand why the mill owners in Britain didn't do likewise. "Because," I said, "they're pig-headed and any assistance that goes towards employees, is viewed as an unnecessary loss of profit." The mill owner responded: "They can't see the forest because of the trees." On-the-other-hand, a considerable amount of Indian employers was the antithesis of this mill owner and cut corners whenever possible, often resulting in unimaginably dangerous and unhealthy working conditions, including cheaply constructed and death-trap factories and mills.

The officers of the Battalion were invited to a three-day wedding ceremony for the youngest son of a local Sikh prince. The first day concentrated on form and ritual; the second on the marriage ceremony followed by a garden party; while the third day was given over to a military parade. There must have been over a thousand guests all beautifully turned out. The Whites looked smart rather than comfortable unlike the Indians, who looked cool, colourful and at ease. The marriage rituals took place under a huge canopy; the bride and groom placed on a raised platform for all to see. The ceremony for this arranged marriage was delightfully simple. Those being wed were aged six and five. An astrologer gave evidence that the date of the marriage was propitious, vows were exchanged, food and drink was catered, and expensive gifts donated. The wedded children then departed, going their separate ways until the age of puberty. The meals served to the guests were extraordinarily good and champagne flowed like water. There was a multitude of servants to cater to the guests' every requirement. During the garden party, I noticed that there was no discussion about the existing political situation and felt that we, the British, were already considered a thing of the past and, quite frankly, so we were.

On the last day, the Prince's own troops, all cavalry in gorgeous uniforms, put on a dazzling display of riding. A regular Sikh unit was also brought in and performed magnificently. Each sepoy carried the Sikh's own weapon fixed at a slant on his pugri. This weapon is a large ring whose outer edge is razor sharp. When the troops on parade turned to face the guests, there was an immense flash as the sun reflected off these rings. It was quite blinding and very impressive. The whole event was regally splendid. Kipling's words come to mind: "Providence created the Maharajas to offer mankind a spectacle."

While the parade was in progress, I sat beside a Sikh officer and we talked about the future of the Princes in India. He was of the opinion that many would continue to wield power due to their enormous influence over their people. Their wealth and control over economy as landowners and industrialists would guarantee such omnipotence. At the end of the parade, he asked me whether I had ever ridden an elephant and on my replay that I hadn't, he insisted on taking me to where several of these magnificent beasts were gathered. An elephant was made to kneel and I mounted by way of a ladder and carefully reached the howdah, a seat with a railing and canopy carried on the elephant's back. I had hardly sat down when the animal rose in two shattering movements that caused the howdah to sway violently while I grimly held on. Even when the elephant walked slowly, I still felt rather precariously on this flimsy seat, but what a view. I could understand why no animal attacked the elephant. The tiger is magnificent and revered by most, but the elephant is without a doubt the true King of the Jungle. Only man is its nemesis for when man no longer needs the elephant, its future will be tenuous.

I had earlier been invited by some friends to stay with them the next time I was in Bombay. During my anti-malaria course at Poona, I contacted them to ensure the invitation still stood and it was agreed that I stay the weekend. During my visit, I was taken sightseeing by car. We toured the British sector of Bombay, a display of regimentally lined assiduously carved buildings of opulent panache and leafy grandeur. It gave me an insight as to the luxury the Raj projected, something my grandfather, James Charles Emerson Branson, the Accountant-General for the State of Bengal, must have been privy to. The tour ended up at a small cove where we had a swim and a picnic tea. Amongst other topics, we also talked about the Indian's philosophy of life and about Ghandi. Unlike many Englishmen in India, the host was a discipline of Ghandi, and thought of him as a reincarnated God. He insisted that not only the simplest villager, but also the highly educated Hindu and Muslim were entirely loyal and devoted to him. I was hardly in a position to add much to the discussion, but was intrigued by the thoughts of my friend's wife. According to her, the Indian's profound feeling for simplicity and restraint made change difficult. I argued that I thought it was more the corrupt system of control at all levels that ensured the status quo. My host thought that the Indian's acceptance of poverty was so ingrained in the peoples very being, that it would be impossible to root it out without doing grave damage to their emotional equilibrium. Behind their lack of ambition was a constant readiness to give up; to be resigned, to be submissive. I offered the thought that education for the masses, that would likely occur once India received its independence, would eventually change such a philosophy. After all, if you know no better you probably don't expect something that otherwise you would miss and strive for.

We also touched on the subject of the bureaucracy, for my friend worked for the Indian Civil Service. He considered Indian bureaucracy as a formidable network. You filled in endless forms and questionnaires and then you waited interminably. He thought that Indian society had an appetite for analysis but not for action and that this was reflected in the civil service. It was the lack of implementation that hampered every initiative. There were plans by the score, conferences and more plans, but sadly there were few Indians trained to implement the decisions of the planners. I asked him about service in the Indian Civil Service. His idea of a suitable recruit was a man with a Public School background, a degree at Oxford or Cambridge, preferably with second-class honours and, if possible, a blue or some other sign of athletic prowess. From 1945 onwards, the job had become substantially a political one rather than that of administration. He went on to say that, on the whole, integrity in public service, good administration and justice were the hallmarks of the British colonial era. Unfortunately, there are always those who leave a bitter taste and there were a few British officials who advertised their arrogance by treating Indians as though they should respond in a sub-servitude manner. This prejudice was particularly evident from the British wives. Nevertheless, there was no doubt that Britain sent to India some of its finest and most dedicated men who gave their best. They were not exploiters. They set an example of administration of which any country could be proud.

On our way back to Bombay, we passed a 'Holy man' who was accompanied by a small boy who carried the man's eating bowl known as a "begging bowl," for such men have to beg for their meals. I would like to see some Christian priest having to do the same – most would starve. I was informed that some Holy men, for a fee, would exorcise the evil demons hovering around dangerous areas such as forests, the jungle, ravines, and such, with the help of prayers and incantations. If only insurance companies could insure you to prevent accidents happening. That evening, we dined at the Gymkhana Club where I was introduced to several people including a number of Indians. I found the Indians had far better manners than the British; furthermore, the manner in which they expressed themselves was charming and without any trace of arrogance or conceit; the complete opposite to the British equivalent. Their sense of humour was refreshing in that it was never directed at someone else's expense.

I had promised myself the luxury of staying at the Taj Mahal Hotel should the opportunity arise and so I made the necessary reservation. Having thanked my friends for their kindness in having me, I immediately moved into this magnificent hotel. One day was enough. It provided me with an insight of the pomp and grandeur of British India in its heyday, but it was extravagantly expensive and full of very old people. For the remaining days of my leave, I stayed at the Gymkhana Club where the costs were reasonable and the company more to my liking. During the mornings, I wandered through the city and in the afternoon, when it became increasingly hot, I remained by the swimming pool where most of the young Brits would also gather.

MAHARASHTRA

Bombay is the capital of the Maharashta State and peopled mainly by Marathis. The city draws unto itself as tens of thousands migrate to its streets in search of wealth, health and glitter, but it is a slippery hold of hope. From all over the country they come: the poor, the jobless, and the hungry; all congregating into an ever expanding and sprawling slum, like some aimless cancer. The language most often heard is Marathi, but there are at least a dozen other languages spoken including English, Hindi, and Gujurati to name the major ones. Walking down any main street is quite an experience. The streets are like a battlefield, pedestrians, bicyclists, cars, buses, and horse drawn vehicles all fighting against inertia. It is only indoors between cool walls that you notice the sudden wall of noise has been eliminated (or at least muffled). Among this throng are countless beggars accosting you for bakshish and interminable street vendors who have set up shop on the pavement like an assembly line. To add to the confusion, hundreds of emaciated and dirty cows wander through the chaos, picking at discarded vegetable matter and no amount of chivvying will make them move out of the way, you simply have to go around them. Walking through the bazaar was unpleasant. The indescribable reek of pan, odorous powders and oils blended in with the stench of unwashed bodies and open drains produced an overall smell that was akin to an open sewer. The concrete walls on either side were dark and smooth with grease where generations of passers-by had brushed their dirty hands. The children, with their vividly painted eyes, keeping watch from the wooden doorways, were in a pitiful state. You needed strong nerves to cope with the endless pestering of the wretched and the unfortunate. The constant sight of such drama and horror is attrition on the DNA of your mental consciousness: pathos, kindness, inflexibility, callousness, resentment, common sense, and fear. The scale of such poverty defies the imagination and seems beyond all remedy.

When you watch Indians at work, you notice that they work at a slow but steady pace. It is said that Indians are lazy; this is too easy an analysis. I believe that the reason for the seeming lethargic manner is often due to poor health, malnutrition and the terrible climate. Given the climatic conditions, the 'system' under which Indians have to work and their poor health, I was always amazed at their capacity for punishingly hard work. I suppose the answer to the people's strength lay in their learning to be content with very little. After my morning walk-about it was surprising how easy it was to accept with no feeling of guilt the ultra comfort of the Gymkhana Club. I would leave one world and step into a completely different one, the two divided by a brick wall sustained by the 'system.' In the quiet of the evening, I sometimes was unable to blot out some of the more obnoxious sights that I had come across that morning, but it didn't stop me sleeping. The same could be said about trying to blot out some of the more obnoxious comments from officers. I was young but I must have also been very callous.

DUSSEHRA

The Gurkha's religion is a mixture of Hinduism and Buddhism that varies from tribe to tribe. Their favourite festival is Dussehra that is for them what Christmas is to Christians. Dussehra is a festival in honour of Durga Puja, the Goddess of War, and takes place in October and lasts for at least four days. Each day of the festival has an important religious significance when the priests come into their own, insisting that long-established rituals are carried out to the letter. From the British officer's perspective, Dussehra was a noisy, cheerful and bloody festival. It was also a bit of a drunken orgy. The festival commemorates two heroic fights: one between Ramchandra and Ravana, the ten-headed demon king. The other fight celebrated being the victory between Durga and Mahishasura, a buffalo-headed mythological warrior. For a start, the men's heads are shaved save for a long tuft of hair at the crown (this 'tupi' is never cut for it is believed that God will pull them up to Heaven by the tupi when they die).

In our unit, junior ranks wore starched white shorts and white shirts. The weapons of the riflemen were arranged to form a hollow square in the centre of the parade ground. Bayonets were fixed to the rifles and jasmine flowers placed in each barrel. On the third day of the festival, the unit's resident bahun (priest) would head a procession in which the effigy of Durga was carried and escorted by an armed guard of about fifty men, their rifles loaded with blank ammunition. At intervals, the armed guard fired a fusillade of blanks, this being a signal for the whole party to call upon the Gods to listen to their prayers. The procession ended at the sacrificial ground where riflemen placed flowers at the foot of the carved and painted post called the Maula, at which a buffalo would be sacrificed at the end of the festival.

Following the procession, the festivities began working up to a climax that came that evening when groups of soldiers gathered about the Maula in a huge semicircle. A number of Gurkha soldiers, dressed up as women, performed several dances including those that impersonated the Godess Krishna. Since Gurkha women were not permitted to dance in public, the 'female' dancers for this occasion were selected from the young soldiers, in particular those with good looks. Several visiting Westerners have been fooled into believing these young men are women. During these dances, everyone drank rum. Whenever an officer's glass was half-emptied, there would be a cry of "Raksi le" by one of the GCOs, whereupon a full replacement appeared. With the rum and the beating of the drums, the party soon warmed up. Occasionally, one of the 'female' dancers would approach a junior officer, enticing him to join the dance. If he refused, then a couple of smiling 'girls' would forcibly drag him onto the impromptu stage and from then on the standard of dancing deteriorated as the air of hilarity increased. Towards midnight a goat was sacrificed. The priest muttering a prayer sprinkled the ground, the executioner and the goat with holy water. The executioner then chopped the head of the goat off while a hymn was sung and more blank rounds were fired into the starry night.

After consuming copious quantities of rum, I had a terrible hangover; thankfully the traditional breakfast of hot, peppery mulligatawny soup with bowls of rice, helped to bring me to a state of normality. After breakfast, the officers returned to the sacrificial ground to observe the spectacle of Mar. The wives were also invited to watch this ceremony. It was now time for Mahishasura to be sacrificed. A buffalo had been chosen to represent the demon and a rifleman had also been selected to perform the role of executioner. He carried a heavy sacrificial kukri, much larger than the service weapon, and wielded with both hands. For the prayers of the men to be answered, the buffalo had to be beheaded with one clean sweep of the kukri – a bit of a challenge. Failure meant misfortune would dog the unit. There was a hush of anxious onlookers as the kukri was raised and with a mighty plunge, the buffalo's head was sliced off swiftly. It was an incredible sight as the silence was broken by loud cheers, the blowing of bugles and the banging of drums. The Commanding Officer would then tie a white turban round the head of the executioner as a public act of congratulations. Then in quick succession further sacrifices followed, each made on behalf of the different Companies and the headless animals would be dragged around the Maula with blood gurgling like spilt ink blots trailing a red river in the dirt. When this part of the ceremony was over, the party resumed from where it had left of and the rum and whiskey flowed as readily as the animal's blood. On the fifth or last day, the men received the holy mark of Tika on their foreheads. Dussehra was then over for another year. As a means of returning things to normal, there was a day given to 'drying out' all ranks. A battalion parade was held early the next morning followed by a twenty-mile grueling march. The march did very little to soothe my aching head.

Once in a while, the battalion would put on a play or a concert that the public was invited to attend. I found these events particularly embarrassing. The Gurkhas produced the show with no help from the officers and the actors were selected from among the NCOs and riflemen. The whole production was generally ill conceived and badly under-rehearsed to begin with.

Half the cast had to be press-ganged into participating and the standard of performance was therefore less than spectacular. The lighting was intermittent and much of the technical apparatus operated badly. Nevertheless, the men enjoyed these shows and so they continued to be produced. A ceremony that took place every quarter was that of "Beating the Retreat" that was held at sundown and attended by all ranks as well as the wives. The event would consist of certain drills performed by an honour guard followed by the playing of the Last Post as the Union Jack was lowered. This ceremony was always taken seriously and carried out to perfection. In a manner of speaking, it was a reminder of the historical past and always had an emotional affect on all present.

Traditionally, the British officers entertained the Gurkha Commissioned Officers in the Officers Mess at Christmas time and the GCOs entertained the British officers at Dussehra. When the GCOs came to the Officers Mess, the Commanding Officier, though not a member of the Mess, officiated as senior host. The event lasted for several hours in which much liquor was consumed, a time enjoyed by all. The GCOs were on their best behaviour, still their sense of humour would take over and the officers were treated to a few tales of past and amusing incidents normally concerning one or more of the serving officers.

On Boxing Day, a soccer match was played between the British officers and the GCOs. The British officers had to wear some form of headdress other than a cap and had to also wear gaudy clothes, while the GCOs had to be dressed in women's clothing. There may have been some rules to the game, but few, if any, were observed. The game stopped occasionally for refreshments and maintenance of dress and continued until all had had enough. No one kept score but I believe the GCOs were usually the winners. To watch a muscle bound Gurkha running after the ball holding his skirt up and shouting the Gurkha battle cry gave all of us a good laugh. Most of the dresses soon split at the seams but the game went on. To head a ball while wearing a topper without first removing the headgear, might be amusing to the onlooker, but I can assure you, is hard on the nose. Following the game there was a party that the whole battalion attended.

New Year's Eve was celebrated at the Gymkhana Club. On one occasion, a large contingent of Parsees who were visiting the area was invited to the New Year's Eve party. The group included some very pretty young women who certainly enlivened the evening's entertainment. In preparation for the party, the British officers had decided to put on a skit based on the 1920's amusing number, *She had to go and lose it at the Astor*. I provided the piano accompaniment and the others, dressed and made up to look like chorus girls, put on the stage show. It was well received by the club members, but was over the heads of the Parsees watching with strained expressions. We danced all night, particularly with the Parsee girls who weren't too keen on dancing cheek to cheek, but we tried anyway. Everyone got very hot and wet with perspiration. It was revealing to see a couple leave the dance floor, the lady's back would have a red or wet imprint of the man's hand wherever he might have placed it.

The New Year brought political turmoil and a number of serious riots and, even in Ahmadabad where, in 1930 Mahatma Ghandi began his campaign of civil disobedience against the British rule in India, there were rumblings of discontent. We therefore took precautions when going into the city. For example, when officers chose to go to the cinema, they went in force and took along a number of Gurkhas who would set up guard outside and inside the cinema. A number of officers, including myself, decided to go to town to see an English film. We had been waiting in a truck outside the Officers Mess for Captain Jock. I told the Mess Havildar in Gurkhali to "Jao, wuk Captain Jock lana karo" thinking that I had said "Go and find Captain Jock." The Havildar laughed and went away. Shortly thereafter, the Havildar returned carrying Captain Jock over his shoulder. He had done literally what I had asked. Luckily Captain Jock also had a sense of humour.

UNREST

Early in 1947, British Prime Minister Clement Attlee, announced that Britain would withdraw from India by a date no later than June 1948 and Rear Admiral Viscount Mountbatten was named Viceroy. Mr. Jinnah was adamant for a separate Muslim state and the Muslim league stated it would revolt rather than accept an all-India (implying an all Hindu) government for they feared the loss of their culture and economic status under such conditions. While the Indian Congress debated the question of partition, lurking suspicion and hate between the Hindus and Muslims, increased leading to further civil disobedience and riots. The violence that had been increasing in the cities had started to spread to the rural regions where the local constable had not the manpower to maintain law and order on his own. British army units were mainly used to keep order in these areas and this they did with some degree of success, but they were spread thin on the ground.

We were alerted to be ready to give assistance. The Commanding Officer thought it prudent that a reconnaissance of the rural areas surrounding Ahmadabad be enforced. In small batches, the British officers toured the region noting potential assembly areas, lines of communication, containment points, etc. During these trips into the countryside, I got a clearer picture of village life. The soil was thin and fertile ground was rare. The farmer's holdings averaged about five acres and he often had to rent this land paying the landlord with cash or part of his harvest. A miserable life, and yet seventy-five percent of Indians at that time, lived in villages. The majority of peasants were illiterate and often ill-fed living close to starvation, besieged by illness, drought and crop failure. The villages were dirty, unkempt and, due to the lack of modern hygienic conditions, smelt badly of sewage and were breeding grounds for untold diseases. The cattle were a distressing sight as they plodded about looking for fodder. They were little more than skin and bones. Half of the cattle, I was told, were unproductive yet they shared the limited food supply with the starving inhabitants. They were saved only by the deep-rooted tradition in the Hindu's religious beliefs. Considering the conditions in which the peasants lived, it is not surprising that most could easily be made to revolt, and activists were ever ready to cause violence between Hindu and Muslims on some pretext or other fabrication.

In the large towns and cities, violence was becoming a common occurrence. Rumours erupted spawned by a combination of idle speculation, hatred and professional agitators that the media unwittingly, or deliberately, provoked resulting in riots between the different ethnic groups. Shops, homes and business premises were systematically destroyed, looted and burnt; cars were overturned and put to the torch; individuals were attacked with iron bars, wooden staves, knives, hammers, billhooks and left for dead, some with their bodies torn limb from limb. What was so illogical about such riots and a tragedy in itself, was the fact that despite their passionate involvement in political affairs, the people involved in the actual riots expected little real change or improvement in their lives, yet they joined the mobs knowing full well that it would inevitably lead to bloodshed.

Given the seriousness of the general situation in North-Western India, the Commanding Officer prepared several plans to meet any emergency that the battalion might shortly have to face. The two areas of most concern were a major riot in Ahmadabad and a series of riots in the local rural areas. Regarding the former, each rifle company was allocated a specific sector in the city for which it would be responsible. For the control of riots in the rural sections, the operation would have to be played by ear for nothing could be planned ahead of time especially without information as to the number of villages concerned: the number of rioters, who had the upper hand, where the main trouble was taking place, and from which direction the rioters emerged.

The Battalion's main preoccupation centred on Ahmadabad, the third most populated city in India and mainly populated by Muslims. It was the capital of the province of Gujarat with, to its north, a mixed Hindu-Muslim and, to the south, a Hindu majority. The general plan for maintaining control over the populace was to stop large groups of people congregating and to prevent reinforcements from outside having the chance to enter the city. As the most junior Company Commander, I was assigned the area of the railway station, usually located in the centre of the city. It is the hub of the wheel with the spokes being the major avenues and roads. My task would be to hold the station and be ready to provide support to any other Company in the other sectors should the need arise.

During the following weeks, each Company built itself a table model (from sand) of their respective sectors and went through countless exercises and prognosis trying to cover every foreseeable exigency. In my case, I had to build a larger model to cover the whole city. Since most of the men had little knowledge of the city, I decided to send them on a reconnaissance mission, familiarizing section by section, particularly where major arteries were concerned. I allocated sectors of responsibility to each platoon and reconnoitered each sector with the Jemadar Platoon Commanders and they, in turn, assigned sectors of responsibility to each section. The Section Commanders then showed each man the position he was to take as and when we were called out. In this way, we were at least ready for action in the city.

From what I had learned during the course at Jodhpur, I decided that I would have a photographer with me and record on film what actually took place rather than have others rely on the local newspapers' biased rendition. I chose an intelligent solider to be the photographer and trained him in the basics of taking photographs, especially in the heat of action. As a matter of fact, the Battalion was only called out once and that was to put down a number of riots that had started in Ahmadabad itself. Most Indians had a healthy regard for the Gurkhas fighting ability and were hesitant to cause trouble and then be faced by these fierce warriors. Maybe this was the reason for there being infrequent turmoil in our area than in other parts of the country. The Battalion was called out in the middle of the night. Thanks to our preparations beforehand, all Companies were in their designated positions within half an hour of being alerted. On arrival at the station, my men went immediately to their allotted positions while I set up my headquarters. Much to the Station Master's disgust, I set up the headquarters in his office, forcing him to find other facilities. The office contained a telephone that could prove useful should unforeseen problems arise. I left my servant and an orderly to guard the place and, together with my Subedar, went to inspect the Company positions and ensure myself that all was as it should be. There was no rioting in my area, but I could hear noise in two of the sectors. My wireless operator kept me advised of the actions of the other Companies as these were reported by wireless to the Commanding Officer. Two Companies were in the process of establishing roadblocks while trying to maintain order in their sections. I had the Subedar organize two small reserve groups should the need arise to support either or both of these Companies. Meanwhile, I sent out roving patrols whose main job was to be seen by the people and to report any suspicious gatherings. A patrol reported some odd behaviour in and around a house some four hundred yards from the station. I decided to investigate and met the patrol Commander close to the house. I called an Indian who was close by and asked him if he knew who lived in the house. He replied, "I reached here quite all right and in the morning itself and so I am no telling who is living there." With this useful information, I told the Patrol Commander to clear the house. As he did so, a number of very irate men and women poured out of the building – it was a brothel. The Gurkhas enjoyed themselves and were quite willing to find other brothels and do some more house clearing, but at a more leisurely pace.

For a time, things quieted down, and I received the order to stand down half the Company. Rather than leave my men among the milling crowd at the station I commandeered several railway carriages to be used as sleeping quarters. Guards were posted and a routine established. I decided to sleep in the Station Master's Office with a one-man guard outside. A hot meal was served to all ranks after which I went to bed. I woke early the next morning and checked the Company positions. All was well except when I went to where the commandeered carriages should have been, but they were not to be seen. Imagine my horror when I couldn't find them. On asking a railway official where the carriages were, he informed me that they had been hooked on to the Bombay Express during the night. What a predicament. I had just lost half my Company. Just then my Subedar turned up to tell me that the carriages had been shunted onto a siding. I pretended not to be perturbed but my heartbeat took some time to calm down. The Station Master had saved face.

Intuition is a great ally and alerts one to the tension that could snap like a dry twig. It begins as a flurry of scattered leaves but through a steady vacuum, gathers momentum. The collective mass surges forward, disrupting everything in its path, attacking the vulnerable while gaining terrifying strength. It has become one voice, one muscle and this cyclone of anger aims right for you because you represent the last defence. Later that morning, the riots started up again. I gathered that one Company was having trouble and soon had orders from the Commanding Officer to send a platoon to assist that particular Company. While riots were going on elsewhere, the people in my sector were carrying on as usual and as if nothing untoward was happening. Trains came and went according to the timetable. Once in a while, there could be heard the clamour of a large crowd and one or two people might stop to listen. It was quite peculiar. By mid-day, the Battalion had regained control and the leaders of the riots had been apprehended. We remained at our posts until nightfall and then returned to camp. There were no casualties among the Gurkhas and no one had had to open fire on the rioters. As is usual in such circumstances, several Indians had been hurt but none seriously.

We realized that the silent majority understood the help we maintained in keeping the city orderly for we received expressions of gratitude from senior officials, businessmen and citizens alike. The City Fathers went as far as inviting the Commanding Officer, the officers and men to a picnic party held in a beautiful park. Huge amount of food and drink were produced, the drink being non-alcoholic much to the Gurkhas chagrin. Games were played and many Gurkhas went for a swim in the park lake until they were warned that the lake was full of crocodiles. This put a damper on swimming but the party continued with gusto well into the evening. It felt good to have been appreciated by the public for a job well done.

During an assistance to civil power operation elsewhere, the military had been forced to open fire on the unruly mob. Automatic fire was prohibited and only the minimal single round fire sufficient to quell a riot was authorized. On a particular case, the young and inexperienced officer in charge of his unit became a little agitated and when required to open fire on members of the mob, gave the following command: "Number Three, front rank, at the man in front wearing the blue pugri, one single round, rapid fire." This became known as 'Hobson's Choicest.' On another occasion when a Gurkha Company was facing a large and angry mob in Calcutta and the situation was getting out of hand, the Company Commander ordered his men to "Draw kukris" and to advance on the maddened crowd. Within record time, the street was cleared and without bloodshed. That is the respect the Gurkhas hold.

Several months after the riots in Ahmadabad, the Commanding Officer received orders concerning the division of Gurkha regiments between the Indian and British Armies. The men were to choose in which of the two armies they wished to serve. Naturally, the choice was going to affect not only the men but also the officers, yet the latter were forbidden to interfere with the men's decision. No decision had yet been agreed to as to how many regiments would be transferred to the British Army. Neither the Gurkhas nor the officers knew what their future was to be. They were kept in suspense for so long that it created intense psychological stress made almost unbearable by the propaganda directed at the other ranks by Indian politicians. Where accurate information was absent, rumour filled the vacuum including one that Indian officers would soon be posted to Gurkha battalions. The Gurkhas disdained Indian regiments and Brahmans looked down on Gurkhas as barbarians. Gradually, bitterness took root and distrust grew. Added to the Gurkhas uneasiness was the rapid turnover of British officers since the end of the War. Many Gurkhas felt that they were being deserted.

The Gurkhas could elect to stay with the Battalion, transfer to a battalion in the Indian Army or take their discharge. Few understood the implications of their choice especially as the British Government had yet to make up their minds as to what they would do with the Gurkhas who transferred and would have to serve outside India/Pakistan. What was to become of their families and what would be the terms of service? The British officers were unable to give firm answers to these questions and were kept in the dark concerning their own careers. They too were apprehensive. The British officer's greatest enemy was depression: his unpredictable future, a detestable atmosphere of hatred that surrounded him, his own career and personal difficulties, particularly for those with families. The British officers and Gurkhas had always seemed bound by the strongest ties of mutual loyalty but now these bonds were sorely tested. The Gurkhas couldn't understand the British abandoning them. Now the British officers were walking out on them during conditions of near chaos; leaving them moreover to be officered by the despised Indians in whose ability and integrity they had little confidence.

The Subedar-Major addressed the men of the Battalion at a special parade to advise them of the situation as best he could. It soon became apparent that his preference was for the unit as a whole to join the Indian Army. Whether this was an honest effort on his part to ensure that the religious susceptibilities of the troops would not be offended or a personal preference was impossible to tell. The men were divided in their choice. Those with long service in the regiment wanted to remain under command   of the British Sah'bs and many of the younger riflemen agreed with the Subedar-Major. Any division in a family leads to trouble and this was amply demonstrated in the number of serious arguments that flared up among the men who previously had got on very well together. In a sister unit, there was serious trouble when an officer was shot by a Gurkha rifleman who had gone berserk and when the Commanding Officer and the Adjutant left their offices to investigate, they were also shot down by the rifleman.

Days later, our Commanding Officer received more details concerning the future of the British officers. First, all officers were asked which British regiment they would prefer to join if their battalion went Indian? The officers were given the option of either resigning at once or within a year and receive financial compensation for loss of career, or join the British Army. I elected to join the British Army and chose the Royal Sussex Regiment since I was familiar with the county of Sussex. Even before the decision as to which Gurkha battalions would be transferred to the British Army, we received word from Army Headquarters that all the junior British officers in the Indian and Gurkha regiments were to be returned to the United Kingdom. The first to go were the most junior officers and these would be sent home in groups of sixty at a time. Not long after getting this unwelcome news, I received my marching orders as did the only other Lieutenant in the Battalion. Prior to our departure, a farewell dinner was given at the Officers Mess where we all got sizzled. I also attended a touching farewell party given by the GCOs and men of my Company that made me aware of what I was leaving behind and how much I would miss the life I had become accustomed to as a Gurkha officer. I left for Bombay accompanied by my servant who took care of my baggage and saw me safely aboard the liner that was to take me to England. It was difficult to say goodbye to the man who had become such a good and faithful friend since my joining the Battalion.

A few weeks after leaving India, I heard that Lord Louis Mountbatten and Mr. Nehru had come to an agreement as to the division of the Gurkha battalions. Out of twenty-seven battalions only eight would be transferred to the British Army, the rest would become part of the new Indian Army. Of the eight battalions were the the 2nd, 6th, 7th, and 10th Gurkha regiments. In other words, had Army Headquarters not been in such a rush to send the junior officers packing, I would still have been in the 2/7th Gurkhas. I was furious on hearing this news and tried to do something about returning to my old unit but the bureaucratic paper was in the mill and that was that. I was tremendously disappointed and fed-up. This was the second time I felt cheated out of getting my due (the first time concerned failing to get the RNC Dartmouth). I felt that luck was definitely not on my side. Ironically, a few years later when Army Headquarters in London was finding it difficult to recruit officers to serve with the Brigade of Gurkhas, I received a letter from the War Office inquiring whether I was interested in rejoining my old Gurkha regiment. My reply, though politely worded, nevertheless must have left the intended message: "Go to Hell!"

The promise by the Labour Government that no Gurkha would be placed under anyone with whom he did not wish to serve was broken. Battalions selected for the Indian Army were turned over intact with no regard for the men who had chosen to serve with the British Army. The whole affair was a hopelessly mishandled business and a shameful way to thank and acknowledge one hundred and fifty years of loyal service to the Crown by the Gurkhas. I left India with much regret, but was thankful for having had the opportunity to serve with the Gurkhas, even if it was for such a short time. It is said, by those with a cynical tongue, that the longer you live in India, the less you understand it. There is a grain of truth in this paradox. The more you get to know it, the more baffled you become by it. The main impression I had of India was the appalling, hopeless poverty. In spite of this, I found more kindness and wisdom in this country than in any other country that I have since lived. I was also left with a profound sense of the magnitude of the Indian's faith in his religion.

Unlike my grandfather, who had been successful to the point of being offered the position of Treasurer of India, and another relative who had a statue erected built in his memory, I left India without leaving a footprint. The ship that was to take me home was the SS Britannic, a magnificent a magnificent, massive four-funnel liner that was on its last voyage as a troop ship and, in fact, was in the process of being reconverted to its prewar luxury status. There were very few passengers aboard and the service was more in keeping with that of a luxury liner than a troop ship. I was not surprised at meeting up again with many of the officers being sent home and we spent many hours during the voyage exchanging the various experiences we had been through during our short stay in India. There was not one who had not enjoyed life in the Indian Army or who did not have a deep affection for the country and its people. "Je hola hola" – whatever will be will be.

Graduation, Indian Army Draft, 13th ITC Miadstone, England. October 1945.

Cyril Branson.
Officer Cadet at OTS Bangalore. December 1945.

Gymkhana Club, Bombay.

"The Three Sisters," North West Frontier (NWF).

"Kassadais" Government employed tribesmen and a downed aircraft.

2nd Lieutenant at Regimental Centre,
7th Gurkha Rifle Regiment. June 1946.

Dam building with other Gurkhas officers at Palampur, June 1946.

Lieutenant, Officer Commanding 'B' Company, 7th Gurkhas.

Subedar Indrahoj Lumtar, my Second-in-Command, with his two sons. Ahmadabad, 1946.

Casualty Clearing Station, Gardia. NWF.

26th Heavy Battery near 'Three Sisters' in NWF area.

The English Club, Ismalia

The Greek Club, Ismalia

Identity Card for Cyril Branson.

Railway Station at Ismala. Main border crossing between Egypt and Palestine.

'Local colour.' Myself and a 'friend.' Ismalia.

Ismalia.

Chapter 7

Egypt

UNLIKE the small vessel on which I had travelled from Liverpool to Bombay, the SS Britannic was a large liner. There were not more than five hundred passengers onboard and these were mostly other ranks. The officers lived in comparative luxury with cabin, lounge and dining room stewards to care for their needs. I shared a moderately large cabin with five other officers who were all submariners. The meals couldn't have been better – sumptuous helpings and well-prepared dishes. The weather was good and the sea remained calm throughout the journey. The conditions were a perfect tonic for a bittersweet end to India. I passed the time playing bridge, participating in all sorts of deck games and discussing with the other ex-Indian Army officers our respective futures. We all came to the conclusion that the future looked dismal. Very few of the officers were happy at the thought of serving with the British Army. A couple of incidents occurred onboard that I vividly recall. One took place as we came aboard. I was registering for the second sitting dinner when suddenly there was an almighty shout. On looking around, I saw an elderly army Captain squirming on the deck in a fit and foaming at the mouth. He was having D.T.s. Those close by, including myself, rushed to his aid and made sure he didn't injure himself. It was a thoroughly degrading sight and humiliating for the individual. The man was removed from the ship before it sailed. It was the first the only time I had seen anyone in such a totally uncontrolled state, except for the time when a boy at my preparatory school had an epileptic fit. The other incident had to do with my cabin-mate, a submariner. He arrived onboard feeling unwell and he progressively got worse, even though the ship's doctor had seen him and given him some medication. The five submariners were disembarking at Port Said. My cabin-mate was assigned Baggage Officer that was completely ridiculous considering the state he was in. He could hardly walk and was obviously ill, but it was none of my business. As we reached Port Said, his party went off to attend their various duties. I helped the sick officer off his bunk but he immediately fell to the floor. I got the cabin steward to fetch the doctor. By the time the doctor arrived, the sick man was in a coma. The doctor had him taken to Said Hospital. A little later, I ran into the Lieutenant in charge of the party and told him what had happened. His lack of compassion surprised me and I surmised that there must have been bad blood between them.

As I was casually watching proceedings from the promenade deck, I noticed several British Army officers and officials come aboard, but soon forgot about them; however, that afternoon, we were informed over the PA system that interviews would be held in the main lounge for any officer interested in being seconded to certain British Army units serving in the Middle-East. I decided it was worth looking into and requested an interview. What a joke. They were looking for volunteers to work with ENSA (the Forces Entertainment Service), or with engineer companies working on the Sweet Water Canal that provided drinking water for the area. I was disappointed and said so to the interviewing officer, indicating that I was expecting something far better. After some thought, the interviewer mentioned that there were a few openings in Palestine. I plied him with questions but he was only prepared to say that he would look into the matter and let me know the answers to my questions the following morning. Since the ship was leaving that evening, I would have to disembark now and he would advise those concerned. If I was not interested in serving in Palestine, I could always take passage on the next ship going to England. I was put up at a staging centre in Port Said. Next day, the same interviewer got in touch with me and told me that Army Headquarters in Cairo could find me a post in Palestine should I still be interested, but that no guarantee could be given as to the length of service or as to which unit I would be seconded. Given the hopeless prospects for an army career in the United Kingdom, I volunteered to serve in Palestine on the off chance of obtaining a permanent commission. I was told to report to another staging centre, this time in Cairo, where I met several ex-Indian Army officers who were also volunteering for the same reasons. We were told that it would take about a week before our movement orders would be ready. In the meantime, we were at liberty to do whatever we liked for we were given no duties to perform. As of that moment, we were on British Army pay and, for a mere Lieutenant that was drastically meager in comparison to our Indian Army salary. Since none of us knew Cairo, we thought it best to stay together. We worked out an itinerary that included seeing the sights and a visit to the pyramids and the Nile.

CAIRO

Cairo, the capital of Egypt, is the oldest and largest city in the Middle-East. Though there are sections of wide boulevards and well polished establishments, speckled with Islamic architecture, most of the metropolis was noisy, dirty and over-crowded. One of the things that annoyed me was the number of touts, scabs and parasites that accosted me in the street. Shoeshine boys would splash black ink over your shoes and then insist on cleaning them at some unreasonable cost. After a pretence at cleaning them, the boy would demand payment and when you put your hand in your pocket, he would grab your arm and pull on it hoping that as your hand came out, it would be full of money spilling like a waterfall which he would promptly try and grab.

If you refused to have your shoes cleaned, the boy would splash your uniform with ink. It was quite apparent that the natives of Cairo had no love for the British. Realizing that the British were soon to leave Egypt, the shoeshine boys (and others) made themselves thorough nuisances, taking liberties from the fact that no action would be taken against them. Having once been sprayed with ink, I took to carrying a two-foot swagger stick weighed at both ends with lead that I had bought in India. Whenever a lay-about approached, I made the motion as though I would hit him. After witnessing my action, an elderly Egyptian apologized for the state of affairs in Cairo. He wondered why more British troops didn't protect themselves as I had done. Merchants and vendors would grab me by the arm and tug me into their kiosk to inspect their wares. "No need to buy, just look," the merchant would say, but if I didn't buy, the vendor would become unpleasant and call out to his neighbours for support as he insulted me. I realize the Egyptians are restless about the U.N.'s partition of Palestine and are against the British involvement in the Suez Canal. The Kingdom's sovereignty is subject to severe limitations imposed by the British, who retain enormous control over Egyptian affairs, (at least until they depart from the country). The Kingdom is plagued by corruption and its citizens condemn it as a mere puppet of the British. To conciliate, the Wafd Government unleashes nationalistic and anti-Imperialism propaganda, but remain anxious about the consequences of independence and growing public discontent that could prove disastrous to their reign. In addition, there is ever-increasing tension between opposing parties - the Muslim Brotherhood and the Ishtarakuja (socialists) - both of which are especially opposed to the Wafd government. Fortunately, Cairo isn't Egypt as we found out during our travels through the northern part of the country, but we did visit the Cairo National Museum and viewed the impressive array of artifacts from as far back as the first pharaoh to the treasures from the tomb of Tutankhamen.

Wherever I went in Cairo, there was a feeling of unrest, of uncertainty as to the future. Everyone seemed tense as if expecting trouble. The political situation was chaotic, mainly due to the antics of King Farouk and his minions. On one occasion, when my friends and I were sitting at a roadside café, we heard the wailing of sirens coming our way. Crowds gathered by the roadside to see who was about to pass. The next moment, a jeep filled with Egyptian military police screeched to a stop beside us and we were ordered to stand up and salute the King as he drove by. We took exception to the manner in which the MPs approached us and while we were all letting off steam, the King and his cavalcade flashed by. For a moment the situation looked grim, but the MPs had to catch up with the King's group and left in a huff cursing us and our ancestors.

Since we were in Cairo, it was a must to go and see the belly dancers. This we did, paying a king's ransom for the privilege. The nightclub was small and the dance floor the size of a postage stamp. The room was full of cigarette and cigar smoke and stank of beer and sweat. There was only one dancer and she had grotesque dimensions. Her brave vibrations gyrating from side to side, freed the very loose flesh about her body so that it appeared to fly about the room in all directions. She continued to undulate with abandon for about ten minutes, watched by an admiring circle of drunken patrons with their mouths gaping wide like bat caves. The event was more amusing than artistic and anything but provocative and especially not seductive.

We soon tired of Cairo and agreed to travel further afield. We had met an elderly Englishman and his wife at the Gymkhana Club and they had offered to take us by car to visit the pyramids and other interesting sites along the Nile. They were both knowledgeable about the places we visited, making the tour that much more interesting. Egypt has better means of explaining its ancient history through organized guides than they do in India. As you travel down the Nile Valley, I had a sense of the country's antiquity and mystique. When viewing the Sphinx at Giza, our guides informed us that the human head on the lion's body was a reflection of strength with a human mind. We were told the Sphinx used to have a beard but were not enlightened as to the reason for its disappearance. The Great Pyramids were simply majestic. Towering edifices of influence, some as high as 130 meters. We climbed part way up one pyramid to get a better view of the surrounding area and were treated to a breathtaking vista. Our guides also took us to Memphis, the city called the "White Wall," but only a few remnants of the XIX Dynasty Temple survived the extensive quarrying carried out by the builders of Cairo; nothing must stand in the way of progress.

The story goes that if you fall into the river Nile as it flows through Cairo and you swallow a couple of mouthfuls of water, your chances of survival are small due to the extraordinarily high contamination due to pollution. But the Nile we saw south of Cairo was beautiful and serene. There were graceful feluccas with vast sails on forty-foot masts, sailing up and down the river as well as the occasional dugout with its lone fisherman standing while steering the boat. After the cacophony of the city, the Nile Valley proved much needed tranquility. Along the river road, I would come across small villages; mud and reed hovels clustered beneath date trees. Strings of camels carrying merchandise were a common sight as was the overcrowded and overloaded buses travelling at breakneck speed, throwing up mini sand storms behind them.

A week after landing in Cairo I received my posting instructions and movement order. I was posted to the 1st Battalion, The Suffolk Regiment that was part of the Infantry Brigade located in the city of Jerusalem where the unit had been for the past year. Packed in tightly, I was thankful the train journey was short. Most of the baggage and equipment was stowed in the passageway, making it difficult to move about the train. As it slowed down to take a sharp curve on the approach to Ismailia, a number of Arabs climbed aboard and began to throw out of the window any pieces of luggage that they could lay their hands on. By the time anyone could get near them, they had fled. Fortunately, my baggage was spared for I had insisted on keeping my things in my compartment. This event taught me to be extra careful with my belongings when travelling in the Middle-East. We were obviously no longer in India. Such actions by these Arabs only reiterated a dubious feeling about the region and the people. When the train arrived in Jerusalem, a military driver introduced himself to me and drove me to the Battalion Lines. I told the driver about the Arabs stealing luggage from the train, but he simply grunted, "Bloody Sand Niggers. You can never trust 'em." I realized a very different chapter in my life was about to start.

Troop Ship, Suez Canal.

Suez Canal.

Ismalia.

Port Said. Statue of Ferdinand de Lesseps, builder of the Suez Canal in 1869.

Port Said. Loading troops and machinery on lighters.

Haifa harbour. 6th Airborne withdrawal route.

Street scene in Cairo.

The Blue Mosque, Cairo.

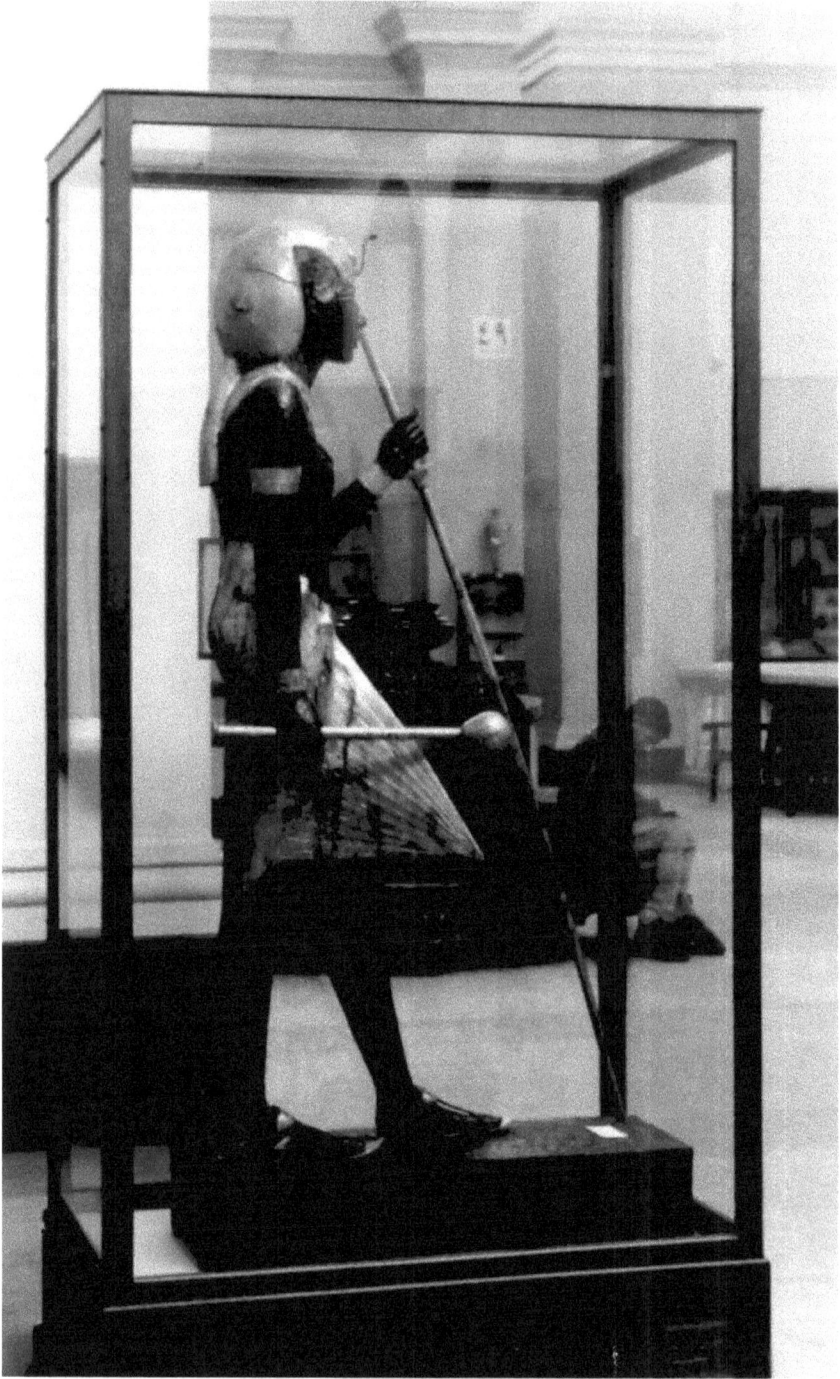

The Museum of Cairo. Ancient artifacts.

The Museum of Cairo. King Tut.

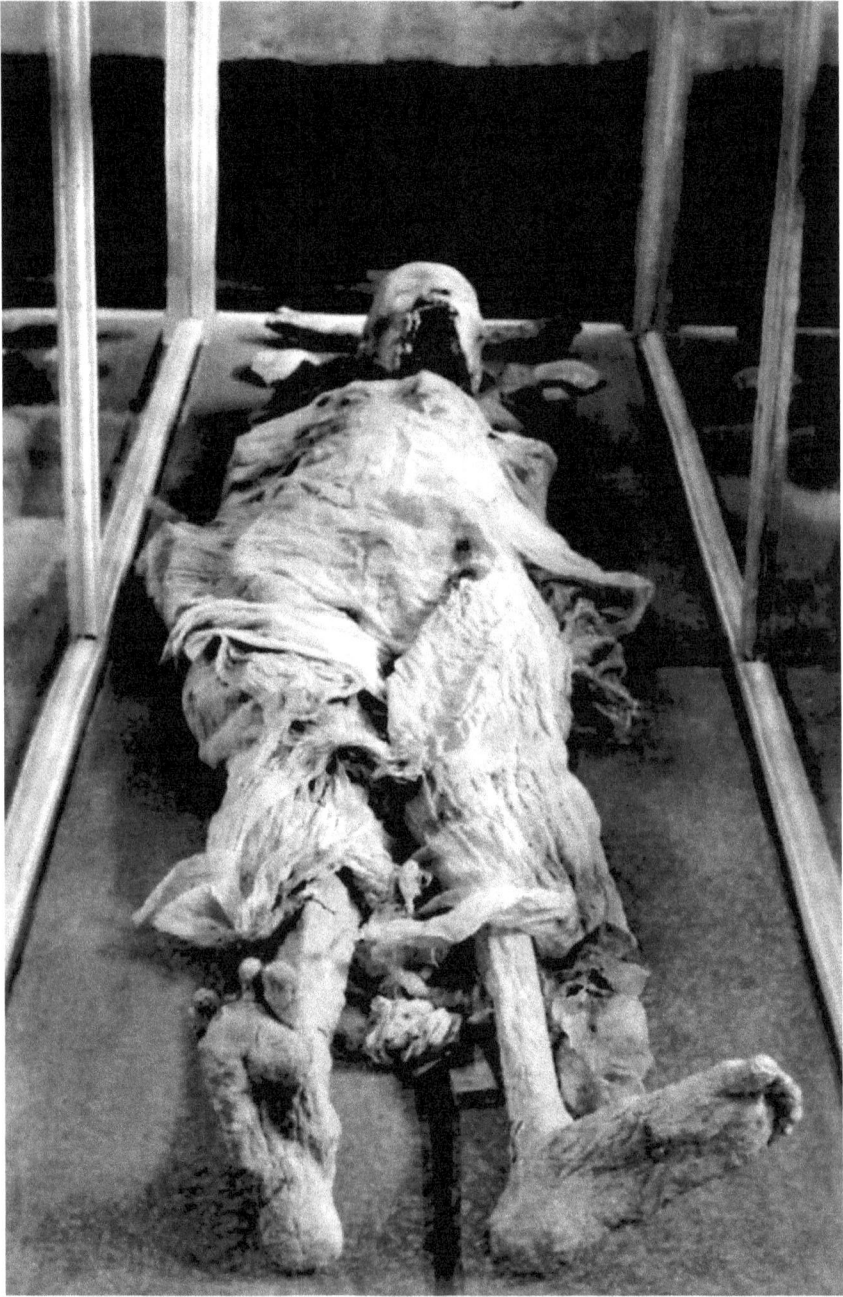

The Museum of Cairo. Mummy.

The Museum of Cairo.

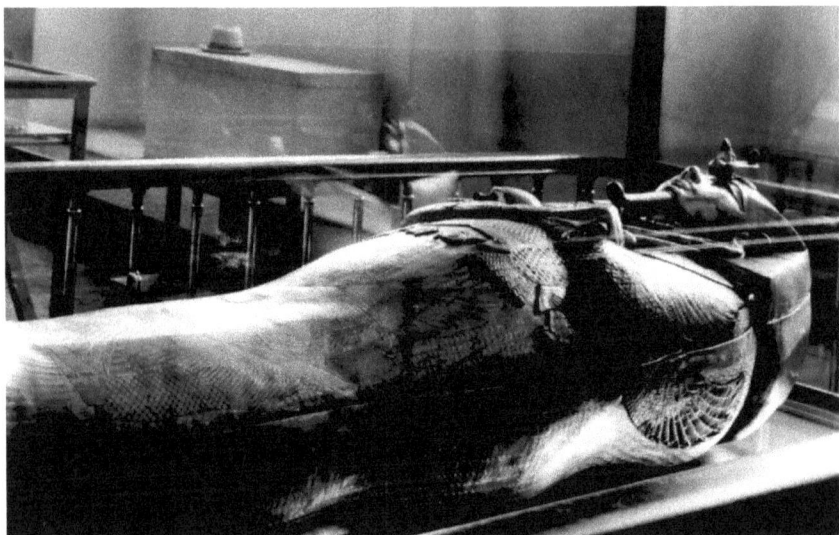

The Museum of Cairo.

Port Fouad. Visiting the town on Messing Officer's Course, Ismalia.

Sweet Water Canal.

Chapter 8

Palestine and Trans-Jordan

THE 1st Battalion, The Suffolk Regiment, formed part of the 2nd Infantry Brigade stationed in Jerusalem. The other two infantry battalions came from the Highland Light Infantry and the Warwickshire Regiments. For operational expediency, Jerusalem was divided into three sectors, each sector being the responsibility of one of the battalions. The Suffolks had the southern sector and was posted close to the Jewish settlement of Mekor Hayim and on the main road leading to Bethlehem.

Of the forty or so officers in the battalion, at least half had been seconded from other infantry units. The majority of Captains and above had seen action during World War II whereas the junior officers were all conscripted into the army from schools or universities and none had any experience as army officers. The Commanding Officer (CO) had been in the Ordnance Corps through most of the war and had transferred to the Infantry Corps in 1944. He was promoted to Lieutenant Colonel shortly before taking command of the 1st Suffolks. A tall, heavy set man but lacking in sophistication, yet his sense of humour was infectious and this counter-balanced his otherwise coarse manner. The Second-in-Command (2IC) was a regular Suffolk regimental officer who was very self-conscious and seemed to compensate this so-called weakness with a lack of humanity. The Adjutant was an ex-Guards officer who was slim and of medium height. He had an inner toughness that I have rarely seen in others. While serving with the 8th Army, he was captured by the Germans but managed to escape. Unfortunately for him, he was recaptured but succeeded in again making his escape. Some months later, he was captured and this time, he was sent to a prison-of-war camp in southern Italy where he was treaty badly by the Italian guards. The Company Commanders, all Majors, were a decent lot and friendly. I was astonished that this mélange of officers with their different regimental affiliations and military backgrounds got along with so little friction. Possibly it was their mixture that deflected any show of disdain for the new boy from the Indian Army, namely, me. We all wore the cap badge and insignia of the Suffolk Regiment and, for the time being, regarded the unit as our own.

The Other Ranks were mainly from the county of Suffolk and about half were country lads. About ten percent were regulars while the rest being conscripts. A large number of Warrant Officers and Non-Commissioned-Officers (NCOs) were regulars and it was they who maintained good order and discipline in the battalion. Most of the conscripts weren't particularly pleased to be in Palestine and were looking forward to returning to England when their 'time' was up. They didn't understand the reason for their being in Palestine and hadn't been briefed on the subject. Generally speaking, the Other Ranks were a pleasant group to work with and quite reliable. I was posted to 'B' Company as a Platoon Commander. My CO was originally from the Queen's Royal Regiment, the same regiment as the one I had been in as a recruit at Maidstone. He was a strict disciplinarian and everything had to be done according to the book. He was very much the schoolmaster: didactic and serious. He was shocked at my lack of knowledge about Palestine and its history and arranged that I, with a few other junior officers, be instructed on the subject by the unit Intelligence Officer (IO), an Anglo-Maltese, who had studied the history of the Middle East at Oxford.

The lecture on Palestine was both instructive and amusing as the IO peppered his talk with different incidents in Palestine that involved himself. It was apparent that he was no admirer of either the Zionists or the Arab Brotherhood organization. In covering the early history of the Jews and Arabs in the area, he exposed the illogical situation of the struggle between these two peoples. After all, the Jews and Arabs are cousins, the children of Isaac and Ishmael, Semitic lines, descendent from the same father – Abraham. Up to the time of the establishment of the Zionist movement in the 19ᵗʰ century, the Jews and Arabs in the Middle East lived relatively peacefully together. It was the Zionists, not the Palestinian Jews, who conspired against the Palestinian Arabs. The Balfour Declaration did little to ease the situation in that it assured the Jews a homeland in Palestine while, at the same time, stating: "nothing shall be done to prejudice the civil and religious rights of existing non-Jewish communities in Palestine." Given that the Arabs owned most of Palestine, and that the majority of the inhabitants were Arabs, the Declaration was impossible to fulfill. Thanks to the support of the American and British governments, a permitted quota of Jewish immigrants was agreed upon; however, the Zionists ignored the agreement and instead, the trickle of immigrants soon became a flood.

The Jewish immigrants, supported lavishly with Zionist funding, made important inroads by buying up Arab property and lands. What had begun as two small streams of nationalism was becoming an ocean of hate and belligerence. At first, the Arabs considered the British to be their major enemy; however, as the waves of Jewish immigrants increased, their hatred was diverted against the Jews. For their part, the Jews considered both the Arabs and British as their enemies, the latter for restraining illegal Jewish immigrants from entering Palestine. The British government was caught in a Catch-22 situation, largely of its own making. Skirmishes erupted between Jews and Arabs and between Arabs and British forces. Later, around the mid-1940s, Jewish terrorist paramilitary groups, such as the Irgun Tzvai Leumi (LZL) and the Stern Gang led by Avraham Stern (who was killed by British forces in his apartment in 1942), attacked British personnel and any others who obstructed with intent of making Palestine the Jewish state of Israel. When discussing the Palestinian situation with other officers, I found that most were sympathetic to the Zionist's cause for 'a land without people for a people without land,' but the violent nature and extreme actions of the IZL and the Stern Gang had made them bitter towards the Jews in general and more in sympathy with the Arabs who were being cheated out of their birthright. It was felt that without a strong Arab leader, no Western government was ready to listen to the Arabs' point-of-view.

It is easy to criticize national or political movements that turn to terrorism to achieve their aims, but in the case of a race of people who have been persecuted over the decades, no matter the reason why, the reasoning that gave birth to terrorism cannot be fully appreciated unless one has suffered such persecution. I could recognize the Jew's frantic efforts to obtain a homeland of their own, yet had difficulty in rationalizing the manner in which they were going about it. For a people known for their patience, the Jews seemed to be in an excessive hurry to obtain what they been promised. In the process, they were antagonizing both the Arab Palestinian and their Arab neighbours. In comparison to the quiet and moderately peaceful Arab Palestinians, the young Jewish immigrants arriving in Palestine by the thousands were an arrogant and tough group of people who were accustomed to harsh living conditions. These young Jews were not likely to give an inch in their attempts to gain a homeland no matter the opposition, be it the United Nations, Britain, or the Arab States. Among the Arab Palestinians were a number of moderates who welcomed a reasonable influx of Jewish immigrants, but as the Zionist movement started to make gains and show its true colours, the moderates were caught in the momentum of events directed by the politicians which they had no means of controlling.

I arrived in Jerusalem shortly before the bombing of the King David Hotel by the IZL. The hotel was used as an officer's club. As the British personnel tried to escape the hotel, IZL terrorists shot them. The result of this myopic action resulted in the British forces on full-scale alert 24/7 and to harden their attitude towards the Jews in the country. One of the Suffolk majors had been on the top floor of the hotel when it was bombed and miraculously emerged from the rubble unscathed. Following that incident, all military personnel were required to be armed throughout the day. Prior to my posting to the Suffolks, I had realized that life as a junior officer in the British army was going to be different to what I had been accustomed to in the Indian

Army and that I would have to make some adjustments in my mental attitude to conform with British Army ways. I hadn't anticipated how great these changes were to be. In the British Army, the onus was placed on 'Rank'. It was not a matter of gaining respect through merit but rather an expectation that any order given by a senior person would be automatically carried out no matter how stupid the order. A certain hubris and pomposity regarding manner was more reminiscent of World War I tactics and attitude. Except everything had to be done in accordance with peacetime procedures even though we were in an operational theatre. In other words, it was a political battle. We couldn't look bad in front of the world. As a junior officer, you were not expected to use too much initiative. As a former Gurkha Company Commander, I cut corners where possible and I was expected to use my imagination at all times. To be restricted to inaction unless otherwise ordered was to cause me problems and I committed several faux pas.

After only three weeks with the Suffolks, I was posted to 3 Divisional Headquarters that was located at Bayt Daras, a few miles from the coast and midway between Gaza and Jaffa. I was to be the Headquarter's Defense Platoon Commander. Somewhat of a come down, but I was 'not to reason why...'

COOKING LESSONS

My supervisor at Divisional Headquarters (Div. HQ) was the Senior Staff Officer Administration (SSO Admin). I reported to him on my arrival and within minutes it was obvious that we were not going to be friends. He was every inch the Colonel Blimp: blustering, rude and a real fat-head. He told me that as Defense Platoon Commander (DPC), I would report directly to the Camp Commander for orders. I was also informed that I was also to be the Messing Officer for the HQ under his direct command and that later, I would be sent on a Messing Officers Course. It sounded like a course in bloody dining etiquette. Following this cheerless meeting, I went to see the Camp Commander who briefed me as to my duties as DPC. At least the

Camp Commander was a likeable, jovial and happy-go-lucky Captain in the Armoured Corps. After having dissected the character of the SSO Admin, we discussed my responsibilities consisting of: establishing adequate perimeter patrols; ensuring the maintenance of the perimeter wire; checking that the sentries at all entries and sensitive areas were alert; confirming the pass system was being adhered to; and establishing a security check system to enforce the overall security of the camp. He warned me that security had become lax and that the previous PDC had been returned to his unit for incompetence. Much of the system had already been established and it only required some further adjustments, tightening up of the procedures, and some fine-tuning. I considered my first priority to be the security of the camp and once satisfied with the system, I would then concentrate on the catering situation.

I made a tour of the camp and was surprised by the number of civilians wandering about without authorized passes. On checking with the guard at the main gate, I was told in a confidential manner not to worry for he personally knew the individuals in question. They were regular visitors and didn't need passes. Conscript soldiers, especially those employed at major headquarters, had a few rungs missing on the ladder and needed considerable coaching. With soldiers like this, who needs enemies? It took some disciplinary measures before matters were put right. I also noticed that there were many holes and gaps in the perimeter wire, some I'm sure made by HQ personnel who hadn't a leave pass. I had the holes repaired and installed numerous trip-flares between the wiring of the fence. Two nights later, the Roving Patrol caught an Arab after he had set off several of these trip-flares while cutting his way through the wire. I suggested several alternatives concerning the issue of day passes for visitors, most of which were approved by the Camp Commander.

As Messing Officer, I was expected to supervise the ordering and distribution of rations to the different kitchens and Messes; oversee the preparation of the weekly menus; ensure that the kitchens met the given hygiene standards; and collect money from each unit within the HQ with which to buy extra rations.

On inspecting the kitchens, I was appalled at their conditions. They had been built at the end of World War I and had been condemned time and again as unfit for use by medical inspectors. Since HQ staff refused to do anything about the situation, the kitchen staff did likewise. I recalled the atrocious food and bad service during my recruit days at Maidstone and was determined that things would be different at this HQ. I gathered the kitchen Sergeants together and explained what I wanted done. One surly individual, with pools of sweat stains under his armpits, told me that he ran his kitchen his way and that he only took orders from the SSO Admin. I more or less read them the Riot Act and informed them that my Standing Orders regarding the operation of the kitchens would be in their hands by that afternoon and that I expected immediate results. Next morning, during the inspection of the insubordinate Sergeant's kitchen, I noticed that my Standing Orders had not been posted and that no change had taken place to improve things. I asked the Sergeant for an explanation. He was a big, overweight man dressed in a sweaty and greasy uniform – a born shop steward if ever there was one. With a cigarette dripping from his mouth, he reiterated that he wasn't taking orders from me. I informed him again of the facts of life and gave him twenty-four hours in which to clean up his kitchen, himself and his staff, and to ensure that everyone knew my Standing Orders and abide by them. I went to each of the other kitchens and gave the Sergeants the same warning.

The following morning, I again inspected the kitchen of the insolent Sergeant and was not altogether surprised to find that none of my orders had been carried out. I placed the Sergeant on charge for willfully disobeying an order given by an officer and told him that he was immediately relieved as Sergeant-in-Charge of the kitchen and that he was to await further orders. I got all the kitchen staff together and announced what I had done and then told the senior Corporal to take temporary control. I warned the other kitchen Sergeants of what I had done and that I would do the same to them if they continued to be insubordinate. About an hour later, the SSO Admin called me to his office. The kitchen Sergeant that I charged had been to see him and had complained about my actions. The SSO asked me to explain what had taken place and I gave him my report and the charge sheet. He was taken aback at my insistence that matters had to be improved and that the management of all the kitchens was positively abominable. I also pointed out that my orders had willfully been disobeyed. Obviously, the SSO was not used to anyone rocking the boat and was irritated at my having done so. He was also a coward (a true bureaucrat) and didn't want to proceed with the charge. He criticized me for the way I had dealt with the kitchen Sergeant. I objected strongly given that I had given the man ample warning. The meeting ended on a sour note with my being told that the matter would be reported to the Divisional Commander. I thought this was extreme, but then, so was the SSO.

Sometime later, I was 'invited' to see the General who asked me what had happened. Having explained the situation (not to mention the lack of discipline), he empathized and then, after a pause, asked me about my background. On learning that I had recently left the Gurkhas, the atmosphere suddenly became more cordial. It turned out that he had also served in the Indian Army. After warning me to abide by the traditional ways of dealing with disciplinary matters, he agreed to approve my action. A few days later, the kitchen Sergeant was found guilty of several offences, demoted to Corporal and posted to another unit. The senior Corporal was promoted to Acting Sergeant and I had no more trouble from the kitchen staffs, who overnight, changed to the better. All this didn't endear me with the SSO Admin, but I wasn't in his good books anyway.

I had brought my batman with me from the Suffolks. His name was Bull and though he was big and strong, he was anything but offensive. In fact, he was the opposite and a most agreeable young man. He had worked on his father's farm before being conscripted into the army. He would regale me with an assortment of amusing tales about 'life on the farm.' He had a craving for the Land Army girls who worked on his father's farm – for *all* of them. As I needed a driver, I made him my batman/driver and was thus able to have him excused from camp fatigues for which he was duly thankful. My quarters consisted of a large tent in the officer's lines. The tent was divided into two sections: an office and living quarters. It was comfortable, but without a stove, it was more often cold than warm at night.

One day, the Camp Commander asked me whether I liked dogs and would I like to see his Alsatian pups? The bitch and her pups were huddled in a corner of his quarters – a Nissen hut. The bitch allowed me to handle the pups but the male would not permit me to leave the hut until ordered to 'sit' by his master. He offered me one of the pups; however, I was not keen on Alsatians and thought that the pup would be a burden. About a week later, an official Mess Dinner was held and when I arrived at the Mess, a little late, the male Alsatian, grabbed my trouser leg and led me to where his master was sitting. On being told to be good, the dog obeyed, let go of me and quietly exited the dining room. Discreetly, I told the Camp Commander that his dog was one of the better soldiers and should be promoted.

SUEZ CANAL

The Messing Officer's Course was held at a school a few miles outside Ismailia and bordering the Suez Canal. I assigned Bull to drive me and he was delighted for any excuse to get away from HQ and to be able to enjoy what the Canal had to offer. The course itself was both interesting and amusing. Most of the instructors had been chefs at different restaurants and hotels in Britain and were awaiting their return home to be demobilized. We were taught the rudiments of how to organize and administer large catering organizations; how to order food in large quantities and inspect it for freshness or spoilage; how to prepare menus months in advance and what to do with small quantities of food left over. This information took little time to absorb. Much of the time was spent on learning how to cook sumptuous dishes that had no bearing whatsoever on the course intent, but the chefs wanted to stay prepared for they would once again be real chefs. The students were happy with this situation for we ate splendid meals. The afternoon classes always ended early, about 3 p.m., allowing us plenty of time to go swimming in the Canal or visit Ismailia. During the last few days of the course, each student had to prepare a meal for all the other students to eat and critique. Some students seemed to be born cooks, but most were poor and we suffered the consequences. Before leaving, the instructors gave us one good bit of advice, never order breaded-meat or breaded-fish in a restaurant as likely as not these dishes are made from stale leftovers or spoiled food.

Ismailia was a very pleasant city with wide, tree-lined avenues. It was the main rail-and-road crossing point over the Suez Canal, and consequently, had some importance as a market town as well as being of strategic significance. There were some very popular and chic European social clubs, but I liked the informality of The English Club that I visited regularly. The French and Greek Clubs were busy places but the atmosphere was very pretentious. One evening, I accompanied fellow students to the Greek Club with the idea of meeting some of the lovely young women, but was frustrated in achieving my aim. Before being able to speak, let alone dance with any of them, a formal process had first to be endured. After the normal introductions had taken place, we were required to spend considerable time in conversation with the much older women – more like a perfunctory questioning whether we were suitable husband material – from one mother or aunt to the next. By the time this was over, our hosts left for it was late. We never did get to dance with any of the girls. I gathered we weren't to be future son-in-laws. Swimming in the small lake beside the clubs was also unappealing due to the highly toxic flotsam and jetsam floating about which had been disgorged by the passing ships. I hired a sailing dinghy and, with a friend, sailed into the greater lake where the water was much less polluted. Vast cargo ships never gave way to our small sailboat and on intermittent times, we were almost submerged by the waves caused by ships coming too close to us. On another occasion, I was swimming across the Canal, which at that time wasn't particularly wide. I spotted a ship coming down the Canal and as it was some distance, I felt that it was safe to swim back. When halfway across, I was shocked at how fast the ship was moving and realized that I had to get a move on. I swam as fast as I could but as the ship passed, the suction caused by the passing ship's propellers was frighteningly strong and I struggled to elude being swallowed under.

Sometimes my judgment in a foreign country can be somewhat bankrupt. It was while I was in Ismailia that I came across a number of coolies towing a fully laden *dhow* and having much trouble in doing so. Wanting to take a photograph of the scene, I got closer. While focusing the camera, I noticed that the coolies were displeased at my presence and were being quite vocal in expressing their objections. Having taken the shot, I unthinkingly threw some *piastres* to the natives who promptly let go of the towing ropes and fell upon the coins. This action infuriated the skipper of the *dhow* as it proceeded backwards and out of control. I thought it best to beat a hasty retreat.

One of my responsibilities as Messing Officer was the procurement of extra rations. I decided that I would shop around for these products rather than delegating someone else as this gave me the opportunity to visit Jaffa, Gaza, and Tel Aviv. I much enjoyed my weekly shopping excursions. Bull drove me to different towns and once in the market, I bartered with the merchants. I would explain that I had just come from Tel Aviv or Jaffa and that the prices were cheaper and the produce fresher. I would receive a knowing smile and be offered another cup of boiling coffee or sweet red wine and be assured that their product was of the best quality hence the price. Of course, I was no match against these masters at the art of bartering, but it was fun and it was *de rigueur*. During these meetings there was always time to discuss local matters and the general political situation. There was little useful 'intelligence,' though I did get some feedback on the merchant's views about terrorists. All the merchants were genuinely against any form of violence. Both the Jewish and Arab merchants seemed to get along together without any outward animosity, but rather with an understanding and respect for each other.

When time permitted during these outings, I would explore the beaches along the coast and go swimming. Sometimes I would invite other HQ staff officers to accompany me. Many beaches appeared attractive but several had wicked undertows to contend with. Whenever we stopped at a beach for a swim, we would take turns at standing guard while the others bathed in case of attack by terrorists. After a few weeks at the Divisional Headquarters, I became bored for there was little left for me to do. I also felt that by remaining at the HQ rather than serving with an operational unit, I was likely to lose any chance of promotion or of getting a regular commission. I therefore discussed the possibility of my being returned to the Suffolks with the SSO Admin feeling certain that he would be only too pleased to see the last of me. For once, luck was with me and I soon received orders to return to my battalion.

THE SETTLEMENT

On my return to the Suffolks, I noted many apparent changes had occurred among the Company officers. I had a new Company Commander, a Major from the East African Rifle Regiment, who had recently transferred to the British Army. He was a charming and friendly individual with whom it was easy to get along. The previous Company 2IC had returned to England and I was made Acting 2IC but without promotion to the rank of Captain. A new Platoon Commander had also arrived and he turned out to be far more effective as an officer than the other two. I was pleased to be back with my Company and even more so at the changes that had developed.

The Battalion was situated on the side of a hill. The camp itself was a temporary affair and had but a few permanent buildings. One of these was used as the Commanding Officer's house and the others as the Battalion Headquarters. Company offices were wooden huts. Nissen huts had been erected for the use of messes for the officers and Sergeants, and as Officer's quarters and storerooms. The Other Ranks slept in tents. When it rained, the camp became a sea of mud. All the camp roads were built of stone as were the vehicle compounds. It was not an imposing looking camp nor was it particularly comfortable, but few complained since the majority of the officers and men spent most of the time out of camp on one form of operation or another. There was rarely more than one rifle company in camp at any one time.

I shared a Nissen hut with one other officer whom I rarely saw for when I was in camp he was away and vice versa, and so we enjoyed relative privacy. The room furnishings for each officer consisted of the bare essentials: a table and chair, a camp bed and a chest of drawers. There were a number of holes in the rounded corrugated top of the hut as a result of the occasional stray bullet or from loose and missing rivets. Consequently, when it rained, water would leak into the room so buckets had to be placed everywhere. The Battalion was given a variety of tasks which involved: manning check points ('Gates'); providing protection for the minority groups in the Old City and elsewhere; carrying out search-and-rescue missions; guarding major routes and providing armoured escorts; maintaining and protecting the main camp; guarding Government House; and clearing mines found on major roads and bridges. Over and above its normal tasks, the Battalion was sometimes called upon to help other units on specific operations or missions. My Company was once sent to help evacuate the wounded from a hospital train that had been attacked and derailed by Arab terrorists. Six wounded men had died and about a dozen others had received further injuries. It was a grizzly business and by the time the last wounded man had been evacuated, the rescuers were in an ugly mood. On the way back to camp, one of the company drivers purposefully rammed a civilian car driven by an Arab injuring everyone in the car.

The Battalion was once tasked with the job of cordoning off a particular coastal area where it was believed a ship bringing illegal Jewish immigrants was about to beach. We were in position in time to witness a small ship plough into the beach, at which point, we descended on them with Palestinian police and rounded up the passengers. As the passengers disembarked by way of ladders and ropes, a large group of Jews, who had been hiding in the sand dunes, rushed forward and mixed with the newcomers.

Obviously, the Jewish Agency had arranged this reception to confuse who the soldiers and police should arrest and detain. In the end, the whole group was carted off under guard and handed over to the immigration authorities. I gather it took days to sort out the illegals from the locals. The illegals were later sent to a camp in Cyprus where they stayed until permitted to enter Palestine as per the agreed quota.

Check points, also known as 'Gates,' were set up at intervals along the major routes and at borders between sectors while mobile patrols were established to police each sector. A 'Gate' consisted of a barrier made from empty oil barrels and concertina wire, covered by automatic weapons from protected positions. All those wishing to pass through the gate had first to stop and show authorization permitting entry into the other area or sector. The purpose of these barriers was to control the movement of undesirables from one area to another, but it would have been hopeless in stopping or deterring a suicide bomber. Guarding such gates was boring work, but sometimes something would happen to enliven the drudgery. Once, a large limousine drove straight through a barrier, the driver disregarding the order to stop. The guard, as per his orders, opened fire on the vehicle smashing the rear window and windshield and puncturing the rear tires. The driver was forced to stop. On checking the occupants, it was found that no one had been injured which was just as well as they were all senior Arab officials. No complaint was made as the occupants admitted that the driver had been at fault. Sometimes pedestrians were turned back much to their annoyance. Those who tried to force their way through the barrier were detained. The Jews and Arabs also established their own barriers in their respective areas.

The purpose of the sector mobile patrols was to 'show the flag' and keep the peace. The patrol would consist of the driver of the jeep or scout car, an officer or senior NCO, and sometimes a machine gunner for protection. The city was already divided into Arab, Jewish, and Christian communities. The Jews and Arabs would send out squads of terrorists or snipers to ambush or kill their rivals in each other's sectors. A vulnerable position of attack was a crossroad where Jewish and Arab areas met. Any person or vehicle travelling through such a crossroad was fair game for snipers. The major fault with this tactic was that other individuals also used the roadways, and when passing through a crossroad were often victims of some trigger-happy hoodlum. While on a mobile patrol, it was quite common to hear the crack of a rifle shot. Though you heard the shot fired, it was difficult to identify the position of the sniper either because it was too dark or due to an echo effect. On one of these patrols, I heard a shot fired from close range followed by a loud clang from somewhere in our jeep. When we got back to base, we discovered that the bullet had been lodged in the crossbar frame holding the canvas hood of the jeep. An inch either way and Bull or I might have been shot in the head. From thereon, I made a point of telling Bull to cross danger points at maximum speed.

Escorting convoys in winter was both tiring and uncomfortable. The escort consisted of a number of armoured vehicles such as jeeps, reconnaissance vehicles, and heavy GMC armoured trucks. The rain would enter such vehicles through small apertures and gather as puddles inside, soaking all of us to the bone. I assisted in a number of these escorts from Haifa to Egypt, from Gaza to Nazareth, and from Jerusalem to Haifa, all without incident. In travelling across the country, the boredom of the job was relieved by the sight of the terrain. We passed through highlands, deep valleys, desert, and fertile farmland.

The Hadassah Hospital was one of the best hospitals in Palestine. It was located a few miles outside Jerusalem. Unfortunately, vehicles on the road to the hospital were shot at no matter whether the occupants were Jews or Arabs. The route to the hospital provided very little cover once a vehicle had left the built-up area. From the outskirts of Jerusalem, the road descended for about a mile crossing a wide-open plain, which meant being vulnerable to snipers. At the bottom of the hill, the road crossed over a small and narrow bridge and then snaked its way upwards along a steep zig-zagging route until it reached the hospital perched at the apex. In the hope of protecting those travelling to the hospital, the Jews would use buses and trucks with steel plates attached to the sides as a form of armour. This proved satisfactory against small arms fire but later the Arabs mined the road and used rocket launchers resulting in an onslaught of carnage. Subsequently, the Jewish Agency requested the British authorities to provide armed escorts so that all vehicles and their occupants might travel along the road in comparative safety. The Suffolks were given this task and, in turn, my Company was given the responsibility of carrying out the mission. I was detailed as Officer-in-Charge of the operation.

Prior to moving any troops into the vicinity, I did a reconnaissance of the ground between the Hadassah Hospital and the nearest built-up area. I went by jeep and took along Bull and a machine gunner and had a large Union Jack flying above the vehicle as identification. After an hour's reconnaissance, I suggested positioning ourselves at a settlement by a bridge as the ideal lookout. The settlement consisted of a dozen or so closely packed houses, most of which were in a state of deterioration. The place was abandoned except for an old rabbi and a half-wit woman. There were several two storey houses and I chose the one with the best all-round view of the area as headquarters. The settlement was on the Jewish side of the road. On returning to my unit, I reported my findings to my Company Commander and asked him for a reinforced platoon, plus three armoured carriers and an armoured car. This was agreed to, the armoured car being the Commanding Officer's Dingo scout car. I was told to be especially careful of the Dingo for it was the only armoured car remaining in the battalion. We moved into position the following night.

On arrival at the settlement, I discovered that several of the houses, including the one I had chosen to be headquarters, had been deliberately damaged. A few houses were still on fire but as it was raining I thought it likely that the fires would soon extinguish the flames. Before moving into the pre-planned positions, I sent a number of foot patrols through the area to ensure it was clear of intruders. There was one heart-thumping moment when two of the patrols suddenly came face-to-face. Luckily no one was trigger-happy and both groups held their fire. Once the "all clear" signal was given, we took possession of a number of the houses and set about reinforcing our own security. The ground floor of my building had been totally gutted, leaving it difficult to secure. As a temporary measure, I had booby-traps installed. Those setting the traps did such a good job that they trapped themselves in and had to make a hole in the ceiling to get into the house. Windows in all the occupied houses were blocked with sandbags leaving only sufficient space from which to shoot.

Once installed in my headquarters, I noted that there was considerable heat in some of the rooms, which given the temperature outside, seemed odd. On touching one of the walls, I found its surface very hot. The walls must have been insulated with straw and this straw must have caught fire, gently glowing behind the plaster. Since it was cold outside, and not wishing to tangle with the booby-traps below, I selected to stay where we were for the night and was glad of the unusual central heating. By early morning, the rain had stopped and steam could be seen rising from some of the nearby houses, but there were no open fires. The fire in the walls of my building had also been extinguished so there was no reason to move. We soon had the ground floor correctly booby-trapped so that entry and exit was now possible. Work continued all day on improving the defenses and in laying tripwires throughout the encampment. I went to visit the old rabbi and to warn him about the trip-flares, but he was not in the least interested. During the day, a number of civilian vehicles travelled up and down the road drawing some sporadic fire. It was not an easy matter to ensure the protection of such vehicles. For a time, I tried pairing my armoured car with one single civilian vehicle. If it was a vehicle carrying Jewish occupants, the armoured car would cover the Arab occupied side and vice-versa for Jewish vehicles. This brought fire on the armoured car that was not sufficiently armoured to stop heavy caliber shots. I sent a message to Battalion HQ to send me a number of small Jewish and Arab flags. When these finally arrived, I placed outposts at both ends of the road with orders to hold up the traffic until several vehicles had arrived. The vehicles were then paired off and a Jewish flag was placed on the vehicles that faced the Jewish occupied side and the same strategy for the Arab vehicles facing the Arab side. An armoured car led each convoy to ensure each vehicle kept its given station. This tactic proved quite successful despite the antics of a few fanatics who chose to open fire on any vehicle that moved. As further protection, I had an armoured carrier patrol on each side of the road. If anyone fired at the convoy and the gunner in the carrier could detect from where the firing came, he would send a burst of machine-gun fire in that direction as a warning.

One afternoon, the quietness was shattered by a shot. I checked with the sentries who reported that the shot had been directed at a lone woman walking up the road. Through my binoculars, I recognized the woman as the half-wit. She was bent over with the weight of a stack of sticks that she carried on her back. She hadn't taken cover and was still slowly walking up the road. To be on the safe side, I sent a carrier to bring her back to the settlement, but she refused to get into the vehicle. The Corporal in charge jumped out, picked her up and more or less tossed her into the carrier where she spent the next few minutes screaming her head off.

Early the third morning, we were woken up by the crack of a high-powered rifle and the yell from the guard who had been standing at the window through which the shot had passed. In following the path of the bullet that had passed through three walls in the house, we were able to deduce where the shot came from. It was a house standing by itself, on the Jewish side of the road and about four hundred yards from the settlement. I decided to pay the house a visit but was shot at as soon as I appeared in the open. I had a Union Jack hung out of the window, but the reply was another bullet through the window. On scanning the house with my binoculars, I was convinced the shots had been fired from the flat roof of the house. There were drain openings and the sun shone through all but one. I ordered fire at the appropriate spot and was gratified to see a man stand up then fall backwards. I had to put an end to this affair and again prepared to visit the house, only this time, I would go with an armoured escort ready to blow the house up. We approached and surrounded the building with three armoured carriers. With a megaphone, I ordered the occupants to come out. When nothing happened, I warned them that in one minute we would fire. After one minute and no movement, I ordered the bazooka gunner to demolish the right base of the house. The impact caused half the building to collapse. Ten young Jews (five boys and five girls) came running out of the building. One of the boys had been hit in the shoulder. I sent in a section of men to clear it. They reappeared with an assortment of American and German weapons, such as mortars, rifles, machine-guns and stacks of ammunition. In addition, they had seized a collection of British Army training pamphlets. On questioning the young people why they had shot at us, they spat out their answers that we were the enemy. We threaten them with imprisonment, but they just laughed and said they would be out of prison in a matter of days. Such arrogance merely made me wonder why we were guarding the Jews. We figured it was a cell for one of the terrorists groups. Arrangements were made to collect the prisoners while we razed what was left of the building: a standard procedure after an altercation.

Every morning, I would send a mine-clearing party down the road to clear any mines that might have been laid during the night. A few mines were discovered but we missed the odd one with the result that a car with some Jewish occupants was blown up. I had brought with me a wireless set to communicate between my headquarters and Battalion HQ. The set was not particularly reliable; nevertheless, it was useful to have a link with the Battalion Intelligence Officer (BIO), as I was able to send daily reports and receive information from him in return. A few days after our moving to the settlement, the Commanding Officer decided to pay us a visit. As I was receiving this news over the radio, I heard a shot fired in the distance. I told the signaler to warn to CO not to leave as there was a disturbance in the vicinity. Too late, the signaler informed me that the CO had already left some twenty minutes previously. This meant that the CO's party might be where the shooting occurred. I realized that the CO would have also heard the shot but I took no chance and sent an armoured carrier to meet the party for I was sure the CO would be travelling in an open jeep.

It was just as well that I took the initiative for the CO's party was the intended target and two individuals had been wounded; a police cadet and one of the drivers. A single shot had passed through one body and penetrated the second. The visitors were brought to my HQ while our medic attended to the wounded. The party included the CO, the Adjutant, the Chief of Police, two police cadets and two drivers. The CO was quite shaken up. The Adjutant was livid, exclaiming how foolish it had been for all of them to make the journey together, especially when accompanied by the Chief of Police, who was thoroughly disliked by everyone – Jews, Arabs and the British. While waiting for an ambulance and more suitable transport to return the visitors to Jerusalem, I gave the CO a rundown of our operations. I mentioned that the Arabs had given us little or no trouble, but that the Jews were causing us problems and were the main cause of the unsettled state of affairs in the area. He told me that he would brief the Brigade Commander of the situation and request that if the overall situation didn't improve, the mission would be terminated. Possibly as a result of this unfortunate incident, we never again were bothered with visitors. This event brought to mind the saying: "There is no guarantee for anything in life except that one day we are all required to leave it."

Every evening a mobile patrol would be carried out of the area. I would share this duty with my Sergeant. For this type of patrol, I used the CO's Dingo armoured car. The Dingo normally carried a crew of two; however, I sometimes added a machine gunner positioned on the outside of the vehicle behind the turret. One evening, I asked my signaler, who was being demobilized back to England the next day, whether he would like to go on one last patrol as the machine gunner? He accepted the invitation somewhat reluctantly. Since it was pouring with rain, we made room for him inside the scout car. This turned out to be a mistake. Halfway through the patrol, we entered a built-up area that was controlled by the IZL. Turning a corner, I spotted directly to our front what looked like a pipe mine stretched across the road. As the noise within the vehicle made it impossible to make oneself heard, I had established a set of signals with the driver. One gentle kick in the back meant 'stop'; two kicks meant 'go ahead'; one nudge to the left or right indicated which direction to go in. I gave what I believed was one kick in the driver's back, but he continued. I couldn't understand and suddenly to my horror, I had kicked the passenger instead. We came to a stop on top of the solid iron bar that had sprung up between the front and rear wheels, making any further progress impossible. It was about 10 p.m. and we were close to an orchard surrounded by a three foot high stone wall on one side and an apartment complex on the other side. The scout car carried no winch so that we had no means of dragging the vehicle off the trap. We tried digging, jacking the vehicle up and levering the vehicle with a crow bar, all to no avail. The vehicle weighed about three tons. To make matters worse, my wireless set was irritatingly out-of-order, so we tried sending an SOS using the vehicle's headlights. We flashed our message across the open ground to a Palestine Police station that we could see about a mile away. We received no response. Frantically, we continued to work at dislodging the vehicle for another half-hour and then gave up.

Given that the Jewish terrorists would do anything to get hold of military weapons and vehicles, and the fact that we were immobilized in IZL territory, I had no doubt we would be attacked and made plans to defend ourselves. The question was when would they attack? To stay in the vehicle was asking for trouble and so I sent the machine gunner to a spot where he could give us covering fire while the driver and I covered the road and apartment building. I remember hoping fervently that neither of my two companions would get hurt for shelter was almost non-existent. It was obvious that we needed to get outside help if we were to extricate ourselves from this predicament. I told the driver to make his way to the police station, get hold of a heavy GMC armoured truck that had a winch and return with it, plus some additional men to help get the scout car off the obstacle. He had a choice: to go by the well-lit road or across the dark open ground. He chose the road. I shall always remember the diminishing sound of his hobnailed boots as he dissolved into the darkness. I kept listening for the inevitable sound of a shot, but there was none.

Ten minutes passed and I picked up a new sound. There was something moving in the orchard. The sound was similar to that made by men crawling slowly forward on their stomachs. The dragging noise would last for a few seconds followed by a longer silence. I moved to where the machine gunner was lying and re-positioned him further away from the wall. My stomach muscles were so tight for we couldn't see the cause of the noise. I had enough of this insufferable waiting and realized that there was no need for anyone to be crawling on the other side of the wall since the wall was high enough to hide from view. I went to the wall and took a quick look over it and suddenly saw a shadow lurking about. I thought that it was too big to be a man. I took a longer look and discovered it was a bloody donkey feeding on the grass and fallen fruit. I went over the wall to assure myself that the donkey was alone and then went back to the Dingo feeling spent and foolish. One's imagination works in double time when under stress.

It was an hour when we finally heard the GMC truck coming our way. The driver was alone which wasn't a complete surprise. He explained that the police had been unwilling to send anyone to our aid since the Jewish terrorists threatened them as marked men if they collaborated with the British. The Superintendent didn't want to even part with his armoured truck, but the driver, no doubt, convinced him with a few unrestrained threats. I believe the driver would have stolen the truck rather than have had to walk back. With the help of the truck's winch, we soon had the Dingo back on the road none the worse for its ordeal. We returned the truck to the police station. On reflection, it was a miracle that we came through this affair in one piece and I still can't understand why we were not attacked.

We resumed our patrol, this time the machine gunner riding on the outside of the vehicle. About a half-hour later we heard the crump, crump, crump of mortar bombs exploding and headed in the direction of these explosions. As we neared the area, the target looked suspiciously like the police station we had earlier visited. Sure enough, the post had been hit and was on fire. We were able to assist in rescuing a few men from the inferno, but soon other police units arrived on the scene and took over. As we were leaving the area, a loose hydro cable that had been snapped by the explosions and wrapped itself around the right rear wheel of the Dingo. This was not our lucky night. It took us an hour to free the vehicle from the entanglement. By now the driver had reached the limit of his endurance, and so I agreed to return to our base. When we reached our settlement, the driver backed the vehicle into a cement barricade by mistake and buckled the car's rear end. If we weren't so exhausted, the irony was amusing. It had been a long, taxing and jittery night. The next day, we were ordered to return to camp. We undid all the booby-traps and tripwires, cleaned up the area as best we could, and departed feeling relieved to be getting back to camp with its more civilized conditions. We had been away for only a week, but it felt more like a month.

Since leaving England in October 1945, I had not had any home leave and after two years abroad was due seven days time off. This I was granted as well as travelling time for the sea passage there and back. The passage to Southampton was by passenger liner departing from Port Said. I remember next to nothing about the journey except that we arrived at our destination at a very early hour only to be met by tired and hostile custom officials. Prior to disembarking, one particular officer onboard had asked a number of fellow passengers to help him smuggle in contraband, including some bolts of expensive cloth. I met him again on the train taking us to London and he was in a flap as he was having great difficulty finding those who had volunteered to help him. In passing through customs, I was behind a pale-skinned army Captain who was arguing with the officials and claiming that he had been in the Middle East for years. I was the colour of mahogany. They took one look at me and then at him and pointed out the difference. He changed his tune. This incident didn't help me one bit. I was hoping to smuggle in five bottles of whiskey and gin, but the officials made me open up my baggage and I ended up paying twice the cost of the liquor. At least one person appreciated the effort, my father, who was with the Royal Navy, and the recipient of the gift.

My parents were then living just north of Edinburgh. Though the train journey was long, I was overjoyed at seeing England again. The countryside was lush and truly magnificent in comparison to the aridness of where I just left. As always, my seven days leave passed too quickly. I seemed to have spent much of my time at parties. The Royal Navy had a large establishment at Rosyth and I was invited several times for drinks aboard different ships. I was invited aboard a boom defence vessel – they don't get much smaller. The night before, I had been to a party that lasted well into the next day and I was still feeling the side effects. On reaching the vessel, I had no difficulty crossing the gangway. My host was most forthcoming with the gin and this, together with the swaying and bouncing of the vessel, only made me tipsy and nauseous. When leaving the ship, I found it difficult to focus on the gangway and practically crawled along it to the pier. I didn't dare look back for I knew the sailors and naval officers were probably all smirking at my condition. 'He proves the army can't hold their liquor!' I felt I let the team down. Though I thoroughly enjoyed my leave, I was anxious to rejoin my unit since I knew that many Captains and Majors were about to return to England and I wanted to be in a position to influence my own future. So it was bittersweet bidding *adieu* to my parents.

During my return journey by ship to Egypt, a curious incident occurred. I was having breakfast as usual, when I noticed a lady at an adjoining table who I was sure I knew. She was my mother's age and had a number of children whom she must have been escorting back to wherever it was. I decided to introduce myself. She was surprised and, I suppose, flattered at being recognized for it turned out that I had last seen her twelve years before. She was the wife of the Commander-in-Chief, Mediterranean Fleet. On arrival in Malta, the Admiral's barge came alongside. She asked me to come ashore and meet the Admiral but I had to refuse owing to the ship's schedule. The incident did give me a certain status for the remainder of the journey.

A few weeks after my return to the Battalion, I was summoned to the Adjutant's office. One tried to keep out of the Adjutant's way as much as possible and I was wondering what I had done to deserve this call. On entering his office, the Adjutant told me, in a curt manner, that I was improperly dressed. I was nonplussed until he got up, came around his desk, and with hand extended, congratulated me on my promotion to Captain. What a glorious feeling to no longer be a subaltern. As a Captain, you felt yourself to be a real officer and were treated as such by the more senior officers and by the Other Ranks. My Company Commander, whom I'm sure had much to do with my promotion, very decently invited me to dine at a first-class restaurant in town. He had selected the menu and wine and it was superb. While we were having dinner, he told me that his illness was worsening and that I would have to take over the company more often. But first, the company was being sent to provide the Guard for Government House.

GOVERNMENT HOUSE

Providing the Guard for Government House was a luxury for the officers and a break for the men. A reduced strength company was required to do the job and each battalion in Jerusalem provided the guard on a rotational basis. During the time I was in Jerusalem, I was twice on this detail. The task included the provision of an armed guard at the main gate; foot patrols within the grounds of Government House; clearing the main roads of any recently laid mines; and providing an escort to the Governor whenever he left the grounds. General Cunningham, who was then the Governor, very kindly invited one of the company officers to dinner each evening. We took it in turn to dine that meant that you dined-out at least twice during the two-week guard duty. You were required to wear 'Service Dress' rather than battle fatigue. I had no British Army service dress and this barred me from attending the dinners. I was damned if I was going to miss the dinners and came up with an idea. Since my Company Commander and I got along well together, I put to him the idea that he loan me his own service dress since we were pretty similar in height and build. He thought the idea excellent but cautioned me that I was not to make any holes in the shoulder epaulettes of the tunic so as to fit my Captain's three 'pips' and would therefore have to attend the dinner as a Second Lieutenant (a single 'pip' which could fit on the epaulette in lieu of the Major's 'crown' insignia). I readily agreed. When it came my turn to attend the dinner, my Company Commander phoned the senior ADC to explain the situation and the latter agreed to go along with the ploy. That evening, I was met by all three ADCs who had come to view this apparition bedecked with two rows of medal ribbons. I think the sight of those ribbons took them all by surprise. We realized that the General could not help but notice these decorations and that he might ask some awkward questions – I was only twenty years old and looked it. We worked out a plan whereby I would try and remain in the background and when introduced to the Governor, I would be carrying a book in my left hand to obscure as many ribbons as possible. It is my experience that on being introduced to senior officers, they spend more time looking at your medals than at your face. If the Governor had been wearing a monocle, it would have popped from his eye as he gazed at the number of decorations displayed. I quickly moved along to allow the next in line to be introduced. He did not seem to register either my age or my rank. During dinner, we went off to play billiards that allowed me to remove my tunic and relax. It was great fun and well worth the risk. At the second dinner, the Governor had as guests Lady Oxford and her niece. I was able to once again escape detection although the niece could not believe what she saw when we were in conversation. I'm sure my appearance made for some interesting conversation behind my back.

The Hounds of Palestine

One evening, our guards reported seeing a huge white animal enter the grounds through the wire. We had heard about these mystical hounds. We believed the reports made by the men when such a hound was seen snatching and carrying off a boxer puppy that belonged to one of the officers. Given the size of these animals, we thought it prudent to double the guard at night for the men's safety. I eventually met up with one of these hounds. I was returning to Government House with some other officers following a Mess Dinner at base camp. We were seated in the back of an open jeep and were about a half-mile from the House when suddenly, out of the night, came forth what we at first took to be a wild pony. It started to chase our vehicle. As the animal got closer, we noticed its fangs and its determined intention to get in amongst us. We were armed with pistols and a few in the group started to shoot at the animal. It took many shots before it veered off the road where we lost sight of it. Next morning, the mine clearing party came across the body of the hound and brought it back to the House. It was as big as a Shetland pony. We made some inquiries about these dogs and the local Arabs confirmed that several such hounds existed in the hills surrounding the city. They were rarely seen by day but foraged by night. No one knew exactly when the hounds first appeared in the area; some thought it was hundreds of years back. In view of the size and ferocity of these beasts, we reinforced the perimeter wire and laid a number of trip-flares close to the wire in the hope of keeping the hounds at bay. It seemed to work.

Misuse of Military Service

One evening, the Duty Officer phoned me from the guardhouse at the main gate to say that there were a number of Arabs at the gate asking for help and would I come down to sort out the matter. When I arrived, I encountered four Arabs of various ages surrounding a woman placed in a roughly made, open coffin. Since I knew but a few words of Arabic, and they knew next to no English, communications was somewhat awkward, but it was obvious that the woman was in labour. I gathered that the baby was dead and couldn't be delivered and that the men wanted to get her to their hospital but was afraid to pass through Jewish terrain and the Jewish gate barriers. I telephoned the Battalion and asked that an ambulance be sent immediately. This was done without any questions. When the ambulance arrived, we placed the woman in it (without the coffin), and told the Duty Officer to take her to the Arab's hospital. Suddenly, all hell broke loose. All the Arab men wanted to travel with the woman. I chose the one who looked the same age as the woman then ordered the ambulance to leave. The Duty Officer had no difficulty in getting to the hospital and back. A few days later, the Commanding Officer heard about the incident and gave me hell for misusing military property. He had also been informed that the Jews had also learned of the incident and were not pleased. Fortunately, my Company Commander intervened and accepted the blame for authorizing the use of the ambulance. He, of course, hadn't since I only told him about the affair after the ambulance had left, but, as he told me later, he would have done the same thing. The husband of the woman came by a few days later to thank me for saving his wife's life. He gave me a brass dish as a sign of his appreciation.

During my second tour at Government House, I was again called to the main gate, this time by the guard commander who fully believed I spoke fluent Arabic. When I got there, a number of Arabs were supporting a younger Arab who had a soiled and bloody rag around his neck. One of the Arabs spoke broken English. On the removal of the rag, I saw that the lad had been shot through the neck. In case I hadn't noticed, his friend placed a dirty finger into the hole. The bullet had passed right through the fellow's neck. I asked the wounded man whether he could move his head without difficulty and I was assured that he could. I then called for the medical orderly with his bag of tricks, who, on arrival, took charge. He cleansed the wound, put some ointment on it and bandaged it up. As a parting gesture, he gave the lad some additional ointment and a bundle of bandages. Before their departure, I warned them to keep their dirty hands away from the wound and to change the bandage frequently. They grinned in a conciliatory fashion, thanked us and left satisfied.

JUSTICE AND THE LAW

On our return to the Battalion lines, the Company was employed on guarding the base itself. In fact, much of the time the men were employed doing a number of fatigues, a task no one enjoyed. To my knowledge, no base camp in Jerusalem was ever attacked by either the Jews or Arabs. While the men were on fatigues, several of the officers, myself included, were kept busy attending a number of court martial cases as members of the Board. Most of the cases concerned the loss of weapons for which, if found guilty, the solider was imprisoned for several months or, if an officer was sentenced, was cashiered.

Since the men, when not on operations, were confined to base, the need for female company became a problem. The Jews and Arabs realized this and would offer the men as many women as they wanted in exchange for weapons. The Band Major and many of the bandsmen succumbed to this tantalizing offer; however, the deal was with the Arabs who insisted that these British thieves also participate in a forthcoming battle against the Jews. They were in the forefront of the battle and were all killed – by whom, is questionable. The Arabs informed us of what had taken place and offered to return the bodies. This offering surprised us immensely for it did little to encourage others to follow suit. To dissuade others from deserting, the Commanding Officer had the men in camp parade in the form of a square and then have the bodies displayed in their coffins. He informed the men what had happened and what was likely to happen to others if they deserted. The level of desertion, which was negligible, dropped to zero. There was one interesting case of desertion that involved an officer. The Transport Officer, a Captain and an excellent officer, had requested permission to return to England where his wife was critically ill. The Commanding Officer was away and the Second-in-Command, who was Acting Commanding Officer, refused the request. In spite of the risk, the Captain took a military vehicle and a few weapons and sold these to the Jews and with the proceeds, made his way to England. He was unlucky for he was caught at Calais whereby he was sent back to his unit under close arrest. At his trial, he was found guilty and later jailed for one year following which he was dishonourably discharged. His wife died while he was in prison. Later, the 2IC was also returned to the United Kingdom in disgrace for the manner in which he had dealt with the situation.

The Quartermaster Branch of the Army, never much admired by the soldiers, had some excellent officers and men who did wonders at producing required supplies and equipment in difficult times without too much concern for the usual protocol. On-the-other-hand, there were too many Quartermasters who abused their position and were caught profiteering in the black market. At this time, the Battalion was suffering from a shortage of all types of equipment and vehicles. We knew that most of the items we needed were held in depot stores in Egypt, but for some reason, our requests were always turned down. Given this situation, you can imagine the satisfaction of participating at the court martial of a Quartermaster whose sins had been uncovered. Dozens of Quartermasters were facing courts martial. I participated in two such cases as the junior member and was quite taken aback by the attitude of the members of the Board, most of whom had served in the war and on the front line. The sentences given to those found guilty were particularly severe, especially to those who had dabbled in the black market. In hindsight, this made sense condemning the self-interest of a few at the sacrifice of so many.

Where discipline was concerned, the men were so occupied that they had little time or opportunity to get into trouble. A good example in keeping a group out of trouble regardless of whether it is in the military or in a prison, is to keep the group occupied and always mentally and physically busy. For those who committed crimes and sentenced, they were placed in a barbed wire cage (similar to that used to hold POWs). The cage contained a small tent for protection against sun and rain. There was one private who spent much of his time in the cage. He was an excellent soldier and kept his equipment in first-class order, even when imprisoned, but each time he was released, he would go after the Regimental Sergeant Major with intent to do as much bodily harm as possible. He never gave reason for the attacks and the RSM was also very reticent about the matter. I believe it was a matter of *cherchez la femme*.

Once, when I was Duty Officer, I was called upon to deal with a serious accident. On reaching the barrack room where the accident had occurred, found a young conscript sprawled across a bed and bleeding profusely from a head wound from the impact of a bullet. Witnesses said that he and another solider had been playing with a rifle when the shot rang out. The soldier who had fired the shot could not explain the presence of a live round in the rifle's chamber. The dying man was immediately sent to the medical orderly room but died shortly thereafter. I placed the man who had fired the weapon under close arrest. He ended up in an infamous Glass House prison in England.

Where justice and law were concerned, to bring known terrorists or their leaders to court was difficult enough, but to obtain a conviction was well nigh impossible. When it was certain that such terrorists would escape justice, a member of what became known as the "Black Gang," would be given the job of eliminating the terrorist – Jew or Arab. As far as I know, only one member of this gang was caught and brought to trial. Ironically, the accused, a Major in the British Army, was found not guilty on the basis of insufficient evidence. Following the trial, the officer was immediately flown to England. I'm convinced our Battalion harboured a member of the Black Gang. He would disappear for a week at a time on some pretext or other, which on closer inspection, did not hold up. On the surface, the man seemed such a kind and mild mannered individual.

SEARCH-AND-RESCUE

Another duty we performed was to carry out search-and-rescue operations after certain violent attacks by terrorist groups.

A tactic used by terrorists to maim "enemies" was to booby-trap bodies. On one such occasion, Jews kidnapped a young British, engineer subaltern. He was hanged from a tree in an orange grove. When the body was found and cut down by his Company, a hidden booby-trap on his body detonated, wounding those around the corpse. Several units were called out to sweep the area and to bring in suspects – any man between the age of 16 to 50. To sweep the countryside, the troops would be spread out in extended lines thus covering a very large area of ground. Other troops were used to prevent suspects moving back into areas previously swept clean. Reconnaissance units in armoured cars would box-in an area to prevent anyone; male, female or child, from leaving the area. It was a long and tedious job that took days. The British authorities didn't expect to find the culprits; however, it gave them the authority to search everywhere, uncovering many caches of arms, ammunition, and other wanted terrorists. The operation also disrupted the lives of the Jews being searched and, it was hoped, this would anger the people sufficiently to turn them against the terrorists, but I doubt that it did.

When clearing a house, we came across several strange situations. In one house, the inhabitants slept in the cellar rather than their bedrooms for protection, even though the cellar was flooded with water. When roused out of bed, they were found to be fully clothed and were still wearing their boots. In another house, we found underground tunnels that linked several houses together. It was here that we rounded up known terrorists who were terrified that we would shoot them. Brave heroes when they pulled off a murderous, terrorist act, but cowards when cornered. In one of the larger houses, we found a big cupboard with a false back leading down into a cellar. The cellar was crammed with very young children and a few women, all of whom became very agitated on seeing us approach. I insisted that they all leave the cellar and return upstairs where no harm would befall them. It took some persuasion.

When searching a town, each sector was cordoned off prior to carrying out the search. On such occasions, the Jews and Arabs would send pregnant women or women with children to break through the cordon of armed men on some pretext, usually the need for milk for the child. Our soldiers by then had become accustomed to all the tricks, and refused anyone passage. When women were refused permission to pass, they would shriek and curse, hoping the British soldier's sense of fair play would weaken his resolve. It didn't. These women would revert to assaulting the soldier by punching him and kicking him. I remember seeing one soldier who had been kicked in the groin by a big fat woman. Instantly, he prodded and poked the woman with his bayonet back to her house and none too gently. I was in full sympathy with the soldier and looked the other way. In some cases where women were particularly aggressive, they were detained and then given a quick search. Occasionally, weapons or secret papers were found.

Though the unit would normally set out at 4 a.m., even this had its colourful side. A large mass of well-trained men marching off in the cool of the early morning, the vast silence broken only by the sound of marching feet, and the sound of equipment banging against another object, produced a keen and desired sensation. The sweep would stretch from the coast to the opposite border. Those lucky enough to be on the coastal side were rewarded with the most magnificent vista at dawn. It was an invigorating feeling being on a sandy coastline without a soul in sight and the stillness of the huge expanse of the sea, produced a calmness among us. I must say, this serenity only happened during these brief moments.

The Battalion Intelligence Officer (IO) understood Arabic and Hebrew and would spend much of the day listening to the operational wavelengths of the two opposing groups. Surprisingly, these two frequencies rarely changed and when they did, they could be picked up again without much difficulty. Through this form of radio interception, we could anticipate and thwart any intended hostile action towards us. Such information we passed to Brigade HQ who, in turn, passed it to the Palestinian police. We were suspicious of the police whose integrity was in question and who, we thought, were informing the Jewish Agency. Our suspicions were proven correct when we sent false information with the assistance of Brigade HQ. The Commander-in-Chief, General MacMillan, was informed of the matter and he agreed that, in future, the Palestinian police would be informed of our actions *after* the fact rather than before. From there-on-in, we had far more success on our 'searches.'

One afternoon, the IO picked up information about an intended Arab attack against a few Jewish settlements located close to the Battalion lines. The CO, using the appropriate frequency, informed the Arabs that if they attacked, we would defend the Jews. Early next morning, we saw thousands of armed Arabs on the hills surrounding our base and the Jewish settlements. They were in no organized formation for fighting but were dispersed across the hills in small groups apparently waiting further orders. Since my Company Commander was in hospital, the ACO ordered me to prepare to defend the Jewish settlements. As two-thirds of the Battalion's strength was out of camp on other duties, very few soldiers remained in camp, and moreover, the security of the camp had to be maintained. I discussed the matter with the ACO. It was decided that we should give the Arabs a display of our firepower and of what dangers they could expect were they to attack. Brigade HQ and the Jewish Agency were informed of our intentions, the latter being told not to interfere other than to warn the inhabitants of the targeted settlements. I grabbed every available man, including cooks, clerks, detainees, etc, and positioned them to cover strategic positions of fire. The firepower was to include mortars, heavy machine guns and tracer fire. The target area chosen was a wide open piece of ground through which any attack on the settlements would have to pass; the whole area being in full view of the Arabs on the hills. Since the noise of the fire display would be deafening, I gave orders that the display was to last exactly two minutes. The ACO warned the Arabs by radio of what we were about to do and when the show was to take place. During this display, we were also going to use rockets to demolish a Jewish house in the centre of the area that terrorist snipers used to shoot at our men in the main camp. When the hour arrived, I gave the order to open fire. The effect was extraordinary. No firework display could have been better. The house was obliterated and the surrounding surface appeared like a lunar landscape. The ACO radioed the Arabs and advised them to withdraw immediately. This they did but in their own sweet time.

The rifle shots directed at us increased as the months passed. It was impossible to tell whether it was Jews or Arabs who were firing, but we thought it likely that both these groups were guilty. The camp was in full view of the surrounding hills, and except for the few brick buildings, there was no adequate shelter against any type of hostile fire. It was decided to send armoured mobile patrols by day to sweep the hills and villages within rifle range of the camp and to set a powerful searchlight on rails to cover the area under the cloak of darkness. The mobile patrols were effective in reducing the number of shots fired at the camp during the day, whereas the searchlight attracted too much attention and drew the enemy's fire. At night, you can see the flash of a rifle shot. A six pounder, anti-tank gun and heavy machine-guns were positioned on the flat roof of the CO's house. When a sniper fired upon the searchlight, the immediate reply was a well placed anti-tank shell followed by a hail of bullets that spat out from the machine-guns. This was rather like using an elephant to squash an ant, but it certainly put the fear of God into the terrorist snipers. Sometime later, when again using the anti-tank gun, its weight and recoil were such as to weaken the roof and the gun and gunners disappeared through the roof to land in the CO's bedroom. No one was badly hurt; however, a new location had to be found for the gun – and for the CO.

THE OLD CITY

My Company Commander's health was steadily deteriorating and his visits to the hospital more frequent. The day before the Company was sent on guard duty to the Old City, he was again admitted to hospital and I again became the Acting Company Commander. To give you an idea of how complex the area is, the Company's task was to protect the minority groups from the Moslems who occupied seventy-five percent of the Old City.

The perimeter is enveloped by high stone walls built in the 16th century by the Turkish Sultan Suleiman, the Magnificent. Behind these ramparts are small stone houses squeezed together like Velcro and only separated by narrow arteries of cobbled streets. At the time, the Old City was divided into four major ethnic and religious quadrants: in the west were the Christian and Armenian quarters; in the north and east and surrounding the Temple Mount (Harim-al-Sharif), was the Moslem quarter; and in the south, was the Jewish quarter. Each sector in the city had its own entrance and exit gate. The minority groups used the Zion Gate while the Moslems used the Jaffa and Damascus Gates. Most of the houses were not more than two storeys high and were either byzantine or flat-roofed. The better homes had inner courtyards. Under many of the houses, were numerous tunnels and passageways leading all over the city and providing safe havens and escape routes. The most important landmarks in the Old City were: the Dome of the Rock, the Western (Wailing) Wall, and the Holy Sepulchre.

The First Temple was built by King Solomon around 960 B.C. and was later destroyed by the Babylonians. On the same sight, the Second Temple began construction in the 6th century under the patronage of the Persian king, Cyrus, and completed by Herod in the 1st century. It was here that Moslems believe Mohammed arrived from Mecca astride his winged horse, al-Buraq, and here that he stopped and tied his magical animal to the Wall before he ascended to Heaven. The Moslem and Jewish religions are so entwined that a remnant of the wall of the Second Temple, known as the Wailing Wall, forms part of the wall of the Haram-al-Sharif, site of the Dome of the Rock. The location of the Dome of the Rock is where Abraham offered to sacrifice his son Isaac. The Wailing Wall, a one hundred foot stone wall, is the oldest and most venerated symbol of the ancient Jewish Kingdom. Jews go there to pray, to touch the heavy stones, to weep for ancient Israel, and to write their wishes on tiny scraps of paper that they then place between the stones of the Wall. The Church of the Holy Sepulchre belongs to six communities each with definite rights – the Greek Orthodox, Armenian and Roman Catholic communities, who have effective residence and individual chapels, and the Syrian (Jacobites), the Coptic and Abyssinian communities. The Church itself is the holiest shrine in Christendom and includes the Tenth Station of the Cross, the Calvary, and the traditional sight of the crucifixion on the hill of Golgotha. Monks of the Franciscan Order are the caretakers of the Church. The Church was built in 335 A.D. by Emperor Constantine to honour the sight of Christ's crucifixion and the Resurrection. The Crusaders added to it in 1149. In the last fifty years, considerable repairs have been made to the Church and it has been necessary to further buttress the walls. I made a number of visits to the Holy Sepulchre and still have a "Certificate of Pilgrimage" dating back to October 29, 1947.

When taking over the guard from the Highland Light Infantry (HLI), I noted that their headquarters was in the house of a Christian merchant. I decided to make my HQ in the Mayor's house for better communication with the Jewish community. He agreed to the idea. The Mayor, a Mr. Weingarten, informed me that the HLI had carried out their tour of duty in an aggressive manner that had caused problems among the Jewish and Arab communities. He hoped that we would behave with more restraint. I promised nothing. I asked Mr. Weingarten whether he could arrange for me to meet the leaders of the Arab community and this he did. The next day, I met two Arab leaders and with the help of an interpreter, I was able to tell them that we would not tolerate any hostility by any fraction in the Old City. Later that day, a few shots were directed at a Jewish home from an Arab house on the border of the two areas. I immediately ordered the Arab house destroyed following which we had no more trouble from the Arab community. It seemed that the Arab leaders had far better control over their people than did their Jewish counterparts, but then, the Jewish community had no say in the goings on of the Zionists and their terrorist gangs.

My men were placed in twos or threes at strategic points along the border dividing the Moslems and the minority groups. The men at these outposts remained there for two days before being relieved by others. Hot meals were brought to them. I also established a roving patrol that kept to the minority group's area and maintained a reserve group to act as an immediate action force in case of serious trouble. The Jewish Agency organized 'food' convoys to relieve Jewish inhabitants of the Old City from potentially hostile Arabs who surrounded the sector. The convoys were made up of buses and trucks. The Jewish Agency demanded protection of these convoys and the British forces provided the necessary armoured escort. As the convoy approached the Zion Gate of the Old City, my reserve group would man the ramparts on either side of the Gate to provide further covering fire. One morning, as a convoy approached the Gate, soldiers on the wall were fired upon by a group of people hidden amongst the rubble of some demolished houses several hundred yards outside the Zion Gate. On seeing some men move about in the rubble, I ordered the machine gunner to fire a few warning shots in their direction. The men wore similar dress to that worn by British soldiers and it was this that gave me some concern. I got in touch with my Battalion HQ to find out whether we had any troops in that area and, some time later, was told that a section of HLI were in fact the ones who had fired on us. I remained discreet about our having shot at our own troops.

An agreement had been made with the Jewish Agency that no weapons or armed men would be brought into the Old City by means of these 'food' convoys, but the Jews broke the agreement time and again. As a result of complaints by the Arab community, and the non-abidance of the agreement by the Jews, the Divisional Commander refused to provide further armed escorts for the convoys. The Jews continued to send their convoys but most of these were ambushed and destroyed by the Arabs.

During my stay at the Mayor's house, I got to know him and his family quite well. He was a kind and gentle man who abhorred violence of any sort. He had two daughters: the one living with them was a nurse. The other was more militant and had joined the Haganah Army much to the family's disgust and fear, for it was very much an orthodox household. In the evening, he would tell me stories of what it had been like to live in Jerusalem in the old days, when local Jews and Arabs worked and lived in

harmony. During the days of Passover, I was invited to partici-
pate in the family festivities as an observer. It was quite touching.
I wonder what happened to him and his family the day after the
British withdrew from Jerusalem?

Though our task was to protect the minority groups, especially the Jews, from attack by the Arabs, we nevertheless suffered casualties from being fired upon by Jewish extremists, who
would fire at us from the top of synagogues or from the flat
rooftops of buildings that gave easy access to escape routes. I had
one man shot in the face and another in the back. We spotted a
sniper firing from the dome of a synagogue and returned fire but
accidently killed a young lad who had been praying below. We
had missed hitting the sniper and a bullet had ricocheted off the
dome and hit the boy.

One morning, explosives were heard going off in the Jewish
quarter. At the time I was in the Mayor's house. Within minutes,
a runner arrived with a grizzly story. Two very young boys had
been badly wounded as a result of kicking some booby-trapped
tin cans that exploded on contact. These booby-traps had most
likely been planted to wound British troops. A few more such
booby-traps were found elsewhere in the quarter. The two
wounded boys were brought to the Mayor's house in severe
condition. The Mayor's daughter gave them first aid but much
more was required. The Mayor asked for my help in getting the
boys through the Arab sectors to a Jewish hospital. I informed
him that I would try but advised him that I could only get them
as far as the Jewish Agency. It was up to the Agency to get them
to hospital. I then called the unit ambulance and when this arrived, I sent a subaltern to accompany the ambulance to the
Agency. The Mayor's daughter accompanied the boys providing
what aid she could. To get through the Arab lines without being
stopped, the subaltern shouted: "Wounded! Wounded!" allowing
the ambulance to get through unimpeded. On arrival at the Jewish Agency, there was a receiving party – no doctor or orderlies -
but a battery of photographers for propaganda purposes. When
the two boys were taken out of the ambulance, no one came to
help. The subaltern was incensed and laid into the photographers

smashing cameras and faces. I later heard that the two boys had died before reaching the hospital. Life is cheap here. My Commanding Officer was again displeased at the action I had taken, but I suppose he had given up trying to change my ways. If everything was "done by the book", why be there at all?

I had thought that once in the Old City I would have felt or sensed the religious fervour of the different religious groups that lived within the confines of its walls. However, this was not the case due to the constant troubles between the Jews and the Arabs that kept everyone in a condition of nervous exhaustion. When I went to the Holy Sepulchre, I was to find that commercialism had taken a strong foothold. The Wailing Wall and its surroundings were filthy. Even the Garden of Gethsemane was nothing like what I had imagined and needed maintenance. Only the Dome of the Rock remained magnificent. In fact, you hadn't time to consider the holiness of the area for you were too preoccupied in looking over your shoulder to see who was following. I certainly didn't feel closer to God in the Old City – anything but, whereas when I was stationed in India, the veneration of the Gods and the observance of religious faiths was constantly on view and became part of your life.

IMMEDIATE ACTION COMPANY

Following our tour of duty in the Old City, we again returned to base camp. The amount of violent incidents in town had augmented to the point where a new and more effective way of dealing with such incidents was required. Someone at Brigade HQ dreamed up the idea of establishing "Immediate Action Companies" for each battalion sector, whose main task would be to contain and suppress those committing the violations. My Commanding Officer asked me whether I would be interested in planning, training and commanding such a company to which I readily agreed. I believe I was offered the job only because I was the only officer with any experience in aid to civil power operations. After some trials-and-errors, it was agreed that the Company should consist of a headquarters, three platoons, a pioneer section (to deal with barricades, mines and booby-traps), and a small administrative team; a total amounting to about 130 officers and men. For transport, we had four large armoured carriers, the CO's Dingo, and four-wheeled vehicles. The intent was for the Company to dash out to wherever the incident had occurred or was still taking place, cordon off the area, arrest the trouble makers and bring calm to the area as quickly as possible. Our first 'baptism of fire' actually took place before the Company had been fully trained and the result was a total fiasco. The Polish Embassy, a stone's throw from the unit lines, had been blown up and it took my Company twenty minutes to clear the camp's main gate. On arrival at the Embassy, it became all too apparent that the Platoon Commanders had little idea about how they were to proceed. I took this opportunity to practice the correct drills and the Company was put through a number of appropriate exercises much to the astonishment of the members of the Polish Embassy. On return to base camp, I established a system to quicken the process of assembly and movement. The men on standby were confined to a number of Nissen huts close to the Company vehicle compound. Meals were brought to and eaten in the Nissen huts. Those on standby slept fully clothed ready to leave at a moment's notice. The vehicles were maintained to a high degree of readiness and all equipment and ammunition was already loaded aboard the vehicles. To give as much warning as possible without necessarily having the men board the vehicles, especially in wet or cold weather, I copied a system used during the 'blitz' by factories in England. When a red light appeared in the huts, the men were to stop whatever they were doing, put on their individual battle equipment and be prepared to move out. On the yellow light, the men were to fall-in beside their respective vehicles where the sub-unit commanders would check their men. The vehicles were covered in oil and grease from constant use and the men's clothing became heavily soiled from clambouring in and out of the vehicles, so we boarded the vehicles only when absolutely necessary. The vehicles' engines were turned on and the convoy formed up ready to depart. On the green light, the men boarded the vehicles and the convoy immediately moved off to a pre-planned rendezvous. On the red warning, I would report to the Adjutant's Office for orders and for a quick briefing by the Intelligence Officer as to where the trouble was and what had happened following which, I would either return to my Company and brief the troops or, if the green light signal had been given, I would depart in the Dingo and hope to catch up with the main group before it reached the rendezvous.

I drilled the troops constantly, even when they were in the process of having a meal or when asleep for we were supposedly ready for action at all hours. Since most of the time the men were on standby, there was considerable time to train them well. Each man was trained to carry out different tasks so as to be prepared for any eventuality. Each man had also to be able to take over the task of any other man in the Company, such as driving the different vehicles, operating the wireless set, giving first-aid treatment, firing the medium machine gun, etc. With the consent of the inhabitants of a Jewish settlement close to the camp, we used the area and buildings to practice the different drills. Within a matter of a week, the Company had become an effective unit that could operate efficiently in most foreseeable situations, regardless of weather or during the day or night. On the receipt of the green light signal, it could now move out of the camp within two minutes.

BATTLE FATIGUE

The Battalion's normal working dress was battledress. Due to the requirements of our job, I received permission for the men to wear loose combat attire consisting of a cotton coverall that looked like a cabinet of pockets, enabling them from enduring heavy additional equipment such as haversacks. In lieu of the cumbersome steel helmet, the men used only the inner liner that was light and gave ample protection against small missiles, such as stones and bricks. By mistake, some earth got mixed up with the paint at the time we were painting the helmets. The result was fortuitous – a dull brown-green, flat colour. We painted at the front and back of each helmet the rank of the individual or the occupation of the man in white paint. For example, a machine gunner would have the symbol 'MG'. These symbols helped to recognize each individual more easily in the dark.

To relieve the monotony when not training or out on a call, lectures on current affairs were scheduled as well as discussions on topics chosen by the men. Soldiers who volunteered to give lectures on their expert fields were often university graduates. We asked one volunteer to talk about his civilian job prior to being conscripted. He was a tall, lean and tough looking Corporal and spoke candidly about life in prison. He spoke with such authority the audience was convinced he was a former warden. It turned out that he had been a prisoner on different occasions, but he never revealed the reasons for his incarceration. He became an excellent section leader.

In late 1947 and early 1948, we were called out at least once every 72 hours. Some calls were false alarms. Every time we heard an explosion or shots being fired, no matter where it might have occurred, we prepared to move out. I slept partly dressed with only my boots and jacket to put on. I became accustomed to keeping one ear open at all times – a habit that has never left me. During these operations, we were fortunate in not incurring a single casualty. We picked up a number of suspects and a quantity of weapons, but exactly how effective we were in reducing the number of terrorist actions is purely speculative. We found ourselves in all kinds of odd places during these maneouvers: down sewers, in underground passages, secret hideaways under the ruins of ancient homes, in orchards or dense undergrowth, etc. It was like guerilla warfare and we got accustomed to working underground and in the dark. There was one occasion as we were searching some underground passages, when we came across several young Jewish women hiding in the dark. I assured them there was no danger and that they should return to ground level. I had become disoriented and was very glad when one of the women was good enough to show me how to get out of the maze of passages. Normally, we were met with hostility and uncooperativeness, which was not altogether surprising.

The Divisional Commander visited the Battalion one day. Since my Company had not been relieved of its immediate action role, and since any damage to one's battledress had to be paid for by the individual, I ordered the men to remain in their 'combat fatigues'. When the official party came to inspect my Company, the General was intrigued by our uniforms and set-up. He asked the men many questions and was obviously impressed by the professionalism demonstrated by the NCOs and men. A month later, the General sent the CO a letter in that he complimented the Battalion, and in particular, the Immediate Action Company on its turn-out and efficiency. The CO was generous enough to show me the letter and thanked me for doing a good job.

The sound of explosions was becoming commonplace, but one day, there was an unusually shudder that shook the ground. The Battalion Intelligence Officer soon picked up reports that the newspaper office of the Palestine Post had been destroyed and that many of the nearby houses had been badly damaged. It later turned out that some disgruntled members of the Palestine Police had done the job. Meanwhile, the Jews thought that the Arabs were responsible and retaliated by blowing up an office of the Arab League. The Palestine Post was anti-British and fanatically pro-Zionist. To be honest, we were quite pleased that it had been put out of commission. Several Jewish inhabitants living close to the newspaper office had been killed or injured and the Battalion sent men and the ambulance to assist with the recovery of bodies, but we were not welcomed and so returned to the unit.

A few days later, the Adjutant and I had to attend a briefing at Brigade HQ. We went by jeep with the Adjutant driving. I wasn't paying too much attention to his driving until he suddenly accelerated at an alarming pace. I looked ahead to see the reason why. About a hundred yards ahead were three Italian State policemen wearing their traditional uniforms. They were strolling down the street and seemed oblivious to the potential danger. The jeep was heading straight for them. I didn't know what the Adjutant had in mind, but I grabbed the steering wheel and turned it to the right. We ended up driving into a wall, managing to just miss driving into the Italians. After a few thoughtful moments, the Adjutant burst out laughing and then thanked me for preventing the impending disaster. We sat in the jeep while he explained that he had wanted to drive the jeep into those Italians for he loathed the Italian police for the way they had treated him as a POW during World War II. According to him, they treated POWs with disdain and without humanity. He had been beaten repeatedly for the amusement of his captors. The three policemen, having got over their fright, rushed over to the jeep and started shouting at the Adjutant, who by then, had calmed down somewhat but not altogether. This Italian outburst was a mistake on their part. The Adjutant took out his pistol, pointed menacingly at them and barked venom to them in Italian. They disappeared in fast order. We watched them scramble down the road and out of sight before we proceeded the best we could given the condition of the jeep.

The powers that be, decided to give the men of the Brigade some relief from their present duties, by sending a battalion at a time to Trans-Jordan for a few weeks 'rest' and training. I was sorry to have to relinquish the role of Commander of the Immediate Action Company. It had been a demanding but exhilarating period. There's a uncanny military shorthand that exists in a soldier's expression and tone of voice, and if you can read it, it's worth a dozen confidential reports. I got to know my men well enough so that I could tell who were anxious about something, who were content, and who were plotting some trouble. On the other side of the coin, the men got to know me, especially as we were living on top of each other. They could gauge exactly how far they could go before I blew my top. As a group, I believe we were a tight, efficient and happy team.

TRANS-JORDAN

The Battalion 'rest' area was a patch of desert some twenty miles north of Amman, the capital of Trans-Jordan. The journey to the 'rest' area covered about ninety miles but took us half-a-day to get there due to the conditions of the route and terrain. We travelled in 2½-ton trucks and in a convoy – always a slow and tiring way to travel. The route took us through Jericho, across the Jordan River via the Allenby Bridge, through As-Salt and on to our lonely destination somewhere in the desert. Jericho has the distinction of being the oldest walled inhabited city in the world. It is located in an oasis, and thanks to the subtropical climate, has splendid gardens. The Jordan valley was a complete surprise. It is about one hundred kilometers long and five to ten miles wide. It was the greenhouse of Jordan with a summer temperature of around 40 degrees Celsius. There is generally enough permanent water to support a rich agriculture of vegetables, fruit and vineyards. Ancient olive trees are everywhere. The crossing of the Jordan River necessitated our following a tortuous road that dipped in switchback loops down to the jade-green river two thousand feet below. On reaching the river, we stopped for a break but found the temperature and humidity so oppressive, that we soon moved on. Once past As-Salt, we came across a sea of dunes between the ever-present stony hills – a very inhospitable land. The Battalion camp was situated in a small depression protected by small, surrounding hills. The camp area covered about one square kilometer. Tents were used for all accommodation purposes.

Throughout our stay in Trans-Jordan, we were plagued by minor sandstorms that would start without warning. These storms, more like small cyclones, caused havoc whenever they occurred. The sand would get into everything: the food, water tanks, your clothing, hair, one's orifices, bedding and into the vehicle engines. It was a curse. Where vehicles continuously passed, the sand was transformed into a sort of floating, ankle deep talcum powder. As a result of the whirlwinds and of the dust kicked up by the movement of people and vehicles, there was a constant flotation of sand in the air reaching to a height of at least a hundred feet. It created a thin, bromine-coloured blanket of air. Within days of our arrival in this camp, we were all complaining of having sore throats. The unit doctor encouraged us to wear protective facemasks. I had brought with me a white

Arab headdress – a *kafeeya* – that I wore to protect my face against the sun and sand. Though warm under such a headpiece, I was at least much more comfortable than I would have been without it. Those not wearing a *kafeeya* suffered considerably. When returning from an exercise each individual's face resembled a death mask – a sheet of powdered and cracked white: A mixture of perspiration and dried mud.

Our training consisted of a number of large-scale exercises to re-accustom ourselves with wartime operations. Several units of the Trans-Jordan Frontier (TJFF), commanded by the Englishman, 'Glubb Pasha', had been invited to participate. They were to be the 'enemy' force for these exercises. Live ammunition was used throughout the course. During the first exercise, the TJFF used an old ruse very successfully. To fool us into thinking that they were making a flank armoured attack, they trailed mats behind a number of wheeled vehicles producing vast clouds of sand and dust – normally a sign of tanks moving in the desert. They also simulated the sound of tanks on the move, which led us astray. While our attention was riveted on this approaching cloud of dust, the TJFF hit us from the other flank with a unit mounted on fast moving camels whose sound of approach was downed by the group on the opposite flank. Their desert tactics were good and they kept us dancing about.

Using live ammunition on an exercise in the desert is to court disaster. There are no obvious landmarks that can be used as reference points and distances are difficult to judge, consequently, errors in placing artillery or mortar barrage on target are common. At one time, I was in a reserve position on top of a hill and was watching live artillery fire falling on another hill where there were some dummy targets. But something was wrong. The dummies were moving. On looking through my binoculars, I saw men moving about among the dummies and the falling artillery shells. I immediately radioed to the HQ who stopped the bombardment. The artillery had mistaken the target. Miraculously, no one was hurt.

On another exercise, my Company was part of a group leading the Battalion in 'advance to contact' operation. On my left flank was another Company advancing, while on my right side, cover protection in the means of heavy machine-gun assault, firing live ammunition on a fixed line. During the advance, the Company to my left lost its direction and closed into my own Company, pushing it further and further to the right where the machine-gun fire was directed. I sent a messenger to tell the other Company to move left, but it continued to move right and my own right flank troops were now in great danger of being hit by our own protective fire. To avoid disaster, I had my group break into a run until we were well ahead of the other Company. This led to a further problem as we now encountered a strong 'enemy' presence to our front whose strength was as great as ours but had the advantage of being well dug-in. I called for non-live artillery fire onto the enemy position, and while the exercise umpires were getting the enemy to withdraw, I went to see the Company Commander who had been causing me difficulties. After some argument, he moved his Company onto its original line of advance and we set off once again only this time, we were to attack a position by first advancing behind a creeping artillery barrage, that is, a constant fall of artillery shells that move ahead of the pace of a walking man. To start with the barrage was about two hundred yards in front of my Company, but every now and then its forward movement would stop. Meanwhile, we continued to advance and as a result were getting perilously close to the falling shells. Once you tell your men to get down and take cover, it is very difficult to get them on their feet again if the danger is still present. Luckily, just before I had to give the order to take cover, the barrage lifted and we were once again able to move forward in comparative safety. Fortunately, the sandy earth took much of the blast and shock of the exploding shells that meant you could get much closer to the barrage than would have been the case on hard ground. That particular exercise was not enjoyable.

The only casualty that occurred during an exercise in which live ammunition was used, at least that I knew of, happened during a mortar fire demonstration. The onlookers were gathered together in a selected position and told to look towards the target area. I was part of the audience. When I heard the first mortar bombs flying through the air, they sounded as if they were coming straight at us. I shouted to the others to get down and fell flat on the ground. A few others followed suit. One bomb exploded a few yards away from the group and blew off the right leg of a young subaltern. We rushed to his aid, but the leg had been ripped off at the hip and it was impossible to stem the flow of blood. He saw his leg lying close by and made some joke about it, then died from shock and loss of blood.

There was a day when the imperturbable Bull lost some of his cool. I still had my large canvas and leather Indian camp kit which normally travelled in my jeep. At some stage of the exercise, the vehicles had to be left behind and we had to travel on foot. I was preoccupied with other matters and had no thought to tell Bull to leave my gear in the jeep. My Company was ordered to hold a high hill behind Brigade HQ. On reaching the top, I noticed that Bull had carried my camp kit all the way to the top of the hill. It was too late to tell him that there had been no reason to do so. During the night, the Brigade HQ was attacked and my Company was ordered to repel the enemy. For the next four hours, my unit was occupied, attacking one hill after another, or taking a defensive position on some other hill. I lost track of Bull during these maneouvers. At dawn, the Company was ordered to take up yet another defense position on another high hill. It was here that I met up with Bull who was quite exhausted, having carried my extra heavy kit from place to place. Shortly after breakfast, we were again ordered to move. This was too much for Bull. He looked at me with a silly look on his face and then gave my camp kit a shove with his foot and watched it bouncing down the hill. After a few moments of silence, I informed him that we were going to move in the opposite direction and that I hoped to meet him again sometime that morning. This remark produced a further silence as we both stared at the kit at the bottom of the hill. This was followed by a magnificent belly laugh from Bull, which felt so contagious, that I roared with laughter. There were very few people as tolerant as Bull. He was one of a kind.

A squadron of tanks had been attached to the Battalion for exercise purposes. These huge machines would kick up a storm of dust whenever they moved. Since it is the job of armour to lead the infantry across open ground, the poor infantry soldier rarely saw what was ahead and constantly had to 'eat' sand until the final assault, when the infantry took the lead. In an effort to make the life of the infantryman less disagreeable, they were sometimes allowed to travel by truck, but this was short lived for the ground was strewn with large rocks that the drivers were unable to see because of the fog or dust and consequently, several accidents occurred. We ended up with some of the infantry riding on top of the tanks while the others followed blindly behind. The infantry didn't particularly appreciate the sight of a tank, whether it was ours or not.

Apart from training, we had considerable time for rest and recreation. Weekends were free for the men to do as they wished. Battalion and Company parties consisted of beans and beer. A sports weekend was organized and tours were planned to visit the more interesting and historic sights of Jordan. The sports weekend included the normal track and field events plus a glorious tug-o'-war match between the officers and the rest. The officers won easily because the judge was an officer and kept moving the cross-line in favour of the officers. To prepare for the long-distance run, competitors would train after work. Dozens of men could be seen each evening rushing about in all directions, quite often in the wrong direction. You would run in a chosen direction either going around or over the sand dunes till you had covered the desired distance and then try and find your way back. More often than not, the camp, which was in a depression, was out of sight. You would climb a hill to get your bearings and then continue your return journey on dead reckoning, only to find yourself off-track or way past the camp. During the sports meet, the most gruesome event was the three-mile race. Given the constant presence of sand in the air and the heat, I soon became exhausted and my throat felt on fire. There were a few men who completed the race in extraordinary good time and with no after effects.

One of our Majors had served in Trans-Jordan previously and was knowledgeable about the country and its history. He organized two one-day tours of the historic sights and I decided to join those. The first day, the trip covered the northern part of the country and on the second, we visited major sights in the southern part. We kept mostly to the King's Highway that stretches from Amman to Aqaba; the route following the crests of the mountains of Moab. The distances are still marked by the original Roman milestones.

Without the benefit of having seen the land or read of its history, I was unaware of how fascinating it actually is. It was one of the great crossroads of the world and trade: a bridgehead between Africa and Asia. Its people witnessed a long series of conquerors, such as the Egyptians, Babylonians, Hittites, Assyrians, Persians, Greeks, Romans, and others. It is a country of contrasts. The east is a vast desert plateau, the west a mountainous region consisting of two tabletop mountains rising to a height of 600 to 1000 metres. Between the two mountain regions lies one of the strangest landscapes, a north to south rift valley from 200 – 400 metres below sea level. Elsewhere, the land is dry with a few green oasis peppered here and there among the arid scrub and sand. Northern Jordan is hill country that looks like raised lava beds.

On the first day of the tour, we were taken to view the remains of a castle that had survived since Crusader times. We then moved on to the town of Jerash, the Pompeii of the Middle East, where we walked around the relics of the one time show place of the Roman Empire. It had been a city of vast colonnades, pagan temples, hippodromes, and subterranean baths. Our next port of call was the city of Amman, the country's capital. In the heart of the city lies a Roman amphitheatre and the remains of a colonnaded street, built on the slope of a large hill. Amman is believed to be the oldest continuously inhabited city in the world. From Amman radiates the country's major highways. A cluster of royal palaces dominates one of the original seven hills on which the city is built. Our next visit was to the pools of Azraq. Here the desert becomes sweet nectar of eucalyptus, date palms and tamarisk. T.S. Lawrence (Lawrence of Arabia), wintered here during the Arab revolt. On our way back to the unit lines, we stopped at Qasr Al Kharana to see one of the string of palaces built for the Umayyad Caliphates. These palaces were known as Desert Castles and served as hunting lodges. The outside structure of the castle we visited was in excellent condition, but the interior had deteriorated considerably and you could only imagine what the living quarters, baths, etc, must have been like. The following day, we headed south for Petra, passing the massive Crusader walls of Korak, a castle that dominated the Dead Sea one thousand metres below. The only access to the hidden city of Petra is along the Sig, a winding thread-like needle of a trail between two escarpments at least 60 metres high. Petra is the most spectacular of Jordan's archeological treasures. The rock from which it has been hewn, is multi-hued but mainly rose-red from which it gets its name the "rose-red city." Houses, temples, tombs and palaces are carved deep into the rock. The Queen of Sheba stayed here and Cleopatra possessed it briefly.

During our tour of Jordan, we came upon several Bedouin camps. The tents were made of black goat-hair ("house of hair"), and these had a certain aroma that was distinctive and not easily forgotten. The Hejaz Railway line that follows the ancient trading trails running north and south, was built at the turn of the century to facilitate the Hadj – the pilgrimage to Medina and Mecca. The highland forest through which the line passed, had been covered in trees but the wood burning locomotives soon ate them all up.

I had the occasion to visit the home of a sheik. One morning, I got into conversation with the Arab merchant who sold us fresh vegetables and fruit. He informed me that he was the Sheik of an area embracing several local villages. Before leaving he asked me whether I would be interested in seeing an Arab village. On showing some enthusiasm, he invited me to bring three or four other officers and said that he would come to fetch us later that afternoon. I found several young officers who were interested, most of whom were university graduates. The young Sheik arrived around 4 p.m. in an old but clean Cadillac. We were taken on a tour of his villages, all of which looked identical. The houses were bungalow-styled structures made of mud and straw bricks with small gardens containing fruit trees. The compound's perimeter was encased in a low mud wall. We were informed that when the rains came, many of the buildings and surrounding walls would collapse. They would be re-built after the rain-season ended, like a 'spring cleaning'. The Arab took us to his own home that was considerably larger than those of the villagers. We never entered the house itself, but were entertained in the coolness of a large, attractive garden with water trickling through a delightful rock garden. He introduced us to his father, who could not or would not speak English, but who spoke passable French. We were amused by the father's fascination for all things American, particularly his great enthusiasm for female Hollywood stars. He asked us questions about Hollywood, its stars and the latest films that we did our best to answer.

A little later we were served a meal of boiled lamb and rice mixed with nuts, yoghurt and butter and were shown how to roll the mixture into a ball – with the right hand, of course – before popping it into one's mouth. This main course was quite pleasant, but too greasy for my taste. The sweet cakes that followed together with the bitter, black and boiling coffee served with cardamom, was more to my liking. The only times we saw any females was when the food was served; the girls being quite young. After the meal, the father recounted stories about the Arab uprisings against the British in the 1930s. I don't think he liked or trusted the British. He explained that the Arabs, especially the Bedouins, consider hospitality a sacred duty and that the traveller is the 'guest of Allah'. If the traveller has 'broken his host's bread and eaten his salt,' he may claim sanctuary for a few days. Between chuckles, he told us that during the troubles in the '30s, whenever a Palestine policeman was on horse patrol in the desert, and happened to spot a Bedouin camp, he always made directly for it, thereby gaining sanctuary rather than the risk of being chased and possibly killed. Our visit was an eye-opener and well worth the time. I was acutely embarrassed the next morning when I saw the Sheik back in camp selling his vegetables and be-ing addressed by the soldiers as "Hey, Wog!"

The expressions of courtesy used by educated Europeans and Arabs are very different. Arabic is rich in its poetic expressions of courtesy. There are a dozen ways of saying 'yes' politely and almost as many of gentle refusal, and always the name of God is invoked as, for example: if an agreement is reached, one might end by saying "in Shallah" ("may God will it") or being offered the inevitable cup of coffee, one might say "Sallim ideeki" ("blessed be thy hands.")

In our wandering about the land, we came across a TJFF De-sert Patrol camp at an isolated watering hole. It turned out that the unit had participated in one of our Battalion exercises. We were invited to visit the camp after which we were served tea – a Glubb Pasha tradition – under the coolness of the trees. The men of the unit had built themselves a swimming pool that looked very inviting. When our hosts saw us looking longingly at the pool, they very generously allowed us the use of it. In seconds, we stripped down and splashed in only to be followed by our new Arab friends. We soon had a friendly game of water polo going. As we left, we invited our hosts to visit our temporary camp explaining its limitations. They graciously thanked us but we never saw them again.

King Abdullah of the Hashemite Kingdom and also a direct descendant of the prophet Mohammed, or so we were told, was invited by the Commanding Officer to an evening gala to be held in his honour. To everyone's surprise, the King accepted the invitation. All the officers of the unit, plus several other invited guests, were looking forward to the event. There must have been about sixty officers and guests crammed into a large marquee tent waiting for the King's arrival. All were getting hotter by the minute, and even worse, were feeling positively dry since the Commanding Officer didn't want to serve alcohol for fear of of-fending the King. As time passed and the King hadn't yet ar-rived, soft drinks and coffee were served. Following the Arab custom, the King arrived late – several hours in fact – by which time, most of the officers had lost much of their enthusiasm for the affair. Eventually, a convoy of limousines arrived and was met by the receiving party. Some confusion arose when no one could find the King for he was a very small man and was completely hidden by family members and a forest of bodyguards. A young subaltern with initiative broke protocol and finding the King, escorted him to where the CO's party was waiting. From then on, all went well. After about half-an-hour, the King left with his bodyguards, but members of the family remained and, when one of them asked for a beer, the party livened up considerably.

Toilet Humour

When not on an exercise, the CO ordered that the troops be given a period of drill each morning lasting about an hour. Small sandy whirlwinds would start up in the area of the parade ground, causing havoc among the men being drilled; nevertheless, the drill period would continue much to the annoyance of all on parade. The parade ground was in the lowest part of the camp whereas the latrines and wooden toilets were placed on the side of one of the bordering dune for sanitary reasons. A hessian-covered fence protected the area of the toilets. One bright morning, when the men were being drilled, an Arab took this opportunity to steal the hessian cover, not realizing that the Commanding Officer was occupying one of the wooden toilets. The CO gave a shout for help that the Sergeant Major, who was in charge of the drill period, chose to ignore. The men being drilled had a front row centre view of the proceedings as the CO, with his pants down to his ankles, tried to chase the Arab away. The Arab, noting his advantage, continued with his task until satisfied with his loot, then wandered off. The drill period continued and no chase took place. Later, we all had a good laugh, including the CO. We remarked on how well the Arab had handled the situation and gave him full credit for a valiant effort.

A less amusing incident involving toilets occurred several days later. The toilets were wooden box-like out-houses fitted to a platform that covered a pit. When using the toilets, the individual would invariably be bitten on his ass by numerous large, red cockroaches. The unit doctor was asked to exterminate these vermin. He emptied all sorts of chemicals into the pit but with no apparent effect on the cockroaches. He had the toilet seats painted with a sort of iodine, but it only left a ring mark on the rear-end. The Pioneer Officer (PO) was then called upon to deal with the matter. He decided to burn the critters. His men emptied about ten gallons of a mixture of gasoline and oil into the pit and then threw a *thunderflash* in to ignite it. There was an almighty whoosh as the mixture ignited and the toilet lid flew up to raucous applause from the men. His next attempt was to use a flame-thrower and this certainly killed off hundreds of cockroaches but thousands were left. Obviously, more forceful means were required. As a last effort, the PO decided to use explosives. Unfortunately, he misjudged the amount of explosives needed and when the dynamite detonated, the whole platform, toilet included, rocketed up into the air, raining down in shattered pieces. The toilets were reconstructed and the cockroaches continued to habitat the pit and aggravate us.

Prior to moving to Trans-Jordan, all personnel had been warned about the venomous snakes that inhabited the desert. We soon forgot the warning until one day a very sick Arab entered the camp complaining of a bite from a snake. He was taken to the hospital in Amman. For a week thereafter, everyone was very careful as to where he sat or walked, especially when getting out of bed in the morning. Underneath beds and all boots had to be checked first thing.

Shortly before leaving Trans-Jordan, I got into serious trouble. On returning from a night training exercise, I went to take a shower, and without thinking, left my webbed-belt on my bed that held my holstered pistol. When I got to my tent, the pistol was missing. This was a serious breach and cost me dearly. I reported the loss to the Adjutant the next morning. Inquiries were made and one of the officers enlightened me that he had seen a certain Lieutenant enter my tent during my absence. I went to see this Lieutenant to confront him why he had entered my tent. It was incredulous suggesting that he had mistaken my tent since his tent was at the opposite end of the officer's lines. On informing the Adjutant of these facts, he asked me whether I knew the serial number of my pistol. Such information would help in the investigation to uncover the weapon, and possibly, the culprit. Among thousands of other officers, I had been issued a pistol prior to leaving Egypt. I wore my pistol during the day and had never stored it in the Company Store; consequently, there was no way of knowing the serial number. The clerk in Egypt wouldn't even try to look for the issue slip. I looked around Amman in the hope of buying a pistol but none was available. I had no proof as to who might have stolen the pistol and no way of buying one to replace it. A Board of Inquiry was convened and I was found guilty of negligence – the case to be reviewed by the Brigade Commander. A few weeks after returning to Palestine, I was summoned to see the Brigadier, who asked me whether I had indeed lost my pistol. I had to admit that this was so (since I couldn't find evidence contrary). He had read the Board of Inquiry report and though he appreciated the situation, agreed with the verdict that I was negligent, and consequently, I had to be awarded some for of punishment. I was reduced from Captain to Lieutenant. I suppose I could say that I was lucky in that this incident occurred in Trans-Jordan and not Palestine, an operational theatre, where the punishment would have been a court martial. This latter punishment happened to a brother officer who had the misfortune to misplace his pistol shortly after our return to Jerusalem. He was cashiered.

This was the third time in a period of a few years that fate had interfered to change the course of my life. I was naturally very disappointed at losing my Captaincy and I cursed my luck that seemed to always turn sour whenever my future looked promising. Any chance of obtaining a regular commission was now gone and so I decided to get out of the army and seek another career. I talked the matter over with the Adjutant who advised me to formally request my discharge from the army explaining that I had served the equivalent of 'conscription time' and that I wished to attend university. He assured me that the Commanding Officer would strongly support my request. After thinking the matter over, I did what the Adjutant had suggested and a week later was permitted my request, signed by the CO and sent to the War Office. The Adjutant cautioned me that such requests often took months to process. The die was cast.

After our return to Jerusalem, there was an epidemic of hepatitis within the Battalion. Most of the officers came down with it, including me. Where possible, those suffering from the illness were sent to the military hospital. When I was sent to the hospital, I found myself in the company of the unit doctor and two other officers. As we were waiting outside the Officer's Mess for transport that was to take us to the hospital, we heard the crack of a rifle as a bullet narrowly passed by. This was immediately followed by a loud whirling and buzzing sound as I suddenly felt a hard thump just above my right hip and experienced a sharp burning pain in that area. The bullet had ricocheted into me. The bullet had lodged into my thick web belt with a portion of the spent bullet penetrating my skin. I immediately removed the belt and the burning sensation ceased. There was a small puncture in my side that the unit doctor, who was now examining me, reassured me that all I needed was antiseptic and a bandaid – no Purple Heart? I removed the misshaped bullet from the belt and was surprised at it still retaining so much heat. I must have kept that bullet for several years as a memento until one day, I realized how foolish this was and threw it away.

THE HOSPITAL

On reaching the hospital, I was placed in a ward with about twenty other patients suffering from the same illness. The unit doctor was in the bed next to me. He made the mistake of administrating himself and came out in ugly ulcers and boils. Since there was a shortage of nurses and orderlies, and given that most of those recuperating from jaundice were not confined to bed and were no longer in quarantine, such patients were asked to help the staff take care of the other patients. Close by were two other large wards, one containing officers suffering from malaria and the other filled to capacity with officers that had been seriously wounded. Our assistance was by way of helping with the making of beds, making bed-sore pads, providing and emptying bedpans, helping those who had difficulty in walking, etc. Every evening, we issued three ounces of whiskey to those with malaria. As 'jaundice' patients, we were forbidden to drink any alcohol but the temptation was too strong and we cheated. To keep us warm at night, the nurses would put hot water in used whiskey and gin bottles as hot-water bottles for our beds. We would empty these and fill them with the whiskey that ought to have gone to the patients with malaria. We had not counted on Matron who checked our beds, and finding the evidence, gave us a good tongue lashing and confiscated the whiskey. The malaria patients were a sorry lot but not as sorry as we.

The patients that had been wounded were a grand lot, cracking jokes and helping each other whenever they could. There was one individual who was suspended from the ceiling in a cocoon with tubes protruding here and there. He had been badly burned when his armoured car had been blown up. Everyone called him Charlie and spoke to him though he could not reply and we could not see his face. When people passed him, they would gently rock him to let him know we were around and sympathized with his injury. Where and when we could, we short rationed the poor malaria patients and provided whiskey 'sippers' to the wounded officers.

We heard that a number of nurses had arranged to attend the religious service to be held at the Church of Nativity in Bethlehem on Christmas Eve. Several of the patients, including myself, received permission to accompany the nurses. Upon arrival at the outskirts of Bethlehem, there was already a multitude of people scattered across the hills since the Church was filled to capacity. Loud speakers had been installed for those unable to get into the Church. The service itself was High Church and very long. From where we were, it was difficult to hear the service, but this didn't trouble me for I was more interested in watching the people and taking in the whole scene which was more theatrical than religious. There were many lit lanterns throughout the crowd and these, together with the bright stars and the quietness of the evening, made a moving scene, even for someone who was not particularly religious.

The day before I was due to be discharged from the hospital, a most peculiar thing happened. I went for a walk in the hospital grounds with a fellow out-patient who had also been recuperating from jaundice. When we returned to our ward, a nurse took our respective temperatures and pulse rates. According to these, we should have been near dead. She told us both to remain where we were and soon returned with another thermometer, but got the same result. This caused a bit of a stir and it was not long before a crowd of doctors descended upon us as though we were a new discovery of a virus. By then, our temperature and pulse had returned back to normal. We were kept over for a further two days during which innumerable tests were conducted. The doctors were at a loss to diagnose the reason for our earlier condition and were intrigued that it had happened to two of us at the same time. Our case must have ended up in some report that likely was published in some medical journal.

When I returned to the Battalion, I heard that there had been a serious riot in Haifa. Jewish terrorists had attacked several British posts manned by paratroopers causing a number of casualties. In retaliation, the paratroopers, rarely well disciplined at their best, went on a rampage and destroyed a number of Jewish shops and vehicles, injuring Jewish civilians along the way. The Jewish Agency made a great deal of fuss over the incident, but other than to send a few paratroopers back to England, the matter was allowed to die through a lack of interest in the United Kingdom.

As the negotiations concerning the partition of Palestine grew more heated, so the number of violent incidents across the land increased, especially in Jerusalem. To assist the Brigade in quelling the turmoil, a battalion of one of the Guards' regiments and a Royal Marine Commando unit were flown in from England. These units took over the responsibilities for manning the gates and guarding Government House. The Royal Marines did their job well, but the Guards were soon in trouble. The Guards knew little about 'keeping the peace,' having spent most of their army service mounting guard over royal palaces in London. A

Guards' unit at one of the gates got itself caught in a shootout with a group of Jewish terrorists. The Guards' battalion sent in reinforcements who also came under fire, causing further confusion. The Brigade Commander ordered us to the scene and my Company was sent to the rescue. The Company boxed in the terrorists and tightened the cordon till the terrorists surrendered. There were not more than a dozen of them. We provided first-aid to the guardsmen who had been wounded and helped to evacuate them to the military hospital. We also left one of our guards at the gate until the Guards were ready to once again resume their responsibilities.

The Commanding Officer was prompted by this incident to invite a few Guards' officers to dinner at our Mess. When these officers entered the Mess and dining room, they wore their caps – a regimental custom. A few weeks later, we were invited to dine at the Guards' Mess. Our Commanding Officer reminded us of a long forgotten regimental custom that we were to observe on this occasion. When the King's health was toasted, all the officers of the Guards rose as one, but the officers of the Suffolk remained seated much to the bewilderment of their hosts. The Suffolk Regiment had once been marines aboard British warships where, due to the low ceiling in the cabins below deck, the King's health was drunk sitting down. So much for customs and traditions.

The American press was firmly in the back pocket of the Zionists where news reports on Palestine was concerned. The American's comments about the British were negative and frequently insulting, not to mention blatant lies. It was, therefore, not surprising that we were less than enthusiastic at the idea of entertaining a group of American journalists who were visiting Jerusalem. The group consisted of three men, a woman and a dog. They should have arrived at 9 a.m., but instead came just before lunch – in time for a free drink. They were escorted to the Officer's Mess where they were introduced to the CO. The owner of the dog made a mistake of bringing it into the Mess. He was told to put it outside. Seeing a large boxer in the room, the owner said he had as much right to have his dog present to which he was told: "Oh, but that's the CO's dog and you better watch it." As dogs are wonted, the other dog went up to the boxer not realizing the latter disliked other dogs. When within range, the boxer leapt on the other dog and viciously attacked it, much to our delight. Its owner agreed to put the dog outside where it licked its wounds. During lunch, the Americans talked without let up, lecturing us on the manner in which we were treating the Jews. It became so tiresome that the CO excused himself saying he had other things to do. We took the hint and did likewise. As you can imagine, all this did little to endear us to the self-righteous American press, but then, nothing would. Zionist propaganda then, as it is today, surpassed that of Mr. Goebbels in its admonishment of others. It brings to mind the Jewish psalm: If I forget thee, O Jerusalem, let my right hand forget her cunning.

Due to the number of unprovoked terrorist attacks against British forces by Jews and Arabs alike, the Divisional Commander gave the order for all units, other than those manning gates and Government House, to remain in camp and not get involved in any skirmishes except in self-defence. Since we now had time on our hands, an energetic sports program was organized. One particular morning when playing a very rough game of rugby (which grew even rougher), I remember seeing one player get hold of another by the feet and bang the unfortunate fellow's head against the ground as if the body was a pneumatic drill. Nerves were obviously getting taught. The game was called off not because of rough play, but because we were getting peppered with a number of over-shots from a fight being fought between Jews and Arabs less than a mile from our camp. The Arabs had ambushed a large Jewish convoy and were in the process of massacring the people in the thinly armoured vehicles. The Arabs were not formed up in any semblance of order and were shooting randomly at the armed vehicles with rifles and rockets. Our CO informed the Brigade Commander of the situation, adding that our own security was being affected. Permission was granted for us to send a negotiating team to the area to try and stop the senseless killing. Our Intelligence Officer got through to the Arabs to inform them of what we intended to do and they agreed to meet our team at an appointed time and place. The CO sent one of the Company Commanders as the negotiator plus two armed escorts. They travelled in an armoured car draped with a Union Jack. The Jewish Agency was informed of the situation and told to keep their people away and that we would bring those Jews, who were still alive, to the Agency. It took about half-an-hour for the shooting to stop. The negotiators met and an agreement was reached on allowing the remaining Jews to be evacuated provided all the vehicles and weapons were handed over to the Arabs. The Jews in the buses did not trust the Arabs and it was some time before they agreed to surrender. They and their wounded were placed in army vehicles and ambulances and taken to the Jewish Agency. We received no thanks for our intervention. Instead, we were criticized for not having brought back the weapons. Mercy.

By May 13, 1947, all British troops in Palestine were packed and ready to move out to the relief of everyone concerned. The deadline for all troops to be out of Palestine was May 15. Prior to withdrawing from Jerusalem, my Company was given one last duty to perform. It had to guard the main Palestine Police Quartermaster's stores, a depot that covered a city block and still contained vast quantities of equipment and stock. We asked ourselves why the stock had not been sent to Egypt since there had been plenty of time to do so? There was something very odd about the whole affair. When the Commanding Officer had asked Brigade HQ the reason for setting up the guard, he had been told to mind his own business and to ensure none of our men entered the store. The CO, an old supply officer, soon came to the conclusion that a deal had been made among officials in high places and determined to inform Headquarters in Egypt as soon as we got there. Meanwhile, he gave orders that should the Company guarding the depot meet with any Jewish or Arab resistance, it was to withdraw in good order. We weren't totally surprised when the CO informed us that he would pay us a visit that evening. For some time, he had been examining ways to obtain good blue, worsted trousers for the Mess waiters. He assumed that the depot had the necessary material to make this apparel for the Palestine Police wore similar blue trousers. At about midnight, a unit truck pulled up beside the Company HQ and out stepped the CO followed by his orderly. He told us he was going inside the depot to check that all was in order. A short while later, he and his orderly returned, the latter carrying several bolts of blue worsted material. Our guard duty hadn't been a complete waste after all.

When guarding the depot, we noted armed Arabs at one end of the building and Jews at the other, patiently waiting our departure before fighting each other for possession of the stores. One of our officers thought it would be a good idea to set the building a fire before we left. Wishful thinking. At 4 a.m. on May 14, we withdrew and took our assigned position as rearguard to the seventeen-mile long Brigade Group convoy that had started its move to Egypt.

We were fortunate in being the rearguard as it allowed us to move at our own pace and to remain several miles to the rear of the main vehicle column that was crawling along slowly and kicking up huge quantities of dust. As the rearguard, our task was to: protect the back of the convoy, collect any personnel from broken down vehicles, and to give assistance to the stragglers. Our route to Egypt took us via Hebron and Beersheba, through the Sinai Desert to Ismailia, where we crossed the Suez Canal, and to a desert tent camp near the Canal between Bethlehem and Hebron. My Company spent the night patrolling the perimeter of the Brigade's encampment area. The next day, the Brigade Group entered Egypt. During the passage out of Palestine, several vehicles had broken down, two disabled by mines, causing a number of casualties. The wounded were sent to the hospital in Ismailia while the men and equipment from the damaged vehicles were transferred to empty vehicles held in reserve for that purpose. We picked up a few solitary individuals who had somehow been left behind. We came upon a Scot sitting and crying beside his broken down vehicle. He had to be physically persuaded to come with us. He gave us trouble for the rest of the journey and we felt like leaving him behind. In crossing the Sinai

Desert, many of our men suffered from sunstroke and sun exposure. By the time we reached our destination, many had swollen legs with the flesh around the knees hanging over their leggings. On May 15, we reached our destination – the desert camp.

The camp was a makeshift affair constructed in World War II. It was simplicity itself, consisting of a number of shallow cemented square entrenchments over which were canvas roofs. For air-conditioning, the tent walls were rolled up. This naturally allowed the sand to drift into the entrenchment. The place was infested with large flies and sand flies. A number of large empty oil drums were converted into flytraps and these were completely filled with dead flies by mid-day. A few men suffered from sand fly fever and had to be evacuated to Cairo.

We were to remain in this ghastly camp for five days prior to embarking at Port Said for southern Greece. The Battalion had very little sports equipment left and it was decided that an officer visit the RAF base that was close by to borrow whatever equipment they could spare. I volunteered to go, and on arrival, was amazed at the base's huge size. There were three different Officer's Messes, two large swimming pools, and a number of playing fields. I eventually found the base sports officer. He was very cooperative and I came away with soccer balls, volley ball equipment and the offer to use one of the base swimming pools. Later arrangements were made allowing the officers and men use of the Messes and canteens. Thanks to these amenities, the five days passed quickly and agreeably.

On arrival at Port Said, we were told that due to an outbreak of cholera in Egypt, everyone had to be inoculated prior to our boarding the troopship that was to take us to Greece. For some reason, rather than enter the date of inoculation in each person's AB-64 (a form of identity book-come-pay account carried by all individuals), as was the normal procedure, each individual was given a small flimsy piece of paper recording the fact. I placed this piece of paper in my AB-64 for safe keeping. We embarked in batches, company by company. We were met at the entry port to the promenade deck by a military policeman who checked our embarkation pass and inoculation slip. On reaching the entry port, I opened my AB-64 to get my inoculation slip, and at that precise moment, a gust of wind snatched the slip, tossing it like a drunken butterfly and out of sight. The military policeman, true to form, refused to let me aboard no matter my protestations and told me to return to the medical orderly room ashore and get a duplicate slip. I kept my equipment in the care of Bull and forced my way down the gangway, colliding with those struggling to climb up. At the medical orderly room, the nurses and orderlies refused to give me the required duplicate slip even after I had shown them the tell-tale lump on my upper arm. I was forced into having a second cholera shot – in the other arm. I did not sleep well that night.

For a change, the troopship taking us the short distance from Egypt to Greece was not overloaded with personnel and the journey was enjoyable. As we left Port Said, the locals gave us the two-finger salute and we gladly reciprocated. There seemed to be hundreds of Arabs sitting about the mouth at the entrance to the harbour, doing absolutely nothing. The Arabs have a wonderful capacity for rest.

I left Palestine with no regrets. I had little liking for the land other than parts of the coastal region. As a peacekeeper, the Jews, in general, gave me little reason to trust them. I felt particularly sorry for the Palestinian Arabs who were being cheated out of their inheritance by the Jews, U.S. media, and the U.S. and British governments. Though disillusioned by events, I did find my tour of duty in Palestine both fascinating and exciting, but I was also very wearing and I was looking forward to a calmer atmosphere in Greece. I was hoping it would be a tonic of sun, sand and sea. I had learned a lot in Palestine, but it was an environment that had become a place of irreparable damage and suspicion. Its soul was permanently soiled and life was merely tit-for-tat.

Lieutenant Branson outside Officer's Quarters, Beit Daras.

3rd Divisional Headquarters, Officer's Mess, Beit Daras, 1947.

Bull, Me, the Company doctor.

Early morning marching.

Bull (standing), Me (seated in foreground).

Military train blown up near Gaza.

1st Suffolk Battalion HQ and Commanding Officer's house. Intelligence Officer's tent.

1st Suffolk Battalion, Other Ranks' accommodations.

6 pdr. Anti-Tank guns and "Pig-Pen."

Arab constable shot by Jews.

Arab unrest over "Partition."

Bren-gunner on guard on top of Commanding Officer's house.

House destroyed by British where Jewish terrorists were shooting from.

Makeshift outpost. Immediate Action Company. Man dressed in special coveralls worn by Company.

Jewish armoured vehicle blown-up by Arabs on the road to Hadassah Hospital. Numerous atrocities occurred along this route to Hadassah Hospital for both Arabs and Jews. It was the responsibility of the British to provide vehicle escorts to the hospital to prevent attacks, but too often this was ignored.

"Dingo." Commanding Officer's armoured car which I frequently used and abused.

Captain – Acting Company Commander, Immediate Action
Company.

King David Hotel, used by British as an Officer's Club, blown-up by Jews.

Cinema blown-up by Jews.

Jewish-owned car blown-up by Arabs outside the Damascus
Gate.

Arab Legion Guard outside Holy Sepulchre, Easter Day.

Arab Legionnaire, Old City of Jerusalem.

Two Arab chiefs – Old City of Jerusalem.

Arab Legionnaires on the outskirts of the Old City.

Bedouin Legionnaire.

Arabs practicing their firing.

Brigade Tactical Headquarters.

Searching for terrorists/insurgents. Waiting for Coldstream Guards to join us.

Entering the village of Hadera.

Rounding up suspects.

Orchard where a British officer was found hanged and bobby-trapped.

Cordoning off sections of town.

The coast. Lunch break.

The "Palestine Post" newspaper office blown-up by some disgruntled policeman. The newspaper was anti-British.

"Palestine Post" in flames.

Arab Headquarters blown-up by Jews.

Reprisal attacks, Jerusalem.

The aftermath of the Jewish Agency attacked by Arabs.

More reprisal attacks, Jerusalem. Jewish Quarter.

Palestinians protesting over "Partition."

Aftermath of the attacks.

Unrest over "Partition."

Polish Consulate (just outside British base), after being bombed by terrorists, 1948.

Zone 'A' outpost. The house was destroyed by the British for having been a sniper's post by the Jews. My Company took over the outpost.

To make sure the Arabs withheld from attacking Jewish settlements, the British put on a firing display across open ground which was sufficient to make the Arabs withdraw.

Another view of the zone where the British fired upon the area to repel Arab terrorists from attacking a Jewish settlement.

British troopers taking a break in Hadera.

My office/accommodations.

Jewish suspects arrested by British troops.

British troops taking Jews to the Jewish Agency.

Jewish victims from an Arab attack.

Another view from the same attack on Jews by Arabs.

Jewish victim of Arab attack.

British leaving Palestine for Egypt, 1948.

Withdrawing from Palestine.

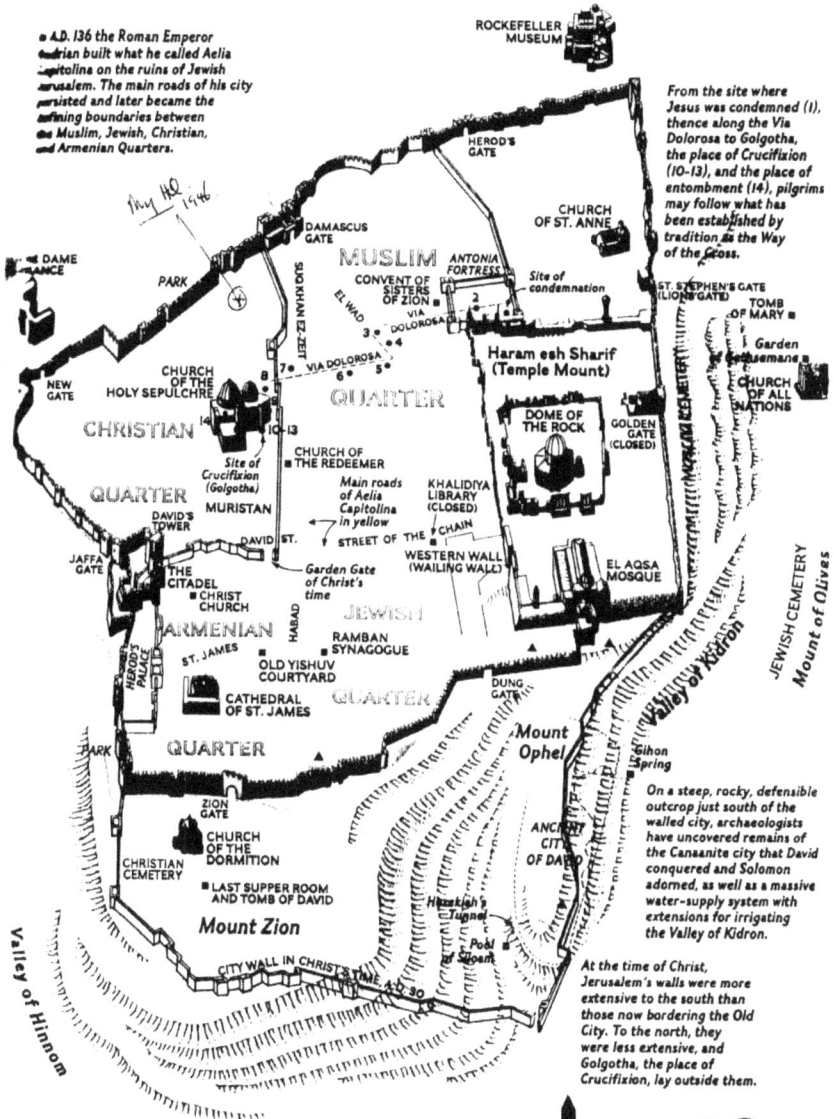

● A.D. 136 the Roman Emperor
Hadrian built what he called Aelia
Capitolina on the ruins of Jewish
Jerusalem. The main roads of his city
persisted and later became the
defining boundaries between
the Muslim, Jewish, Christian,
and Armenian Quarters.

ROCKEFELLER
MUSEUM

From the site where
Jesus was condemned (1),
thence along the Via
Dolorosa to Golgotha,
the place of Crucifixion
(10-13), and the place of
entombment (14), pilgrims
may follow what has
been established by
tradition as the Way
of the Cross.

HEROD'S
GATE

CHURCH
OF ST. ANNE

DAMASCUS
GATE

DAME
FRANCE

PARK

MUSLIM

ANTONIA
FORTRESS

Site of
condemnation

ST. STEPHEN'S GATE
(LION'S GATE)

TOMB
OF MARY

CONVENT OF
SISTERS
OF ZION

VIA
DOLOROSA

Garden
Gethsemane

NEW
GATE

CHURCH
OF THE
HOLY SEPULCHRE

VIA DOLOROSA

Haram esh Sharif
(Temple Mount)

CHURCH
OF ALL
NATIONS

CHRISTIAN

QUARTER

DOME OF
THE ROCK

GOLDEN
GATE
(CLOSED)

QUARTER

Site of
Crucifixion
(Golgotha)

CHURCH OF
THE REDEEMER

KHALIDIYA
LIBRARY
(CLOSED)

DAVID'S
TOWER

MURISTAN

Main roads
of Aelia
Capitolina
in yellow

DAVID ST.

STREET OF THE
CHAIN

WESTERN WALL
(WAILING WALL)

EL AQSA
MOSQUE

JAFFA
GATE

THE
CITADEL

CHRIST
CHURCH

Garden
Gate
of Christ's
time

HABAD

JEWISH

ARMENIAN

ST. JAMES

RAMBAN
SYNAGOGUE

HEROD'S
PALACE

OLD YISHUV
COURTYARD

CATHEDRAL
OF ST. JAMES

QUARTER

DUNG
GATE

JEWISH CEMETERY
Mount of Olives

QUARTER

Mount
Ophel

Gihon
Spring

PARK

ANCIENT
CITY
OF DAVID

On a steep, rocky, defensible
outcrop just south of the
walled city, archaeologists
have uncovered remains of
the Canaanite city that David
conquered and Solomon
adorned, as well as a massive
water-supply system with
extensions for irrigating
the Valley of Kidron.

ZION
GATE

CHURCH
OF THE
DORMITION

CHRISTIAN
CEMETERY

LAST SUPPER ROOM
AND TOMB OF DAVID

Mount Zion

Hezekiah's
Tunnel

Pool
of Siloam

CITY WALL IN CHRIST'S TIME A.D. 30

At the time of Christ,
Jerusalem's walls were more
extensive to the south than
those now bordering the Old
City. To the north, they
were less extensive, and
Golgotha, the place of
Crucifixion, lay outside them.

Valley of Hinnom

Valley of Kidron

▲ ARCHAEOLOGICAL EXCAVATION
● STATION OF THE CROSS

0   KILOMETER   ¼

0   STATUTE MILE   ¼

DRAWN BY ISKANDAR BADAY AND DOROTHY MICHELE NOVICK
COMPILED BY DAVID B. MILLER
NATIONAL GEOGRAPHIC CARTOGRAPHIC DIVISION

Jerusalem
The Old City

Map of the Old City of Jerusalem.

1st Suffolk Regiment. Camp Zurqa, Jordan.

Me in front of my tent, Jordan.

A British attack against an Arab strong point. Palestine.

Chapter 9

Greece

OUR port of arrival was Piraeus, the third largest city in Greece, boasted the largest port in the country. It was a glorious and sunny morning; not too hot and the port was teeming with activity. Numerous ferries were coming and going while fishing trawlers were unloading their catch. It was a picturesque scene and a welcome sight after that of Egypt. We had returned to European civilization.

The port of Piraeus is located 7 miles south of Athens and is situated on the Saronic Gulf and is part of the Attica Basin. The plains lead to Mount Aegaleo. On disembarking, we were immediately taken to our new base that was at Cape Aixoni, some four miles south of Piraeus. Cape Aixoni was a small peninsular of about eight hundred yards long by three hundred yards wide with sandy beaches at its base and rocky terrain bookmarked on either side. During World War II, the Germans used the area as a coastal battery site, and later by the allies, as a convalescent centre for wounded officers. The guns had been removed and the concrete emplacements demolished. Still remaining were the camp bungalow or ranch-styled buildings, all of which had large, wide windows and spacious rooms. It was a very clean and comfortable camp with adequate space for the Battalion. There was a sea breeze that not only rid the place of mosquitoes and flies, but provided a constant clean and refreshing air.

The junior officers occupied a couple of large bungalows, each officer having his own room. The Officers' Mess was perched on a promontory some fifty feet above sea level and had a magnificent view of the Gulf and of the bays to either side of the peninsular. Given the accommodation, we had put up with in Palestine, Trans-Jordan, and Egypt this was the height of luxury. The next day, I was detailed to see to the Battalion's baggage that had been left under guard at one of the docks. There was no problem in moving the baggage to the camp; however, the Regimental Colours and the King's Colours, that were also part of the total baggage, were missing. As we were searching for the Colours, someone noticed a Greek lay-about pointing to something in the water beside the dock. On investigating closer, we discovered a sunken barge containing several cases. I had one of the baggage party dive in to take a closer inspection. When he resurfaced, he confirmed that the cases belonged to the Battalion and, furthermore, he had found the Colours tucked between the cases. The Colours were quickly retrieved from their watery resting place and cleaned up as much as possible. No apparent damage had been done for the Colours were still incased in their leather holders that had protected them to some degree from the polluted waters. Our Battalion Colours which had been mended time and again by the good women of Suffolk, were the oldest in the actual possession of any battalion. The Colours were the old six-foot size version as compared to the modern smaller size. Once back at the base, the Colours were thoroughly washed and then placed in the Officers' Mess. On any hot night, a rather unpleasant smell emanated from the flags, but we pretended not to notice. It was during the Battalion's tour of duty in Greece that the smaller version of the Colours was presented to the Battalion by King Paul of Greece on behalf of King George VI. The old Colours now rest in Colchester Cathedral, England. We never did find out how the barge sank.

There was only a single British Brigade in Greece at the time. The Headquarters and two infantry battalions were stationed at Salonika and we, the third infantry battalion, were also part of the Brigade. This was an ideal posting. We were a very long way by road from Brigade Headquarters and were therefore rarely troubled by that august body. Our task was mainly one of "showing the flag." The Greek government was still having problems with the communist-inspired ELAS and the ELAM; respectively the military and political wings of the Greek Liberation Movement, but we did not participate in any action against the communists. The centre of Greece, all mountainous terrain, was almost completely controlled by the communists or 'bandits' as referred to by the Greek governing party and the military. The economy of the country was rapidly deteriorating and the rate of inflation soaring, though there were plenty Greeks who were living in the lap of luxury while turmoil surrounded them.

Other than showing the British government's support for the Greek regime, we had very few duties to perform. This, in fact, was not as desirable as at first seemed. The men of the Battalion had been fully occupied on aid to civil power duties for several years and now there was little to keep them occupied. As often occurs in such circumstances, many of the men got into trouble. To add to our problems, the Battalion had been given one ridiculous task, that of guarding a large supply depot on the outskirts of Athens. On a rotational basis, each Company provided the guard for one week. One quick look inside the depot was sufficient to confirm that very little remained other than a few derelict vehicles that had been stripped of all useful parts. The Greeks or the Ordnance personnel, had stolen or sold whatever the depot might once have contained. In spite of guarding virtually nothing of value, we continued to guard only the depot reducing the guard as a token force.

Normal operational training was maintained and, since there was insufficient room at the base itself for field training, all operational training was carried out in the coastal plains and mountains close by. Our Training Officer, convinced that we should be introduced to mountain warfare, planned a Battalion-sized exercise in one of the higher mountains some ten miles from camp. He had failed to conduct a reconnaissance of the route and of the area and the result was a fiasco. We found ourselves slowly zig-zagging our way up the mountain in 2 ½-ton trucks to be met halfway up the side of the steep mountain route by heavy mist that completely enshrouded us, obscuring any view, including the narrow road. We persevered and, with a man walking ahead of each vehicle to give directions, finally reached what we supposed was our destination – a flat piece of ground! No one in authority seemed to have realized that it would be cold in the mountains especially when they were enveloped in heavy fog.

We were clad in shorts and short-sleeved shirts. On disembarking from the vehicles, we were at odds as to what to do next for we couldn't see more than a few yards. No field or mountain exercise was possible under such conditions. Everyone was feeling the cold and I sent men to collect firewood. It had taken us considerable time to get to our site and darkness was closing in as we lit the fires. We cooked a warm supper and afterwards, set up small patrols to look for a better area to spend the night, one that would protect us against the natural elements. Sometime later, one of the patrols reported sighting a large establishment about a mile from our position. A couple of officers were sent to investigate and the "establishment" turned out to be a large sanatorium. We were invited to spend the night, three large rooms being placed at our disposal. There was insufficient room for all our personnel, so shifts were organized. Those outside continued to practice mountain patrols as a means of keeping warm. The mist had not cleared by next morning and too many men were now suffering from exposure. We couldn't continue to stay in the mountains and so it was decided to forego the training exercise and instead, return to camp. Our passage down the mountain took twice as long to complete as the one up. As you can imagine, we were relieved to get back to the camp and to the warmth of the sun.

One night, my Company conducted a patrol exercise in the high hills overlooking Athens. Our patrol route took us through vast vineyards guarded by Greeks with shotguns. We had been told that we were entering 'bandit' country, so everyone was very much on the alert. We obviously made too much noise or possibly the guards were extraordinarily vigilant for several guns went off, making lots of noise and forcing us to keep our heads and bottoms down as we crawled through the vineyards. Later, when on a patrol with two men, we stealthily approached the Company Headquarters for I had heard someone approaching the HQ from its opposite side. On reaching the HQ, I found the sentry asleep and shook him. He jumped at the sudden awakening and immediately took me for a bandit. I was covered in dust and dirt and was wearing a non-regulation uniform. The sentry immediately grabbed hold of his rifle by the barrel and, swinging it over his shoulder, struck me on the temple with the butt end. I was unable to avoid the blow. I recall the contact making quite a noise in my head. He was about to repeat the attack when I grabbed the rifle and for a while there was a bit of a scuffle during which the only thing I thought of saying was: "You stupid man!" It at last dawned on him who I was and he calmed down. When hit on the head, copious amount of blood gush forth. This happened to me and I started to feel weak from shock and from a loss of blood. The first-aid man was sent for and he quietly cut the hair from around the wound, now the size of a lemon and a small hole in my scalp. He dabbed antiseptic on the affected area and bandaged me up, saying I probably received a concussion. I was placed on a stretcher that was strapped to a jeep and taken to the military hospital in Athens. The route down the hillside was bumpy that did nothing to help ease my throbbing head. On arrival at the hospital at around 2 a.m., I was administered on a cold marble floor in the hallway and seen to by the duty doctor. After, what seemed an interminable time, the doctor came by accompanied by the duty nursing sister. Both seemed off put at being disturbed at that hour of the morning. The doctor, bless him, kept prodding me where it hurt most and on asking if it hurt and my answering in the affirmative would mutter, "that's bad." Having been concussed several times prior to this accident (at school, playing rugby), I was rather concerned that my skull might have been fractured. The doctor's utterances gave me no encouragement. Finally, the inspection over, the doctor told the sister to clean up the wound and bandage it correctly. She had much trouble bandaging my head and gave it up as a hopeless task. The first-aid man, who we still present, came to the rescue. He asked for a large bandaid and stuck it over the wound. The next morning, I was x-rayed by some brut from the Medical Corps who took delight in shoving my aching head hard against the metal plates of the x-ray apparatus. The x-rays showed no abnormalities and I was permitted to return to my unit the next day. The soldier who had hit me, was grilled as to why he had done it and was fearful about his future. Though I had little sympathy for the man, I assured the Board of Inquiry that there was no malice intended and explained that the man had instinctively reacted in self-defence. The matter was dropped.

I happened to be at the Piraeus docks one morning with a party of men loading equipment onto a cargo boat when a small convoy of vehicles pulled up alongside. The officer in charge of the group, a Captain in the Military Police, came up to me and informed me that my Adjutant had agreed to take responsibility of the persons aboard the vehicles until they're assigned ship embarked that afternoon. The passengers turned out to be about forty, hard-case military prisoners, including murderers that we were suppose to guard. I explained to this officer that I didn't have the manpower to guard such a large group of criminals and, furthermore, none of my men were armed. He regretted being unable to help and said that I would have to do the best I could. I managed to get him to loan me a number of manacles and with the help of his men, had the prisoners stand in a large circle. The men were handcuffed one arm to another man's leg till we completed the circle. The trouble was that there weren't enough manacles and so we roped up the others and placed them in the middle of the circle. Fortunately, there was no incident with the prisoners and it remained so until it was time for them to board the ship. Unfortunately, I forgot to collect the keys to unlock the manacles. The ship's Captain was delighted and had the convicts board chained together as they were. It was a sight reminiscent of a Hollywood film about the slave trade.

As Company Second-in-Command, it was my responsibility to pay the troops every week. The men were paid in Greek currency. At that time, the inflation rate was chaotic and rose every hour. The value of the drachma was in the neighbourhood of D 42,000 to the pound sterling. I had to travel to a bank in Athens to get the money and by the time I got back to camp, the exchange rate sometimes had changed. The men knew all about the exchange rate and would insist on receiving the correct rate. Obviously, this became on ongoing dilemma. It was the custom to deduct a small amount to pay from his earnings to cover extra messing and damages. I came to an agreement with the Company

Commander and the men to pay them at the going rate at the time I collected the money and that any difference would be taken out of the Company Funds. There were no more complaints. One of my other responsibilities was that of being the Camp Security and Fire Officer. All fire equipment had to be tested once a month. By pure accident, it was found that the foam in the fire extinguishers killed the little beetles that lived in the outer walls of the buildings. The foam was also an excellent whitewash. With this in mind, I had the men test the fire extinguishers by spraying the outside walls of each building, and regrettably, killed several birds with the same stone.

ANYONE FOR CRICKET?

When not on training or attending to administrative duties, sport was the ideal tonic for fitness as well as combating any sort of boredom for the officers and the men. Sports usually consisted of cricket, soccer or going sailing. Sea trips in hired fishing boats were also arranged, but this soon came to an end as the men were inclined to seasickness. The Unit cricket team was the champion of the Eastern Mediterranean Cricket Association. One day, a British frigate paid a courtesy call at the port of Piraeus. We had some of the officers to dinner and learned that the ship's company was the cock-of-the-fleet at water polo. We resolved then and there to have two matches the following day; one being a cricket match and the other of water polo. As fate would have it, the Navy won the cricket match and the Army won in water polo. In neither match were the rules adhered to. The outcome of theset matches called for an evening in town where officers and men did their utmost to liven things up. The following day, the frigate departed and made a point of passing close to our camp, giving us a salute on its siren. At its yardarm a cricket bat was displayed. Long live the Navy.

In days gone by, an East Anglian Regiment had liberated the Corfiots from the Turks. When the anniversary of this victory was about to be celebrated, the Battalion was invited to Corfu and whilst there, play two one-day cricket matches. The Corfiots played regularly, having learned the game from the East Anglians. The General-Officer-Commanding the Eastern Mediterranean decided to make this event an occasion and invited members of our cricket team to participate. How could we decline? He picked us up in, of all things, a captured German U-Boat (the fact that he kept it infuriated the Ordnance Corps who insisted that all booty be returned to them.) As there was insufficient cabin space for all the guests and the cricket team, we gallantly volunteered to stay on deck though we never anticipated bad weather. That night, I woke up thinking that I must be in Hell for I could only see a thin grey line above my head surrounded by millions of red dancing lights. We were in the abyss of the Corinth Canal and it was still dark. The grey light was the top ridge of the deep channel of the canal while the red lights were hot cinders emerging from the short funnel of our sub that, on coming into contact with one's clothes, left a scorch mark. Once through the canal and into the Ionian Sea, we soon encountered heavy swells that threw the submarine about, making us all seasick. When we arrived in Corfu, we had considerable difficulty in mooring. Thanks to the Skipper's excellent handling, we were able to come alongside the quay for a few seconds at a time and each time a number of us would jump ashore.

The palace where Prince Philip was born was being used as a rest centre for British officers. It was there that we stayed. We arrived tired, disheveled and green from seasickness only to be met by a glamourous young woman, our hostess, who was dressed in tight shorts and a thin blouse; and this at 4 a.m. We were shown to our respective suites where we forgot our tiredness, had a quick bath, shaved and changed and made for the dining room where a glorious breakfast awaited us. That morning, we were taken on a tour of the Paleokastritsa, visiting chapels, old forts and ruins and other antiquity, and then stopped for lunch at a bay almost completely enclosed by high cliffs. For lunch, I was invited to wade out into the bay that was only knee-deep at its greatest depth and catch crayfish. Lunch was served in the only café in the area. The owner boiled the seafood and this delicate meal, washed down with either beer or local wine, was gastronomic nirvana. On our way back to Kerkyra Town, we saw miniscule dwellings clinging precariously on high cliffs where monks stayed for days at a time to mediate and pray. To collect food, the monks would lower a basket to the road where a merchant would fill it up with sufficient sustenance for the monks' needs. Goodness knows how the monks got to and from these small monasteries.

The first cricket match was played that afternoon and we lost. Given our outward bound journey, the storm and the morning tour, this was hardly surprising, but to add to our problems, the members of the opposing team came, unexpectedly, out onto the field and presented to each of us with blue and white flowers; the colours of Greece. We were at a loss as to what to do with the flowers and for several overs, kept them in one hand while trying to catch or field the ball with the other. We felt as stupid as we must have looked. That evening, there was a grand buffet/dance held at the palace. Guests included nobility, dignitaries and our Greek hosts. It was great fun and we only got to bed around 3 a.m., feeling decidedly tipsy. The next day, the second match was played, but this time, we won. We had discussed what to give the Corfiots to reciprocate their presentation. It was decided that each member of the Corfiot team would receive a bouquet of red and yellow flowers in remembrance of Minden Day (the Suffolks had fought at Minden and celebrated the date of the battle each year.) The Corfiots and other onlookers applauded this gesture, but I noted that the members of the Corfiot team soon rid themselves of the flowers since the stems were covered with thorns. During the match, the King and Queen of Greece arrived and stayed to watch the match for about half-an-hour. I was in the outfield and standing directly in front of the Royal couple. I decided to move to the side out of politeness but was told, in no uncertain terms, to get back to where I had been first positioned. It was somewhat embarrassing for me. One can't win them all.

LIQUID DIET

We left the island late that afternoon on a calm sea and made for the hilly island of Levkas. To reach the main harbour of Levkas, we had to travel through a mile of high sea grass, the weeds standing some two to three feet above the water level. It was quite an odd sensation. It was at Levkas that the boat was to refuel with high-octane gas. Since we weren't allowed to stay aboard during refueling, the passengers decided to visit the ruins of an old castle situated on a high hill overlooking the harbour. Our journey up the hill had brought on a thirst and on our return to the boat we stopped off to have a drink. The drink became several drinks, in fact, I believe we visited every bar along the route, sampling the local brew that turned out to be extremely high in alcohol content. As we progressed further down the hill, we started to collect souvenirs. Before long, we were carting away mugs, tablecloths, even a chair or two, and not surprisingly, an irate group of islanders following close on our heels. The boat's skipper, sizing up the situation, brought calm to the area by dragging out his bagpipes and playing the instrument while marching up and down the quay. He told us to leave our playthings on the quay and to quickly get aboard. We left in some disgrace and were even more off put when we realized that we were hungry and that there was no food on board. Sometime during the night, we arrived back at the port of Piraeus. It had been an excellent weekend and a good break in the routine of camp life.

MARINE LIFE

The beaches to either side of the peninsula where the camp was located were inviting but heavily polluted and had been placed out-of-bounds. Fortunately, swimming from the rocks was permitted where the water was delightfully warm and crystal clear. Though the waters were peppered with jellyfish and octopi, the most interesting sight was at night when the bioluminescence of organisms rose between the surface layers of the sea. Anything that swam through this body of organism left a green neon streak or trail. When we swam, our bodies were outlined in green. Phosphorescence of the sea can be observed everywhere except in waters of very low salinity. The Greek fishermen who went fishing at night always used lit lanterns to draw the fish into their nets, particularly effective in luring squid. As we sat outside the Officers' Mess facing the sea, we would catch sight of the dozens of lights bobbing in distant inky black. For all their efforts, the fishermen rarely brought home a good catch.

I was invited by an old fisherman to accompany him and his son on their next crab and octopus hunting. Their extraordinary method to catch octopi was to use himself as bait. Having dived overboard, the fisherman-hunter would cling to the rock face near a probable octopus hideout. When the creature came forth to investigate, the hunter would grab it and bring it to the surface and dash its head against the side of the boat until it was dead. The old fisherman asked me whether I would like to try my hand at the game, but I declined explaining lamely that I didn't have the breath to stay down more than a few seconds. Besides, I preferred seeing the octopus underwater than on my plate; nevertheless, it was regarded by the locals as a great dish. The tentacles were chopped up and fried as calamari and when cooled, served as an accompaniment to an aperitif.

By 4:30 p.m. the sun over our camp was usurped by a mountain's shadow overlooking Athens. This particular peak was three thousand feet above sea level. Some of us used to complain about the loss of the sunlight at this time of afternoon. A Major told us to stop complaining and climb the mountain instead. For the fun of it, I accompanied three subalterns and our batmen for a weekend climb. To make it more of a challenge, we chose to travel in a direct compass line rather than use any existing trails. We planned to establish our base camp about five hundred feet short of the mountain's peak. Each man carried a 40-pound pack and two filled water bottles. On the Saturday morning, we motored as far as the base of the mountain and then started to ascend. To our surprise, there were many hidden crevices and valleys that we had to cross. This we found exhausting, particularly when trekking in the deep and airless valleys. At one point, we encountered a huge convex rock approximately sixty-feet in height that we had to scale. It took more than an hour to mount it. The surface was bald with few footholds for support. I would climb a few feet only to slip down again before coming to a sudden, jerking stop. Our passage left a white scratch on the rock's surface illustrating where we had slid. Once on top of the boulder, we stopped to admire the view. It was fantastic, allowing a panoramic vista of the sea. One could gauge the various depths of the sea by the different shades of blue. The air seemed very pure and the slight breeze was refreshing after our hardship in the gullies and valleys. We found a grassy area some fifty yards from the edge of the rock and decided to spend the night there. Supplied with quantities of food and cooking equipment, I've never tasted a better meal; however, we used up all our water. We slept well that night, using our mosquito nets as a form of hammocks. The next morning, after a dry breakfast, the four officers set off for the peak, leaving the batmen, who preferred to stay at base camp. Only three of us made it to the mountain peak, the other officer, having become dehydrated, was unable to continue and returned to base camp. On our way to the peak, we twice thought we had reached it only to find that there was a further climb, one that was hidden from view due to the mist. The final part was tricky for it required covering about one hundred yards of a razor edged rim with a thirty-degree slope. We had to pull ourselves along the ridge 'a cheval,' that is, with our legs dangling over the two sides of the ridge. This was both hard on the nerves and on the bottom. I once again went through bouts of vertigo, but as I was in the middle of the group, there was little I could do but struggle on. From the vantage point of the peak, we spotted the campsite of a goatherd and decided to pay the camp a visit. We noted the best way to get to them was to return to our own base camp and collect the others. By following existing paths, we soon came to the goatherd's camp where we were made welcome. The shepherd understood sufficient English to communicate and offered us goat's milk and cheese. In return, we gave him loaves of white bread, butter and bully beef; a luxury as far as he was concerned. Since we were in dire need of water, he sent his very young daughter, much to her chagrin, to fill our water bottles. It turned out she had to walk a total of six miles so that we could have water. We rewarded her with several bars of chocolate that seemed to satisfy her. The shepherd had fought the Germans with a partisan group and he recounted a few anecdotes about that time, all of which were pretty grizzly tales. When asked his views about the 'bandits' in the mountains, he feigned his inability to comprehend, which spoke volumes. Much later, we descended the mountain in semi-darkness, using the trails guided by the lights of the port of Piraeus. During the descent, there was a beautiful view of Piraeus and the sea, dotted with fishing boats, as a backdrop.

To meet some of the other officers in the Brigade, the Commanding Officer arranged a special Mess Dinner. The Brigade Commander and an assortment of officers from Brigade Headquarters and the other two infantry battalions, descended upon us on the appointed day. The dinner was a success even though the Unit Band insisted on playing regimental marches that meant that officers had to stand up whenever their respective regimental march-past was played; a sort of jack-in-the-box atmosphere. After dinner, some 'games' were played all of which were pretty rough, resulting in a number of injuries. The two visiting Commanding Officers had to be removed to hospital by ambulance as well as our Adjutant who suffered a double fractured leg. To end the evening, we 'escorted' our Second-in-Command, who was even more plastered than the rest of us, to the edge of a cliff and tossed him over into the sea forgetting that there were numerous rocks below. Lady Luck was with him that night. He clambered onto a rock and from there, burst into song. He bore us no grudge the following morning, probably because he couldn't remember what had happened the night before.

Local dignitaries were occasionally invited to lunch or dinner and in return, a number of officers were invited to different social events given by these same people. The Commanding Officer once received an invitation to a dinner given by a very rich businessman in Athens. The CO took along with him a few officers, including me. On arrival at the palatial house, we were ushered into a large reception room where we were introduced to further guests. Among those were some very pretty young women. At the dining room table, I was seated between a pleasant older woman and a delightful young one. The wines must have been excellent for I can't remember what I ate and I certainly chatted away to both women. Before leaving, I asked the young woman whether she would have dinner with me some night and, to my delight, accepted my invitation on condition that we went as a group. A week later, we went out to dinner; the choice of restaurant I left to my partner. It happened to be the most expensive place in town and it cost me more than a month's pay. How do I get into these jams? Anyway, it was worth it.

THE RIDE OF MY LIFE

To get to Athens from Piraeus, you follow the route better known as the "Mad Mile." The route was still pitted with badly filled shell craters and in complete disrepair, as were most of the roads in the neighbourhood. The bus drivers, in vehicles that were only just hanging together, made little effort to miss the potholes and would drive as fast as the vehicle permitted. Whether you were sitting or standing, the result was the same – a feeling of being perpetually suspended in mid-air. All buses were crowded to overflowing and I was convinced it was a catastrophe in the making. The driver was also the ticket collector and he would get off at each stop, shove the last passengers into the bus – rather like a Tokyo subway official – and, when unable to return to the driver's seat due to the human congestion, climb through the driver's window. To collect the fares, the driver would cart around a large canvas sack that, due to the continual rate of inflation, was filled to the brim with almost useless money. I handed him two fistfuls of paper money and expected no change. What bills fell to the floor remained there; they weren't worth the effort of bending over to pick up. The passengers would sing all the way, though I can't imagine what they had to sing about for these were hard times for the average person. The singing perhaps distracted everyone from the dangerous driving. As songs poured out of everyone's mouths, so did the garlic, not to mention the acute body odour from a busload of unwashed bodies. It made for an unforgettable experience.

ATHENS

Whenever I found myself in Athens, I could not resist the temptation to go to a particular restaurant that served the most delicious ice cream, accompanied by a tall fluted glass of pure lemon juice and iced water. A sip of lemon required a taste of ice cream, the richness of which required a further sip of lemon. I must have spent much of my pay at that restaurant. The traffic in Athens was constant and even more frenetic than in India. Drivers refused to stop at stop signs and pedestrians crossed the road at their peril. The trams, like the buses, were overflowing with people, many of whom were clinging precariously to the outside of the swaying vehicle. I took a taxi once but was a nervous wreck by the time we reached my destination. How we missed hitting pedestrians I do not know. The driver kept cursing both pedestrians and motorists with equal venom. As far as he was concerned, he had the right of way. Not surprisingly, almost all vehicles had badly dented fenders – if any at all.

Other than for the magnificent Roman ruins, the city of Athens was not particularly attractive or interesting. More functional than aesthetic. It was dirty and smelly. The people, on-the-other-hand, were quite fascinating. In the evening, it wasn't uncommon for citizens to put on their best clothes and, like first loves, promenade up and down the avenues. The men seemed to go in for 'Quink ink' blue coloured suits. Both men and women were liberally doused with perfume and cologne that, I'm sure, could be smelt from the island of Rhodes. Though few of the citizens had classic beauty reminiscent of the Greek Gods and Goddesses, there was nonetheless an air of pride and confidence about them. I liked the majority of the Greeks that I met for they were full of life and gusto, but I felt sorry for those who were struggling to make ends meet. From time-to-time, I would have supper in town, choosing a small restaurant where I could dine cheaply and in the open, under a vine-covered trellis. Invariably, a violinist or an accordion player would come to my table (why I don't know for I was alone) and play, hoping for a tip, but only received a weak smile, hoping he would move on.

We got to hear about the expected appearance of a well-known prima donna who was to sing at the Roman Amphitheatre in Athens. I was determined to hear her sing. On the evening in questions, I and two other officers attended the opera. In some ways it was more of an opera comique. The conductor was very late and the star refused to wait for him. She strutted onto the stage, whispered something to the leading violinist, who appeared apprehensive as she took her place front and centre and began to sing. The orchestra soon caught up with her and joined in the fun. When the conductor finally turned up, he rushed up to the star, kissed her hand, picked up his baton and went to work, all this without the slightest disruption in the performance. Rather wonderful, really. Could you imagine that happening anywhere else?

Several months after arriving in Greece, I received orders to report to my parent Unit, the Royal Sussex Regiment, located at Chichester, England and to await my release from the British Army. I was very sorry to be leaving the Suffolks. It seemed I had to leave far too soon wherever I was happiest. Had I known that the Battalion would shortly be posted to Malaya to assist in the struggle against the communist insurgents, and that they would be in action alongside my old Gurkha battalion, I would have tried to postpone my departure, but that's life. After a farewell dinner given by my brother officers, I packed my belongings and the following day, embarked on the liner that was to take me home to England. As the coastline of Greece receded into the distance, I had a sudden feeling of loneliness and felt at a loss as to where I was heading. I was saying goodbye to a way of life that I had known for over four years; a life that I had got to like. But to make up for this initial misery, the trip home was most relaxing: the company onboard was good, the food was excellent and the weather, calm. By the time I arrived at Southampton, I had accepted my fate.

Chapter 10

The Royal Sussex Regiment England

THE Regimental Centre of the Royal Sussex Regiment was located in the city of Chichester. I imagined the Centre to be a magnificent establishment with a full complement of personnel. To my disappointment, I was met by a slovenly private who was not even armed and who, had I not stopped to speak to him, would have let me through without a challenge. He directed me to the Adjutant's office where I reported my arrival. There were only four officers on staff, one, I discovered, being me. The Commander of the Centre was a Lieutenant Colonel. There was also a Major, a Captain (the Adjutant), and another Subaltern. The twenty-two other ranks consisted of clerks and administrative personnel. The main responsibility of this staff was to process those being demobilized. Most of the officers were a good, welcoming lot, though more often than not, found reasons to be absent.

The Centre was a large establishment capable of accommodating several thousand men and women, but since the end of the war, most of the buildings had been closed up for lack of personnel. Each officer had a house to himself. Given the shortage of fuel, none of these buildings was heated. The orderly provided me with a large number of blankets, but I was still cold at night due to the ever-present dampness. While waiting for my release, I was given the job of training the Junior Training Corps consisting of boys from local schools. This training was similar to that I had undergone at Bedford School and was easy to organize and fun to conduct since the youth appeared eager. And so I had come full circle – from Bedford JTC to Sussex School JTC.

Some three weeks after my arrival at the Centre, I received my release together with authority for about six-month leave. The few officers remaining at the Centre took me to dinner in town as a farewell gesture that I considered very kind and thoughtful. I spent my termination leave with my parents in Scotland. I have occasionally wondered what would have happened to me had I remained with the Suffolk Regiment until I was officially released (at his Majesty's pleasure), but, I believe in fate, and now consider that my decision in getting out earlier was the correct one.

The four years I spent in the Indian and British armies were filled with a great deal of interest and some excitement. Each country where I served, the situation and conditions I experienced were completely different and my actions were governed accordingly. The trials and tribulations encountered and the knowledge gained, helped me to mature. I learned as much about the army as I did about myself. It was an education on human psychology and how we react under trying conditions. Though there is obvious good and bad in all races and peoples on earth, I became completely tolerate of other people's religion, but also disillusioned with 'organized religion' as compared to 'faith.' I had by necessity taken an interest in the politics that led to the given circumstances in each place I served. My opinion of the politicians responsible for the chaos I encountered was low and cynical. Subsequent events with the withdrawal of the British in India were proof that the whole program was far too rushed, resulting in the massacre of half-a-million Hindus and Muslims that I'm sure could have been averted. The Palestine question was examined without due regard to the future of the Arab Palestinian. The consequence of that disastrous policy continues to haunt us today with no resolution in sight.

Wherever I served or was posted, the Union Jack and British presence came to an end – an end to Empire. While serving abroad in these different countries, this "end to a era" was always in the back of my mind. It was a very odd time to be serving in the forces and rather depressing for anyone hoping to embark on a military career since the future was so uncertain. Nonetheless, I wouldn't have missed it for anything. For the most part, one usually remembers the good and exciting times rather than the bad. I had my share of excitement and certainly more than most young men under twenty-one. Having been a soldier, I can say that it doesn't matter what happens to you thereafter, you never forget that ageless Company you once belonged to. It remains a part of you for life. The manner in which I lived when in India is a thing of the past and can never be recreated; I was therefore exceptionally fortunate to have had the opportunity to experience such a wonderful time. I do not regret serving in the Army during 1945-1949, in fact, it changed my life for the better.